Business Etiquette For Dummies, 2nd Edition

D0520170

Shaking Hands with Skill

Handshakes are the physical greetings that go along with your words, and they're an important part of the first impression you make — good or bad. For complete details on shaking hands, head to Chapter 5.

You're expected to shake hands in the following situations:

- When meeting someone for the first time
- When renewing an acquaintance
- When a client, a customer, or someone you don't know well enters your office, cubicle, or home
- When greeting a host and being introduced to people at an event
- When meeting someone you already know outside work or in your home
- When ending a transaction or leaving a business or social event

In American etiquette, a handshake requires the following:

1. **Hold out your hand.**

   Don't hold out your hand too soon; you'll seem nervous. And don't wait too long; you'll seem unfriendly. Shake hands when you've just met the other person. Lean forward ever so slightly, and hold out your right hand.

2. **Grasp the other person's hand.**

   Fit your hand into his — not too loosely and not too tightly. Push your hand all the way into the other person's hand, to a point where both hands meet web to web (the area between the thumb and index finger). Never grasp just the other person's fingers. Keep your fingers firm — never loose and limp.

3. **Squeeze firmly — not too hard — and shake once or twice for 2 to 3 seconds.**

   The range of motion should be 2 or 3 inches. A proper handshake is done from the elbow, not the shoulder; you want to be relaxed, not stiff.

4. **Let go.**

   That's it!

Giving Business Gifts with Savvy

Gift-giving between companies or between individuals in different companies is a thorny issue — so thorny, in fact, that most organizations have explicit rules governing the practice. The following tips outline a few important elements of business gift-giving; for complete details, see Chapter 15.

- When selecting a gift, be careful to abide by your company's policy concerning gifts. A bit of research and thought can make the gift-selection process a whole lot easier.
- Should you decide to give a business gift, make certain that it's not too personal. Be careful with humorous gifts as well. If you aren't sure that the recipient will be pleasantly amused, don't send it.
- Extravagant gift-giving is both bad strategy and in poor taste. Others may not share your love of lavish gifts and may be embarrassed by them — or, worse, resent you for going overboard.
- Professional gifts can be quite varied, from food to wine to small conveniences (such as a business-card holder or a pen) to office items (such as a picture frame or a computer accessory).
- Giving a material gift isn't the only way to go, even in business. The gift of your time for volunteer work or for helping a colleague's or client's company charity might be appreciated more than a material item.

Business Etiquette For Dummies®, 2nd Edition

Cheat Sheet

Gracefully Traveling Abroad for Business

You should observe every courtesy when you're traveling, especially abroad. The faux pas you may commit while working in a culture unlike your own could cost both you and your company business and relationships. If you want your business trip to be as successful as possible, the following travel tips can help; see Part V for full details and guidelines on business travel abroad.

- ✔ The ugly American isn't just a creation of fiction. Develop enough awareness of cultural diversity to avoid exposing yourself as a person who may not respect another's culture and customs. Your way isn't necessarily better, and every new experience you have makes you not only a greater asset to your company, but also a better global citizen. Before you leave for your destination, brush up on its geography, beliefs, customs, culture, religion, sports, weather, and attitude toward Americans. Remember the adage "When in Rome, do as the Romans do."

- ✔ Before you embark on your trip, practice the greeting rituals or additional key words of the language.

- ✔ Always dress conservatively and appropriately when you're in a foreign land.

- ✔ You can never go wrong by using titles and last names when you first meet people. Academic titles often add a great deal of luster. A handshake is practically universal, and worldwide, everyone relates to a smile — which always makes a positive impression.

- ✔ Know the protocol and ritual involved in presenting and receiving a business card. If necessary, prepare business cards in proper languages.

- ✔ Schedule and confirm business meetings before you leave for your trip. Pull together a checklist of action items and send them to your business contact ahead of time. Your checklist should include items such as meeting locations, agendas, equipment for presentations, and meals. If an interpreter is required, make arrangements to have one prior to leaving.

- ✔ Brush up on the country's cuisine and dining etiquette so that you'll be ready to tackle the local food without embarrassing yourself or causing offense.

- ✔ Find out the appropriate etiquette and protocol involved in business gift-giving, especially if you're doing business in the Pacific Rim, where business gift-giving is an integral part of business culture.

- ✔ Watch your body language so that you don't make gesture-related mistakes.

- ✔ Don't take rude incidents personally, even if you are pushed and shoved. Practice patience! What may be considered rude in the United States may not be elsewhere in the world.

For Dummies: Bestselling Book Series for Beginners

Business Etiquette FOR DUMMIES®

2ND EDITION

by Sue Fox

WILEY

Wiley Publishing, Inc.

Business Etiquette For Dummies®, 2nd Edition

Published by
Wiley Publishing, Inc.
111 River St.
Hoboken, NJ 07030-5774
www.wiley.com

WILEY

About the Author

Sue Fox has provided etiquette products, educational material, group training, and private consultations to business professionals, celebrities, corporations, and educational institutions since 1994 through her company, The Etiquette Survival Group, which has offices in California. She has set up many Etiquette Survival consultants throughout the United States and internationally. Before that, she was employed in the high-tech industry, with 10 years' experience in sales, marketing, and event planning at Apple, Inc.

Sue has traveled extensively and is well acquainted with various international cultures. Her travels have taken her to East Africa, Central America, and Europe. Sue and her company have provided etiquette programs throughout the United States, Singapore, Malaysia, Hong Kong, and India.

Sue is a professional member of the International Association of Protocol Consultants (IAPC) and has an additional background in image consulting and makeup artistry, with 20 years of fashion-modeling experience in television and print.

Sue is also the author of *Etiquette For Dummies,* published by Wiley Publishing, Inc. She is executive producer of *The Etiquette Survival Kit,* a series of educational videos and DVDs featuring dining and social etiquette and proper table settings for adults and teens.

The Etiquette Survival Group and its affiliates MCE (Los Angeles, California) and Global Adjustments (Chennai, India) have formed strategic alliances and currently are developing etiquette and diversity products and programs. They are working together to create a better understanding of people in diverse business and social environments by emphasizing the importance of respect, diplomacy, and civility in every aspect of life.

Sue and her businesses have been featured in many national and international publications, including *Woman's Day, Vogue, Ladies' Home Journal, Real Simple, American Baby, Newsweek, Fortune, New York Magazine, US Weekly, People, Los Angeles Times,* the *New York Times,* the *Wall Street Journal, New York Post, Chicago Tribune, Washington Times, San Francisco Examiner, Boston Globe, USA TODAY, Sunday London Times, Australian Financial News, Folha de S. Paulo, Brazilian Daily News, Nikkei Business Journal, Times of India,* and *The Hindu Businessline.*

Sue's media credits include radio interviews and feature stories on CNBC, KRON-TV (San Francisco), Knowledge TV, *San Francisco Mornings on 2,* KOVR-TV (Sacramento), ABC *World News, ABC News with Sam Donaldson,* KQED-TV (San Francisco), CNET.com, and KABC-TV (Los Angeles).

Sue is the mother of two grown sons, Stephen and Nathan, and she has two grandsons, Joseph and Michael Fox.

Find out more about Sue and her business by visiting her Web sites: `www.susanannefox.com`, `www.etiquettesurvival.com`, and `www.etiquettesurvivalgroup.com`.

Dedication

To my sons, Stephen and Nathan Fox, for their love and encouragement.

Author's Acknowledgments

I'd like to express my sincerest thanks to the dedicated team at John Wiley & Sons who generously contributed to the preparation of this second edition. My continued gratitude goes to my acquisitions editor, Tracy Boggier, and my project editor, Georgette Beatty, for their guidance and expertise.

Big thanks go to my copy editor, Kathy Simpson, for her meticulous editing, and to the additional talent at Wiley, illustrator Liz Kurtzman and cartoonist Rich Tennant, who helped shape this book.

My sincere appreciation goes to my technical editor, colleague, and friend, Syndi Seid, for her editing expertise and knowledge. A special thank you to my agent, Reid Boates, and my colleagues Millie Drum, Gayle Downs, and Cheryl Dandridge for their generous assistance during this project. It has been a privilege to work with all of you!

To my friend and business partner, Linda Cain, thank you for your ongoing support and encouragement. My appreciation and gratitude go to all my colleagues, clients, students, and Etiquette Survival consultants, who motivate me to continue in the quest of raising awareness about treating others respectfully.

I gratefully acknowledge the love and support of all my family members and friends. You have been there for me through thick and thin. Thank you! To my two adorable grandsons, Joseph and Michael Fox, you bring me so much happiness.

Finally, I would like to thank all of you who read this book. May we all strive for a more civil society.

Publisher's Acknowledgments

We're proud of this book; please send us your comments through our Dummies online registration form located at www.dummies.com/register/.

Some of the people who helped bring this book to market include the following:

Acquisitions, Editorial, and Media Development

Project Editor: Georgette Beatty

 (Previous Edition: Tim Gallan)

Acquisitions Editor: Tracy Boggier

Copy Editor: Kathy Simpson

(Previous Edition: Ben Nussbaum, Tamara Castleman)

Editorial Program Coordinator: Erin Calligan Mooney

Technical Editor: Syndi Seid

Editorial Manager: Michelle Hacker

Editorial Assistants: Joe Niesen, Leeann Harney

Cartoons: Rich Tennant (www.the5thwave.com)

Composition Services

Project Coordinator: Lynsey Stanford

Layout and Graphics: Stephanie D. Jumper, Laura Pence, Christine Williams

Special Art: Elizabeth Kurtzman

Proofreaders: Laura Bowman, David Faust, John Greenough

Indexer: Cheryl Duksta

Special Help: Alissa D. Ellet, Christy Pingleton

Publishing and Editorial for Consumer Dummies

 Diane Graves Steele, Vice President and Publisher, Consumer Dummies

 Joyce Pepple, Acquisitions Director, Consumer Dummies

 Kristin A. Cocks, Product Development Director, Consumer Dummies

 Michael Spring, Vice President and Publisher, Travel

 Kelly Regan, Editorial Director, Travel

Publishing for Technology Dummies

 Andy Cummings, Vice President and Publisher, Dummies Technology/General User

Composition Services

 Gerry Fahey, Vice President of Production Services

 Debbie Stailey, Director of Composition Services

Contents at a Glance

Table of Contents

Introduction

・・

The need for etiquette has not disappeared just because we live and do business differently from the way we did 1,000 years ago. In fact, knowing how to treat other people well is more important now than ever. In the past 40 years, fundamental changes have occurred in the makeup of the workforce and the way people do business, and some of the rules have changed forever.

By examining how good manners apply to the work world, you benefit yourself and everyone around you. After all, who you are shows in how you behave and in how you appear to others. How you look, talk, walk, sit, stand, and eat — in other words, how you present yourself — speaks volumes about who you are and creates the impression you give other people, not only in your personal life, but in your professional life as well.

Although the basics of etiquette remain the same, many business situations now need redefinition and rethinking. How do you promote the right sorts of relationships in the global office? How do you foster general goodwill and success with your peers and managers? How do you handle gender, race, and sexual orientation in the boardroom and in the workplace? What are the new rules for interviewing, supervising, and changing jobs? Are there new rules about dressing and about conversing with colleagues, clients, and bosses? Do new rules apply to business entertainment, conferences, trade shows, and travel?

Think, too, of the enormous impact of computers and the Internet on the business world. Whether you work in the vortex of Silicon Valley or do business far from the high-tech tornado, the Information Age and its technologies have permanently changed most businesses. Do you know the rules for online etiquette; e-mail; and the use of cell phones, laptops, PDAs, and MP3 players?

The essential soft skills of good manners are critical to advancing your career. Not only do they give you added credibility, but they also ensure that you are an exceptional representative of your company. Having these skills often means the difference between being pigeonholed in your current position and being offered an attractive promotion or the opportunity to start your own company. You may even find yourself becoming a model for others in your business by setting a standard of respectful behavior and kindness toward others. People around you will appreciate your graciousness and follow your lead.

Proper etiquette is now understood to be vital to career and professional growth, and it is important to personal growth as well. Integrating civility into your behavior allows you to stop worrying about what to do in complex social and business situations. When good manners become part of who you are, they provide a foundation that you can take for granted when you encounter stress and anxiety. More than that, etiquette helps you recognize the importance of other people and the ways in which you can be a presence without being a burden.

The world has changed dramatically during the past few years; cross-cultural awareness is crucial, and social and business niceties aren't nearly as pervasive or clearly defined as they used to be. Knowing how to behave courteously and professionally is far from trivial. Etiquette and protocol really do count in the business world. No matter how brilliant an employee may be, any lack of social grace will make a bad first impression on clients and business associates.

About This Book

Business Etiquette For Dummies, 2nd Edition, guides you through the new rules of business etiquette. You soon find that good manners are far more than just superficial observance of social customs. You see that graciousness and civility are sincere and come from the heart.

My intention for this book is not only to answer the technical hows and whys of etiquette and protocol, but also to show that the core of etiquette is really a way of life — one that emphasizes attention to the needs of other people and recognizes diversity. A person with good manners is someone who always tries to be generous and attentive.

Read on to rediscover the good manners you may have misplaced. Perhaps you'll pick up a few new tips that you can incorporate into the way you work. As you read this book, grade yourself on how you conduct yourself at work right now, noting where you can improve.

You may use this book as a reference guide, reading any section that interests you. You can start at the back or in the middle. I hope that I have avoided dogmatism, but because I think certain things are really important, I have repeated and overstated them for emphasis. This book discusses some difficult parts of life. The tough issues can't be trivialized, but neither do I want to be overly serious when it's not necessary. Remember: "Life has to be lived forward, but it must be understood backward."

The book is wider than it is deep. In the effort to portray a panorama of business etiquette, I have tried to include virtually all the topics that affect it. Yet no single book can provide every detail. I encourage you to join me in exploring the rules of etiquette. Perhaps you will be encouraged to check out some of the many other excellent books on this subject.

Conventions Used in This Book

Here are a few conventions to help you make your way through this book:

- *Italics* highlight definitions and emphasize certain words.
- **Boldface** text indicates key words in bulleted lists and actions to take in numbered lists.
- `Monofont` points out Web addresses.

When this book was printed, some Web addresses may have needed to break across two lines of text. If that happened, rest assured that I haven't put in any extra characters (such as hyphens) to indicate the break. When you're entering one of these Web addresses, just type exactly what you see in this book, pretending that the line break doesn't exist.

What You're Not to Read

Throughout this book, I share some information that may be interesting to you but isn't essential to your grasp of a given etiquette topic. This information appears in sidebars (shaded gray boxes); feel free to skip them.

Foolish Assumptions

It's never too early or too late to learn about etiquette. Everyone has to interact with others to succeed. This book is great for new players in the working world, but it's also great for those who have been in the workplace for a while and want to clear up some confusion about the complexities of social interaction in culturally diverse business environments. In short, I assume that those of you who pick up this book seek to understand or brush up on appropriate manners for the workplace; for work-related events; and for business travel, both domestic and foreign.

How This Book Is Organized

This book is divided into six parts, with 24 chapters and an index. Cross-referencing is provided between the chapters.

Part 1: Conducting Yourself Gracefully in the Business World

What's all this fuss about business etiquette? Can it really help you get ahead in business? In Part I, I explore these basic questions and share the secrets of contributing positively to the office environment and building good relations with people above and below you on the corporate ladder. I also navigate cultural diversity in the workplace. Finally, I talk about appearance, how much it matters, what people read into your style of dress and body language, and what you can do to give yourself every grooming and style advantage.

Part II: Building Better Communication Skills

"What we have here is a failure to communicate."

How often have you heard those words? Communication is key in business, just as it is in personal life. In Part II, I help you get started by tackling one of your most common challenges: meeting and greeting other people. Many of us get tripped up on introductions, so I set you on the right path of who to introduce to whom, how to use titles, and the all-important firm handshake. Then I give you tips on making sparkling business conversation that everyone will want to be part of.

Speaking on the telephone is another situation in which manners seem to slide, so I cover how to speak and listen considerately on the phone. I explore new tactics for handling voice mail, call waiting, caller ID, speaker phones, and cell phones. Next, I look at the written word, and I close with brand-new advice on electronic etiquette.

Part III: Behaving in the Boardroom and Beyond

Meetings are chances for people to size one another up, make judgment calls, and decide who they want on their team. In Part III, I help you shine in the boardroom. I hit the potential highs and lows of group gatherings, from seating arrangements to chairing a meeting. I give you words of wisdom on surviving trade shows and conferences, and on representing yourself and your company to your best advantage. In addition, I show you what to do if the responsibility for planning a special event falls to you.

Business isn't all about meetings and industry events, however; entertaining is also key. Business entertaining has expanded far beyond the traditional business dinner. What about golf games, rock climbing, and hang gliding? In this part, I put you through a real etiquette workout, reviewing everything from table settings and wine choices to buffet lines and company retreats. Then I help you figure out the office-party minefield. Should you give a gift? And if so, what? I also include a reminder about combining alcohol with work functions, and I give you some tips for handling them both gracefully.

Part IV: Overcoming Work-Related Challenges

Every office has at least one challenge: the difficult person. How do you handle that person and wind up on the high ground? What are some tactics for dealing with difficult people? In Part IV, I offer tips and strategies to help keep you sane. I also cover office conflicts and help you decide when and how to get involved. Then I tackle the subject of stress and how to keep your cool under pressure. I discuss some ethical dilemmas that occur at work, and use real-life scenarios to illustrate the right and wrong ways to handle them. I close with a discussion of office romance and sexual harassment — and how to draw the line between the two situations.

Part V: Doing Business on a Global Scale

As communication and business travel increase, people are working more and more with colleagues overseas. You have to know how to get along in Minneapolis and in Mumbai. Having to know so much can be intimidating, but in Part V, I give you some universally helpful pointers. From traveling with colleagues to surviving airline travel to knowing what to pack and how to speak when you get there, I get you through international business travel with dignity. I examine international etiquette by region, explaining ways of adapting to other cultures, customs, foreign attitudes toward women, and ways in which business is conducted around the world.

Part VI: The Part of Tens

This part is where you find my best advice, concisely given — quick, tried-and-true tips for the transition from college to career and for job interviews.

Icons Used in This Book

I use little pictures, called *icons,* to flag bits of information throughout the book. Here's what they mean:

This icon indicates a story that helps explain an important concept.

Beware of the potential missteps highlighted by this icon.

This icon points out take-home messages to last a lifetime.

Wherever you see this icon, you find small hints that help make the bumps easier.

When you see this sign, pay attention!

Where to Go from Here

The introduction is the end of the beginning and a broad template of the rest of the book. I hope that as you read, you pick up ideas and information that allow you to be yourself while being considerate of other people. Start by becoming aware. So keep reading!

Part I

Conducting Yourself Gracefully in the Business World

The 5th Wave   By Rich Tennant

"Apparently, no one told you about the dress code here, Mr. Dunn, but we don't wear ties."

In this part . . .

In this part, I give you the secrets of contributing positively to the workplace while building good relations with others above and below you on the corporate ladder. You find solid advice for surviving job interviews and ways to make a positive impression. This part also helps you respectfully navigate today's culturally diverse work environments. Finally, I talk about professional appearance, how much it matters, what people read into your style of dress and body language, and what you can do to give yourself every grooming and style advantage to look sharp.

Chapter 1

Displaying Good Manners at Work

∙∙∙

∙∙∙

*B*usiness etiquette is vitally important for creating a harmonious work environment and for representing your company in the best manner possible. Although many people consider their technical skills and intelligence to be their most important job qualifications, many employers consider the ability to get along well with colleagues and clients even more important. Being well mannered means two things above all else: respecting others, and treating people with courtesy and kindness.

Whether your company is a highly caffeinated startup, a small gift boutique, or a large law firm, good manners at work are important because they emphasize your willingness to control your behavior for the benefit of others. I introduce you to the basics of business etiquette in this chapter.

Conducting Yourself with Class

As a representative of your company, you stand not only for yourself, but also for the company as a whole. If you are poised, courteous, and respectful to your company's clients, they will extend their approving judgment to other employees of your company. If you are inconsiderate, insolent, and rude to your company's clients, you will be out of a job soon.

Acting with grace and tact is also crucial within your workplace. In the following sections, I introduce you to three important concepts: making a positive impression on your colleagues, working well in a diverse environment, and dressing appropriately.

Making a good impression

Your considerate behavior in the office and with clients makes a big impression; it's instantly recognizable and beneficial to both you and to your company. When a courteous employee works with others, including his peers, staff, and superiors, his grace lends an air of professionalism to the workplace that others emulate and that employers reward.

Being a well-mannered business professional is harder than memorizing a bunch of stuffy rules. The greatest challenge is to incorporate the rules of good behavior so readily that you don't have to think about them at all. For details on how to make a positive impression on the job, see Chapter 2.

Working in diverse environments

In today's increasingly global business environment, people of various physical abilities, races, ethnicities, and genders work together. But misunderstandings, thoughtlessness, and poor attitudes create barriers among colleagues and cause fear, hurt, and isolation. The use of appropriate language is crucial for respectful and dignified communication. Education and considerate thought are needed to remove misunderstandings and unnecessary discrimination in the workplace. See Chapter 3 for full information about acting gracefully in diverse work environments.

Dressing well

Psychologists say that most people form impressions of others in the first four minutes and that 80 percent of an impression is based on nonverbal signs. In other words, what comes out of your mouth has very little to do with how people judge you. Also, after you make a first impression, getting people to change that judgment is hard.

How you dress, how you groom yourself, and how you handle your body language in the workplace are all part of your "packaging." As in product packaging, you can present yourself to be most appealing, and you can present yourself differently according to the time and place.

A well-mannered person always considers the impression communicated by clothing, body language, and grooming. Always be thinking about what your appearance says about you. Never pretend to be anything you aren't. You should not be uncomfortable or present an image that is not you, but you should present the best you that you possibly can. For more on appropriate business attire and professional presence, see Chapter 4.

Communicating in the Business Arena

Clear communication in business is an essential part of being courteous to others, whether you're conversing in person, talking on the phone, writing a letter, or chatting on the Internet. What you say reflects who you are, so you want your words to build others up rather than tear them down in any way.

Polishing your introductions

In the business world, you meet new people all the time, for many reasons and in many situations. Being able to introduce others makes everyone feel comfortable and is one of the most useful skills you can acquire in business. The ability to remember names, shake hands properly, and graciously accept and receive a business card demonstrates that you're at ease and in control, which sets others at ease too.

Knowing how to make a graceful introduction not only allows you to concentrate on making a good impression, but also gives you the confidence and power to nurture relationships from the get-go. To discover more about practicing these skills and using them properly, see Chapter 5.

Mastering the art of conversation, in person and on the phone

So many people work in front of a computer screen all day that they tend to forget the usual social graces of conversing. A conversation occurs when two or more people discuss a topic, exchange ideas, share information, and give one another an opportunity to contribute. Having a conversation is the best way to find out what other people like, think, and need.

Every time you make or receive a telephone call at work, you're representing your company. Many times, the first contact a person has with a company is over the phone, so the impression you make on the phone may be a lasting one. Therefore, you want to sound professional.

Take the opportunity to reinforce your business contacts and improve your work relationships by exercising your best manners when conversing in person and using the phone. For more on improving your conversational skills, both in person and on the phone, head to Chapters 6 and 7.

Understanding business writing, online and off

Just like a handshake or good phone skills, business correspondence can tell people a lot about you. Anything that you mail out is a reflection on your company, so make sure that you correspond professionally. Selecting appropriate stationery, crafting a business letter correctly, and remembering to send thank-you notes not only makes you look good, but also shows that you care about the impression you make for your company.

Communicating by e-mail is no different from writing on company letterhead. A business communication is business, period. A certain degree of formality is required. Just because e-mail tends to be more immediate and personable doesn't mean that it needs to get personal. Just thinking about how the other person is likely to receive your communication can go a long way toward preventing misunderstandings and offenses. A simple test is to ask yourself, "How would I feel in these circumstances if I received this message?"

To find out more about how business correspondence can be the best way to accomplish your business goals, see Chapter 8. I discuss the rules of proper work e-mail in Chapter 9.

Taking care when using technology

The Internet has developed its own unique rules for proper behavior. Although the Internet may seem to offer a perplexing array of new etiquette situations, the old rules still apply. Basic courtesy always means considering others' needs first; it requires you to make others feel comfortable, which forms the basis of what's called *netiquette*.

One of the main principles of Internet etiquette is remembering that you are interacting with real people in real time. Even though you see only words on a monitor, a flesh-and-blood person is behind them. This live human being deserves the same respect that you would offer him face to face.

The manners associated with these new devices have taken a turn for the worse. The problem isn't the technologies, but the ways they are being used and abused. Technology has made communication easier, yet at the same time, people have created a need for instant gratification. For guidelines on minding your manners with technology, see Chapter 9. Although the information there may not be totally new to you, knowing the rationale behind it is always helpful. Either way, being able to distinguish yourself online as a considerate person to your colleagues and coworkers is important.

Behaving No Matter Where Your Business Takes You

In business today, you must know how to conduct yourself properly in a variety of situations. From company parties to the boardroom, your behavior is observed and judged daily by employers, clients, and coworkers. Knowing how to behave properly and respond in certain business situations puts everyone at ease and builds self-confidence. Your ability to establish effective working relationships wherever your business takes you can make or break your career.

Meetings

Business meetings are one area in which poor etiquette can have really negative effects. No matter what your job entails or where you work, knowing meeting-etiquette rules should be a priority. Meetings provide you an opportunity to shine in front of your clients, coworkers, and superiors. You can demonstrate your meeting manners in quite a few ways with positive results. If you haven't thought about what goes into being an effective meeting chair or participant, or about how knowing a few meeting guidelines can improve your chances of success, check out Chapter 10.

Business meals and parties

The business world can be quite overwhelming, even if you never leave the office. When entertaining enters into the business mix, it's easy to get confused about what is appropriate and what is not. The goal of mixing business with pleasure is to create a warm social atmosphere even with the necessary business undertones. Business entertaining is a way to foster personal trust and confidence in others and is the fastest-growing way to do business. From staff breakfasts to working lunches to cocktail receptions for clients, being in your best business form at any meal really pays off. See Chapter 11 to find out key strategies for entertaining.

Table manners can make the difference between getting that promotion or not, and between closing that business deal or not. Fortunately, old habits can be changed if you want to change them; all it takes is some effort. For a thorough discussion of proper dining etiquette, see Chapter 12.

Conferences, trade shows, off-site activities, and other events

Conferences and trade shows may masquerade as chances to update the status of a project or to catch up on industry developments, but they're really a way to find out about and measure other people. These events give you an opportunity to shine in front of your superiors and your peers. Industry events are also great places to make contacts in your field and find out more about what's going on at other companies. No matter how you feel about these events (some people love them, and some people hate them), guidelines exist. For details on attending special work-related events, see Chapter 13.

Most would agree that off-site company activities are an effective means of team building and a big part of today's work environment. But, knowing how to be a team player and balance work with play requires a few skills. Whether you're hosting a group activity, playing golf with a client, or attending a business retreat, make your way to Chapter 14 for a few key etiquette elements that can help you when taking part in a variety of off-site activities.

Life's major passages

Special occasions, such as a coworker's wedding or your boss's birthday, can put your manners to the test. Even though you may encounter these situations less frequently in business, they often require you to be aware of a different set of etiquette rules. Whether you're attending a christening, a funeral, or a graduation, what counts most is that you are there for your coworkers, colleagues, and clients and that you show you care. Head to Chapter 15 for more on making it through life's big events with grace and style.

Overcoming Challenges at Work

Your success in getting along with others in your workplace has a major influence on your career success. You can have excellent job skills and good productivity, but if you don't fit in with the people you work with and your colleagues find you difficult, you'll have a much tougher time winning promotions and advancing your career. On the flip side, you may have to work with someone difficult or manage conflict among colleagues. In this section, I introduce the basics of overcoming these and other challenges.

Dealing with difficult people

Sometimes, folks who work together don't get along. Some people are difficult because of their personalities; others are difficult because of their positions in the company. You may never know why certain people are difficult, but the reason could be a lack of self-esteem or confidence.

For better or worse, what goes on at work comprises the most significant portion of your social life. You most likely spend more time with coworkers than you do with friends outside work, and in many instances, you spend more time at your job than you do with your family. Mastering the techniques of understanding various personality traits and group dynamics will make your work life a lot less stressful. See Chapter 16 for complete guidelines on dealing with difficult personalities.

Coping with conflict

You can manage office conflict effectively in lots of ways. Practice active listening, ask clarifying questions, be willing to compromise, look at the bigger picture, watch your language, and put yourself in the other person's shoes. When the temperature goes up, actively look for ways to cool it down. Vent if you must (just not at work).

Believe it or not, some conflict is actually helpful. In Chapter 17, you find out why. That chapter also introduces some effective conflict-management tools to help you and your colleagues get along better.

Managing ethical dilemmas

Countless unfamiliar situations can arise in the workplace — situations in which you simply don't know how to behave. Knowing how to handle every situation that comes up is impossible, but there are ways to handle the ups and downs of life on the job. See Chapter 18 to learn how your ethical manners can be your trademark.

Handling sexuality

Know your company's policies *before* you get into any situation involving more than day-to-day contact with another employee. Your company may have rigid rules about fraternizing and may have special provisions designed to head off suspicions of harassment. The etiquette of office romances involves a combination of good judgment and discretion, but company rules are absolute. Yield to temptation of the wrong sort, and you may find yourself out of a job or transferred to a remote location that's snowbound eight months out of the year.

Assuming that both you and your prospective partner are unencumbered and officially eligible, and that your company has no policy against it, there's nothing shameful about a blossoming romance. But no etiquette exists for illicit romances — just sad consequences. To learn more about handling sexuality in the workplace, check out Chapter 19.

Traveling Near and Far

You can't find a tougher test of your manners than when you're traveling, especially when you're traveling abroad. No question, travel — especially business travel — can put people under tremendous stress. But being away from home doesn't give you permission to abandon politeness. Good travelers are always ready for the unexpected.

Packing up and heading out

Being a model of good manners means that when you leave home, your manners travel with you. Knowing a few key elements for having a safe and successful trip is essential. What does that have to do with etiquette? The better prepared you are for a trip, the better your experience will be. Head to Chapter 20 for details on traveling *anywhere* with your manners intact.

Acting gracefully after you arrive

After you arrive at your destination, you have to adapt to the local ways of getting around, time changes, unusual foods or table manners, and means of communication. Feeling completely comfortable in another culture can take months or sometimes years, but with just a little research, you can lessen your chances of committing a minor error or a major faux pas.

To acclimate yourself to a different culture and avoid offending your host or business colleagues, try to blend in, dress conservatively and appropriately, keep your voice low, refrain from showing strong emotions in public, and behave in a pleasant manner no matter what happens. Also, when you're asked to taste some exotic food, do your best to be a good sport! For more on ways of adapting to another culture, see Chapter 21.

Minding your manners in different regions of the world

A wide variety of appropriate behavior exists for building business relationships in different areas of the world. By discovering and understanding the
customs and cultures of the country you're visiting, you show that you have
respect for the other side, and respect is crucial in building a rapport and
developing business relationships. For complete details on regional business
etiquette, travel to Chapter 22.

Chapter 2

Making a Positive Impression on the Job

A successful career does not come only to those who have worked the longest or the hardest, or to those who have the most impressive résumés. These days, many corporations are unwilling to send someone to the front lines unless she has a little polish, style, and finesse. (And a little finesse goes a long way!) This is the new competitive edge.

In this chapter, you are introduced to the skills required to be respectful and polite in your professional life, from your job interview to everyday life in the office, classroom, hospital, or wherever you work. Among other things, you discover how to respect others' privacy, how to handle criticism and compliments, and how to be a good visitor. By the end of the chapter, you'll know what it takes to be a gracious and generous colleague.

Surviving the Job Interview

So after days of networking, you have an interview with the company you most want to work for. Congratulations! Your next response is likely dread. How can you make the best possible impression? What will make you stand out above the others? You want to be polite and charming, but you don't want to come across as overly confident or arrogant. You want to negotiate a great starting package, but you don't want to seem greedy. Bottom line: You want the company to like you, and you want it to convert that affection into cash while everyone maintains professional decorum.

If you're like most people, job interviews are on your list of least-favorite activities. Just as you're meeting a whole group of people for the first time, you're also trying to assess them as potential colleagues, as well as to determine whether all those nice things they're saying about the company and how much they love it are really true. You're also trying to assess the job and how it compares with your other opportunities. As though those things weren't enough, you suddenly need to brag about your many accomplishments — something your mother told you never, ever to do. All this pressure is enough to send you around the bend.

Relax. This section doesn't guarantee you that dream job, but it can help you make a positive impression while maintaining your dignity.

Soul searching before job searching

First of all, you need to put some serious effort into deciding what kind of job you really want. You're in luck. An entire industry is dedicated to helping you find the perfect job. Start on the Internet, or at your local library or bookstore. You can also check out job-search Web sites such as www.monster.com or www.careerbuilder.com. These sites not only give you guidance about different lines of work, but also provide job counseling, interviewing tips, and outstanding advice on composing an effective résumé.

Before you secure an interview, read and learn as much as possible about the company. Test flagship products, read annual reports, memorize the names of the top executives, and know the stock price. You can gain this information by searching online for relevant articles, looking in business journals, or reading a company brochure or Web site. This not only gives you added confidence and prepares you to answer questions or ask questions about the company or the products, but it also helps you decide whether it's a company that you truly want to work for.

In the very unlikely event that the company doesn't have an online presence or that its site isn't very informative, start with what you know:

- **Query the person who referred you to the company for information.** Does the boss have any pet peeves? What are they? What is the company culture? Is the company formal or casual? Is there a dress code? What should you wear to the interview?

- **Do a news search for the past few months, and see what you can find.** Being aware of recent press releases gives you a better understanding of the business, and it also shows you're interested in the company, the new products, marketing strategies, or other activities. You'll also be better prepared to answer questions.

- **Track down the friend of the friend who used to work there.** Most people like to talk about their careers, and almost everyone is pleased to help a job-hunter.

Writing appropriate cover letters and résumés

Unless you're using a job-search company, most employers today request that you e-mail them a résumé and state that they'll contact *you* if they're interested. When you send your résumé to a company, either via e-mail or as hard copy, you should always attach a cover letter. Cover letters are so important to the application process that many times employers or HR managers reject those résumés that arrive without one.

The cover letter should be on personalized stationery, with your address, telephone number, and e-mail address (if you have one) at the top of the page. Include this basic information even if the letter is an e-mail message or e-mail attachment.

WARNING!

Do not use unusual fonts or brightly colored paper. Use fonts such as Times or Arial. And stick to cream-colored paper and black type. You want your résumé to stand out — but in a good way!

TIP

Stick to the communication medium you start with until the employer changes it. If you begin the correspondence on the Internet, you may continue on the Internet. If the company starts to call you, you call the company back. (See the next section for information on how to handle yourself on the phone with a potential employer.)

Your cover letter should follow these guidelines:

- ✔ **Keep the letter short and to the point.** Even though your résumé took you hours to write, hiring managers typically spend one minute reviewing it. Keep the cover letter to one page and make the most of it by briefly highlighting your qualifications, giving a short explanation of any gaps in your employment, and providing information that will *entice* the employer.

- ✔ **State your interest in the job, and provide contact information.** If you have names to drop, now is an appropriate time. ("Our mutual friend, Dr. Phil Thomas, told me you have been golfing together for years, and he suggested I get in touch with you about entry-level accounting positions.")

- ✔ **Don't go into unnecessary detail or discuss personal interests.** The same goes for your religious affiliation, height, weight, sexual orientation, or any other facts that could possibly be used against you. Until you're in an actual interview, potential employers are unlikely to be interested in any type of personal information.

- ✔ **Don't be too generic.** It's important to customize your résumé and cover letter for each employer and job for which you apply. By tailoring your information and materials, you can show that you will be a perfect fit for the position.

✔ **Avoid grammatical and typographical errors in your résumé and cover letter at all costs.** Your sloppiness, however unintentional, may be interpreted as a character trait. Use spell-checking and grammar-checking software, and have at least two people you trust proofread both résumé and letter before you send them. Use Standard American English, please — no shortcuts or text-messaging vocabulary!

Your résumé should be long enough to include all pertinent information that is relevant to your current career. One page is just fine if it allows you to present a complete picture. If not, don't be shy about adding an extra sheet, but your résumé shouldn't be longer than two pages.

One reliable format is a modified chronology, listing skills first, followed by work experience in reverse chronological order (most current first) and then education.

Unless you already have permission to do so, do not e-mail large or complex attachments with your cover letter and résumé. Although attachments may be appropriate if you're applying for a position as a Web designer, never assume that the other person has time to download your creations.

For more information, check out *Cover Letters For Dummies,* 2nd Edition, and *Resumes For Dummies*, 5th Edition, written by Joyce Lain Kennedy and published by Wiley.

Making the most of phone calls

After you send a résumé and cover letter, the next step normally is a follow-up call to make sure that the résumé was received. However, this depends on the manner in which you have applied for the job. If you send a résumé for a job opening on a job search Web site or on a company Web site, check first to see what policy is in place. Many times it states that you will be contacted if there is an interest. If you've spoken with a potential employer or had any communication before you've sent your résumé, normally you can follow up with a call. Prepare for the call by practicing what you want to say. Your goal is to sound and speak intelligently — no shakiness in your voice, stammering, or (worse) rambling on out of nervousness. You want to sound confident, so practice until you feel completely comfortable, and use the following tips:

✔ **If you're calling the company for information or to follow up on a sent résumé, always introduce yourself first.** Say something like "Hello, this is Ron Johnson. I'm calling for Harold Haynes" or "Hello, this is Ron Johnson. I'm calling to find out the name of your vice president of marketing."

✔ **Be patient.** Receptionists often must put you on hold momentarily to address other incoming calls or to transfer the call.

✔ **Provide additional information politely if the person with whom you're speaking requests it.** Most receptionists and assistants try to screen calls; however, they normally have no problem with providing the information you need to send a résumé or to follow up after sending one. Let the person you're speaking with know your availability (and flexibility) should an interview be requested.

✔ **Explain the subject briefly when making follow-up calls.** Say something like "I had sent Mr. Haynes my résumé, and I'm calling to make sure he received it."

✔ **Leave a brief message if you get the person's voice mail.** Include your name and phone number, and explain your reason for calling. At the end of the message, repeat your name and number slowly.

✔ **Find out the name of the person who has helped you before hanging up, in case you need to call back.**

✔ **Always say, "Thank you"!**

Knowing what to wear (and what not to wear)

Dressing for a job interview used to be very simple: navy suit, white blouse or shirt, and well-polished black shoes. If you're interviewing in a traditional office and/or industry, these rules still apply. Pick a conservative tie or scarf to match your suit ensemble, snip off errant price tags, lose the flashy jewelry and excessive perfume or aftershave, use a comb, brush your teeth, and you're home free.

In recent years, however, dress codes have become much more relaxed at many companies and nonexistent at others. In this case, your decision is a little more difficult.

Many employers explain that their casual dress policies recognize that job performance is more important than appearance. At the same time, most of the people who will interview you — whether they admit it or not — would like to see some sign that the interview is worth some special effort on your part. Dress is one way to convey that impression.

Even though workplace dress codes have relaxed in the past few years and you have more choices regarding what you can wear, it is still important to step it up a notch. If you're not wearing a business suit for the interview, your attire should reflect that you respect yourself. Beyond that, you may want to consider a few subtleties that can affect your choice of outfit. For example, to make a good impression, wear an outfit that would be suitable for the work you would be doing. If you would be doing computer work in an office environment, neat slacks and a well-pressed, button-down shirt or blouse will do.

If the job calls for a uniform, business casual for the interview is appropriate. For an outside sales position, men should consider dressing in a tie and business suit. Women clearly have more options, but a jacket and skirt or slacks will suffice. Remember, business casual isn't the same as "casual" and can vary from company to company. Just make sure you're within the boundaries of the company's standards. For more on dressing professionally, see Chapter 4.

As a general rule, tattoos and piercings shouldn't be visible during the interview, especially in conservative business settings. Remove your piercing ornaments ahead of time.

Practicing for the interview

The best person for the job must be able to communicate to the interviewer that she is the *best* person for the job. To effortlessly navigate through the interview process, practice is required.

Careful thought about your job search will keep you from wasting others' time. Doing practice interviews is an excellent strategy — if you can't hire a professional coach, rehearse interviewing with friends, family members, friends of the family, or at least at companies you have some interest in, even if you consider them to be last resorts. If you can't get anyone to listen to your interview, do an interview with yourself and videotape it if possible.

Face-to-face communication is 58 percent body language, 35 percent tone of voice, and 7 percent words used. Your body doesn't know how to lie. Find out as much as you can about your body language by *being aware* of your posture and breathing, the positions of your hands and feet, and your facial tensions. (See Chapter 4 for more about the importance of body language.)

There are numerous Web sites on the Internet that give you everything you need to know for acing that interview! These job search sites include recommendations and suggestions on what to wear, relaxation techniques, how to get mentally prepared, what *not* to say, questions for you to ask, sample dialogue, common questions interviewers ask (and answers to sell yourself), tips for group interviews, and much more. For an interesting array of resources, check out the following Web sites: www.careerbuilder.com, www.monster.com, and www.hotjobs.yahoo.com.

If you can't videotape your rehearsal, use an audiotape so you can hear your responses. What you say is important, but how you say it is just as important.

Once you're prepared, rehearse the interview from start to finish — from greeting the interviewer, to exiting confidently. Here are a few pointers to keep in mind when practicing on your own:

- ✔ Dress in the attire you plan to wear to the interview.

- ✔ Practice while sitting in a chair in front of a full-length mirror so you can observe your mannerisms. Observe your posture while standing and sitting, as well as your facial expressions and hand movements.

- ✔ Don't fidget, tap your fingers, wring your hands, or touch your hair, face, or jewelry.

- ✔ Read through a list of common questions and respond to each as though you are really in the interview.

- ✔ Don't ramble on; keep answers short and on track.

- ✔ Remain professional and upbeat, but don't be overly friendly or get too comfortable by discussing health problems or sharing personal information.

- ✔ If it's an interview over a meal, practice your table manners.

For additional help, purchase a copy of *Job Interviews For Dummies,* 3rd Edition, by Joyce Lain Kennedy (Wiley).

Painting a rosy picture on the big day

Everybody's nervous about a job interview. What should you do? If your hands have a tendency to sweat, apply some hand sanitizer with alcohol just prior to entering the office or, in severe cases, apply antiperspirant to your palms just before leaving the house in the morning and again just before entering the interview building.

Next, *relax!* That's right — relax. If that seems impossible, just concentrate on breathing deeply. The idea is to keep oxygen flowing to your brain so that you can remember all the reasons why you deserve this job. Deep breathing also prevents you from losing consciousness and waking up underneath that big ficus tree in the lobby.

You have a great deal on the line in a job interview, of course, but your display of nervousness may thwart your ability to negotiate the best deal and may even harm your chances of getting the job. Does that fact not make you feel any better? Take more deep breaths, and read the following sections. (For additional help, see *Job Interviews For Dummies.*)

Arriving at the office

Here are a few pointers to get you started:

- **Be on time.** If you get lost easily (or even if you don't), allow a few extra minutes for construction delays, traffic, and a pit stop. If you've never been to the building before, get specific directions, including where to park, which entrance to use, and where to go when you get inside. Write the information down, and look at a map. Better yet, drive over a day or two in advance so that you know exactly where you're going.

- **Be early.** There's no crime in arriving early. Arriving early will help you relax, allow you to review your notes, and give you time to freshen up in the restroom and perhaps get a drink of water before the interview.

- **Get the correct pronunciation of your interviewer's name.** You can ask for this information when you're asking for directions. If the name is difficult, practice.

- **Know your interviewer's title, if any, and use it until asked to do otherwise.** You do not call your interviewer by her first name until your host informs you that you can drop the titles and surnames.

- **Bring a folder with a few clean copies of your résumé, some paper to write on, and a pen.** A leather portfolio adds a nice touch.

- **Leave unnecessary items in your car.** When the interviewer shows you to her office, you don't want to spend time packing for the trip. Women in particular sometimes find themselves loaded down with purses, tote bags, briefcases, and enormous zippered day planners.

- **Be pleasant to the receptionist, assistant, security guard, or anyone else who may be helping you find your interviewer.** If this person is on the phone, be patient. Find something else to look at until she finishes, and don't tap your fingers on the counter or succumb to other nervous tics. At the very least, this person is another working professional who deserves your respect.

  Try not to be overly friendly, however. Take your cue from the employee. If she strikes up a conversation, go with it. If she seems busy, don't bother her. Now is not the time to line up a date. (If you don't get the job, you can always call back.)

- **Don't chew gum, smoke, eat, or drink on company premises unless refreshments are offered.** Your water bottle, handy though it may be, does not belong on the interviewer's desk — even if you're very thirsty, and even if your doctor has advised you to drink lots of water.

Acting appropriately during the interview

If you've been practicing your etiquette, then good behavior has already become habit. If you have not been practicing, you may want to skip around to other pertinent chapters of this book to refresh your memory.

Also, do the following:

- ✔ **Dress appropriately.**

- ✔ **Start with a smile and firm handshake.**

- ✔ **Stand up when your interviewer approaches.**

- ✔ **Greet the interviewer by name, look him in the eye, and thank him for this opportunity.** Refer to the interviewer as "Mr. Nguyen" if you have never met. If you have met, and if he indicated that calling him by his first name is okay, you can do so.

- ✔ **Give the interview your full attention.** This opportunity may be your best chance not only to sell yourself, but also to notice important details about the interviewer and the company. Minimize possible distractions by turning off cell phones, watches, and other beeping gadgets.

- ✔ **Watch your language.** Swearing is never appropriate at the office and never appropriate during an interview. Even if the interviewer swears, you don't have to.

- ✔ **Be as specific as possible in answering the interviewer's questions.** Anticipating possible questions (again, with the help of the many available resources) is helpful and allows you to prepare your answers. Whenever possible, cite actual examples from your experience. Give yourself time to think about your answers before you speak; they don't have to be automatic.

- ✔ **Add other comments and ask questions at the end of the interview.** When the interviewer finishes answering questions, she almost always gives you the opportunity to add other comments and ask questions. If you feel that the questions she asked didn't allow you to explain why you're the right person for the job, now is the time to volunteer that information.

Be positive, and always paint a rosy picture of previous jobs and bosses. You should always have some upbeat questions. Even if you feel that you know everything already, ask something like "What is your favorite thing about working here?" Avoid questions on a negative topic for the company or questions that you can answer easily through a Web site or annual report; if you ask them, the interviewer may conclude that you didn't take the time to research the company.

Closing the interview

When the interview is over, do the following:

- ✔ **End as you began, with a firm handshake, good eye contact, and a big smile.**

- ✔ **Tell the interviewer now that you'll call her to follow up, and specify a time period that's reasonable based on your discussion.** If she indicated that the company will be interviewing for another three weeks before making a decision, tell her that you'll follow up with a call near the end of the three weeks.

- ✔ **Thank the interviewer again for her time.**
- ✔ **Walk out confidently.** You did it!

Sealing the deal

You must always, *always* write a follow-up note immediately after an interview. Compose your note in your very best handwriting in black or blue ink, on quality cream or white paper — no cheap store-bought thank-you notes or decorated stationery, please.

And yes, if you interviewed with several people, each person gets a note. You should make an effort to vary the wording a little, just in case these people . . . well, compare notes!

Your note can be very simple: a salutation, a thank-you, a specific point of some kind, and a closing. Figure 2-1 shows an example.

Even if your handwriting is atrocious, a handwritten note has far more impact than an e-mail or no note at all. At the very least, the interviewer will put you on the list of people who took the time to follow up. If the hiring decision is a close contest among several candidates, your graceful good manners could give you the edge.

In many instances, you may apply for a job via e-mail or a Web site and then be interviewed via e-mail without ever speaking to a human being. In that case, you may e-mail your follow-up note. If you've had a telephone interview, however, your note should still be handwritten. The only other time an e-mail follow-up/thank-you note is appropriate is when the length of time until the decision to hire is less than the time your handwritten note will take to arrive by regular mail. In this instance, do make mention of this in your e-mail by indicating that although your preference would have been to send a nice note by regular mail, because of the shortness of time, you had to send it via e-mail.

You even send a short thank-you note to someone who gives you a screening interview. You may not get beyond the screening interview, but your good manners will be remembered if any other job for which you're qualified comes up in the future.

Last, follow up by phone as you said you would. If you don't get a return call right away, don't be a pest. Let a couple of days pass between calls, or alternate between telephone calls and e-mails. Most people are busy but committed to getting back with you. If someone refuses to call you back, you're probably lucky not to be working with that person!

April 18, 2008

Mr. John Hedren
President
Hedren Technology
1949 Fairmont Avenue
San Francisco, California 94131-2700

Dear Mr. Hedren:

Thank you for the opportunity to discuss the open accounting position with me. It was a pleasure meeting you and Ms. Martin.

Our discussion and tour of the facilities gave me a good understanding of Hedren Technology and the job requirements. I was particularly impressed with your warehousing accounting procedures.

I believe my background and accomplishments to be a very good match for the position and my proven track record an asset to the company. I would consider it a privilege to join your team.

I look forward to hearing from you and to the possibility of joining your staff.

Sincerely,
Danielle Rogers

Figure 2-1:
A simple
thank-you
note after an
interview.

Being a Positive Part of the Workplace

Everyone knows people who are easy to work with and people who are not so easy to work with. Whether you're just starting a new job or have been with the same company for years, you're likely to ask yourself at some point just why some people are so much harder to work with than others. Psychological explanations may help you understand, but they don't always help you work with difficult individuals. For that, you need patience, respect, and consideration. In short, you need good manners.

The prime directive in office or basic work etiquette is treating each person with courtesy and respect. Having good manners in the workplace means working with others so that you're a positive part of the work environment, even when the environment is stressful, even when others aren't being helpful, even when some people are being out-and-out rude. I explain how to interact with colleagues, staff, and superiors in the following sections.

Problems that start small can become big if you let them go on very long. Small slights, swearing, peevishness, and forced smiles have a way of getting under everyone's skin. More-outrageous behavior — such as temper tantrums, yelling matches, crude displays of power, and harassment of any kind — simply shouldn't be tolerated by anyone.

Developing good relations with your peers

You can do many things in a work environment to irritate people, just as you can do many things to make yourself a prized worker. In the following sections, I explain how to foster happy, well-mannered work relationships with your colleagues.

Understanding personality types

Part of respect is knowing enough about others to know what they're likely to like and dislike. The polite person is sensitive to differences in personality types and acts on that knowledge. A work environment has lots of personality types. Watch for the behaviors that each personality type exhibits, and appreciate the diversity. People's quirks are inherently interesting, and acknowledging them can help increase harmony.

- ✔ **The control freak:** This personality wants to do it all herself. She doesn't easily trust others but will do a great deal of work. You can identify a control freak by her impatience with others on tactical and strategic decisions and by her constant desire for more challenges.

- ✔ **The appreciation fan:** This person wants to be recognized by others. You can identify her by her self-promotion and her promotion of her team. She gets sulky if her hard work isn't recognized publicly on a regular basis.

- ✔ **The obsessive:** This person wants to get things right. She's an information junkie and may be a loner. You can identify this person by the way she devours information — the more, the better! She'll do outrageous amounts of work, but she doesn't like to make decisions because she is afraid that the decision she makes may be wrong.

✔ **The consensus-builder:** This person wants everyone to get along. Not given to making quick decisions — how could there be such a thing when everyone has to agree? — the consensus-builder is inclusive and compassionate. She enjoys working with others but gets nervous when asked to take the initiative by herself.

✔ **The socialite:** This person wants everyone to have a good time. You can identify her by her preference for chatting while others are around and having fun. Although she works best after hours or at home, the socialite generally improves other people's motivation.

✔ **The steamroller:** This person wants to get things done now. You can identify her by her willingness to make decisions, even when information is incomplete. On a team, the steamroller keeps the group moving at full speed and won't tolerate seemingly meaningless discussions.

Most people are combinations of these basic types, and each of these personality types is helpful in particular situations. Need a quick decision? Go to the steamroller. Need to put a team together for a project? Make sure that you include a consensus-builder. Need someone to sift through a long report? The obsessive person is your choice.

The idea behind looking at personality types is not to pigeonhole people, but to recognize certain strengths and weaknesses. One of the keys to etiquette is paying enough attention to others to be able to modify your behavior to accommodate them. Appropriate responses to particular personality types are helpful for anyone who wants to be an effective colleague.

Using the right office manners

All the different personality types have to live together in a small space, of course. Keep the following tips in mind for surviving life in a workplace environment:

✔ Dress in a manner consistent with company culture, and make sure that your clothes are always clean.

✔ Treat a cubicle as though it has a door and a ceiling. Speak calmly and with an even cadence in person and on the telephone. Personal telephone conversations should be kept to a minimum if you inhabit a cubicle. No one wants to hear your arguments with your spouse.

Confidential business conversations should also be kept to a minimum if you're in a cubicle. You don't want to spill the beans prematurely about some important deal.

✔ Face forward in elevators. If you're getting off near the top of the building, move to the rear of the elevator. If you're getting off on a lower floor, stand close to the front.

✔ Say "Hello" or "Good morning" to those you encounter in the morning and "Good night" to those you encounter as you leave.

✔ Shower or bathe every day.

Avoid these faux pas:

- Don't interrupt others unnecessarily or visit their offices or cubicles while they are working.
- Don't bring odorous food to the office.
- Keep music low so as not to disturb others.
- Heavy use of perfume or cologne is a no-no.

Developing good relations with your staff

Your staff helps you do your work. They're not your slaves, and they're not drones; they're people who deserve your respect. Praise them when their work is excellent. Comment on their work (in private) when it needs improvement. Above all, acknowledge their existence and their hard work, and treat them with courtesy. Without them, you wouldn't get your work done. In the following sections, I show you how to work well with your staff.

The best way to earn respect is to treat others with respect. As the boss, the things you say and do have consequences for others. Do your best to make these consequences positive:

- Ask, rather than tell, others to do things.
- Be clear.
- Be polite.
- Learn people's names, and use them.
- Recognize that everyone has a life outside work.
- Show sensitivity, be accommodating, and don't pry.

Remembering the right names

Get names right. Learn other people's names and how they prefer to be addressed. Memorizing names is hard for some people and easy for others. If it's hard for you, admit it up front. If you make a mistake and call someone by the wrong name, apologize, and blame yourself. Say something like "I'm terribly sorry, Juan. I'm so bad with names sometimes. I'll get it right from now on." Then make an effort to get it right.

Repeat the name to yourself as soon as possible; then find a pen and write "Juan in Information Technology" 30 or 40 times. This trick works!

As far as your own name goes, let your staff know how you prefer to be addressed. Say your name slowly and clearly when you meet new employees so that others will understand the proper pronunciation. Spell your name if you think it will help.

Acting calm, collected, and respectful

An oppressive boss is a nightmare. Someone who thinks her employees need to be blamed for her mistakes, or someone who thinks her assistants should understand that her violent temper is simply part of her creativity, is a notorious figure. Follow these guidelines for harmonious working relations with your staff:

- ✔ You want your employees to respect you, and you want them to be willing to give their best for you and the company. You will get both only if you treat them with respect and hold yourself to the same standards.

- ✔ Keeping an even tone in your voice helps everybody work efficiently. Dictating a dismissal letter in a calm manner is better than venting your rage while you dictate. Correcting errors is best accomplished privately, politely, and precisely. Yelling at people — even people who deserve it — is rarely effective.

- ✔ Try to give precise and clear instructions. Vague and ambiguous instructions are stressful for anyone who's trying to fulfill them. Rather than saying "Do you understand?" say, "I'm not sure I've covered everything. Can you think of anything that I've left out?"

REMEMBER

No one is perfect, of course. If you make a mistake, admit it. If someone else makes a mistake, remember that your irritation is rarely another person's motivation. Instead, focus on the situation and its solution.

Developing good relations with your superiors

Unfortunately, plenty of bosses expect a level of servitude that is utterly unreasonable. Whether you're in business, entertainment, academia, or banking, you find oppressive superiors who enjoy watching people squirm. I talk about how to deal with some kinds of bad bosses in Part IV. Here, I discuss general guidelines for appropriate behavior toward those who are higher than you in rank.

Newcomers at a company often believe that they can establish themselves in a company's culture by being unfailingly outgoing and friendly. The trouble is, business culture is based on rank; friendliness, even if well intentioned, is sometimes at odds with rank. Your primary function at work is to do your job. Too much friendliness can actually hurt your effectiveness.

One way that friendliness unleavened with manners can be unproductive is in your relations with your superiors. Slapping them on the back and assuming that they're interested in your latest adventure may get you nowhere fast. And talking to them as though you are their equal may be seen not as friendly, but as bumptious and pushy.

So curb your chumminess, and check your sense of humor enough to avoid humiliation. Take the following tips as your first lesson in cultivating good relations with your superiors:

- ✔ Follow the boss's lead.
- ✔ Do your job.
- ✔ Treat your boss with respect and understanding.
- ✔ Call your boss "Mr. Garcia" if everyone else in your position does so. Don't assume that you have the right to call him "Spike" unless he asks you to do so.
- ✔ Don't assume that your boss is your friend. Don't venture into your boss's private life unless you're invited.
- ✔ Don't confuse business entertaining with social events.

Interacting with superiors requires that you be aware of certain subtleties. Although your company may have a friendly "backyard barbecue" culture, your boss should be the person to introduce more-personal subjects. If you're in a social situation with your boss, general small-talk topics are permissible until your boss takes the lead and introduces other topics. See Chapter 6 for more on business socializing.

Offering compliments and criticism

Compliments and criticism are unavoidable in the workplace. I cover both in this section.

Praise and criticize the work, not the person.

Compliments

Compliment others when they've done exceptional work, when they've done more than you've asked them to do, and when they've done you a favor. Don't cheapen compliments by offering them willy-nilly, like a kindergarten teacher. Give compliments when people deserve them. Think of them as little gifts.

A compliment shows appreciation for someone else's work. Focus the attention on the other person, not on yourself.

Giving compliments should be easy, but surprisingly, most people need practice to do it right. Always compliment

- ✔ **Politely:** Be sincere, and use a genuine tone of voice. Insincere or snarling compliments are pointless.

- ✔ **Precisely:** Be precise and detailed. Say something like "Jane, you did an excellent job on the Millman project. It was accurate and extremely well written, and I really appreciated receiving it before the deadline. Thank you for such a great effort."

- ✔ **Promptly:** Be timely. No one wants to hear "Oh, by the way, Ralph, the work you did on that contract for what's-his-name last year was good."

- ✔ **Publicly:** Usually, it's best to praise in public. But shy people and those with cultural prohibitions against public praise are best praised in private.

Delivering compliments in person or in writing is largely a matter of personal style. Some people prefer face-to-face contact; others prefer e-mail. One nice thing to do is to compose a handwritten note, seal it in an envelope, and deliver it to the person with a handshake and a quick "Good job." A hand-written note from a superior is a pleasant surprise that is long remembered.

Receiving compliments is even easier but is done poorly even more frequently. There is one — and only one — rule for receiving a compliment. When getting a compliment, always say, "Thank you." That's it! No other comments or qual-ifiers need to be added. Be genuine. Accepting praise is hard. But thinking of a compliment as a small gift may help.

Don't apologize, belittle your accomplishment, or amplify the compliment by adding your own self-praise. If you apologize or belittle your accomplishment, the person giving the compliment will think you're fishing for something more. If you congratulate yourself after someone else does, you appear to be an arrogant so-and-so who doesn't deserve compliments at all! Just say, "Thank you," perhaps smile, and be done with it.

Criticism

Giving and receiving criticism are difficult. Unfortunately, they're necessary parts of working. If you have to give criticism, make it constructive criticism. Avoid anger and irrelevant detail. If you need to give praise and criticism, give the praise before the criticism and follow up with an uplifting and posi-tive close.

The *only* reason to give criticism is to improve performance. Criticizing is not complaining, and it's not attacking. Criticize in the following manner:

- ✔ **Privately:** Make comments only to those who need to be criticized, and do so away from all others. Nobody else needs to hear what you have to say.

- ✔ **Politely:** Assume that the other person has feelings that will be hurt when she hears your criticism. Focus your comments on the problematic work and not the person. Avoid identifying what she did as "stupid," "brainless," or worse. And never call anyone names.

- ✔ **Precisely:** Criticism should be specific and constructive. Identify the problem, and look for a solution. Say something like "Chris, last week's order for Arete Systems was shipped in error to Hexis World instead. This is the third time this month that one of their orders has gone astray. Let's discuss what happened and figure out how to prevent this problem in the future."

- ✔ **Promptly:** Hand out criticism as soon as possible. If you're mad, take a few deep breaths and count to ten. Repeat as necessary! If you need time to formulate your criticism, take it. But procrastinating only increases the chance that the problem will be repeated and makes you feel worse. Deal with it now.

Being criticized is difficult. When someone is criticizing you, follow the four cardinal rules, and always take criticism

- ✔ **Professionally:** If the criticism is appropriate, accept responsibility. Avoid excuses or blaming others. Apologize, assure the other person that the mistake won't happen again, and then live up to your word.

- ✔ **Politely:** Assume that the other person doesn't mean to insult you when she gives criticism. If she calls you names or is rude, redirect the discussion to the work itself. Avoid retaliating in like manner; you'll almost always make the situation worse. If necessary, you may say something like "I can see the problem here. Please accept my apologies. I'd like to think about what you're saying and think of a solution. May we talk again after lunch?"

- ✔ **Positively:** Assume that the other person has something helpful to say. Listen. Try to understand the issue. If you're too mad to understand, count to ten. Repeat as necessary! Ask for clarification. Ask for assistance.

- ✔ **Appropriately:** If the criticism is unfair or misplaced, say so, so long as you're polite and do so in private. The workplace is neither a family nor a therapist's office. You're no one's punching bag, and you're not responsible for accepting other people's mistakes or poor performance.

Visiting Another Office

Visiting someone else's office is generally not a complicated affair, and the rules are fairly simple. Nonetheless, tales of churlish behavior by visiting colleagues have inspired these tips:

- ✔ **Make an appointment.** If you choose not to make an appointment, leave quietly and cheerfully when your colleague doesn't have time to see you. When setting the appointment, specify how long you would ideally like the meeting to last. This way you aren't thinking one hour when your colleague is thinking only 30 minutes.

- ✔ **Look up your destination on a map before departing.** Internet maps and auto GPS systems have greatly reduced the risk of getting lost. Better yet, call the office and talk to an expert — someone who drives to work there every day. That person can also tell you where to park, which entrance to use, and so on.

- ✔ **Don't bring any food or drink with you to someone else's office unless you've been asked to provide food for the meeting.** No one wants to watch you eat or dispose of your lukewarm latte after you leave.

- ✔ **Be polite to everyone at the office.** If the office has a reception desk, state your name, whom you're visiting, and the scheduled time of your appointment. If the receptionist is on the phone, be quiet and wait your turn.

- ✔ **Don't touch things in someone's office without asking, even if they look like toys.**

Chapter 3

Working in a Diverse Environment

*T*he fact that people are different isn't a news flash. Why, then, do people spend so much time belaboring the obvious? People love to talk about other people. Perhaps curiosity makes others a natural topic of conversation. Perhaps differences are an easy source of cheap humor. But this kind of cheap humor can get you into trouble, especially in the workplace.

Stereotyping, ridiculing, demeaning, or insulting other people is always a mistake. At work, this behavior can be disastrous. You should not assume that the women in the room are secretaries or nurses, or that the men are bosses or investors. Neither should you assume that the person on the other end of the phone shares your ethnicity. The man using the wheelchair may be the CEO, and your potential client may be gay.

These differences are simply not always that interesting and shouldn't be the subject of comment. Even when the story behind the difference may be interesting, remember that prying is rude. Regardless of individual particulars, you have a job to do that brings you together. Focus on the job, and treat other people as important. In other words, treat them with respect.

In this chapter, you find out how to be a respectful colleague to people who are physically, ethnically, and culturally different from you. You also are introduced to some straightforward principles regarding gender and sexual differences in the workplace.

Respecting Physical Differences

The United States is home to more than 54 million people with disabilities, and more than half of all Americans say they're a bit unsure around people with disabilities. Pretty clearly, life at work can be tough if you're among the

54 million, and getting over your uncertainty about people with disabilities is a matter of urgent importance if you're one of the others. The following sections help you work more comfortably with your colleagues or clients who have disabilities. If you have a disability, take the initiative by giving your coworkers, employees, or boss some guidelines for working with you.

Starting with a few general guidelines

When you work with someone who has a disability, you may think that he should be treated differently. This thought is a mistake, for the most part. People are people first and disabled or nondisabled second. In the following sections, I provide a few simple but helpful general guidelines for working with people who have disabilities.

Making reasonable accommodations

Federal law requires that employers make reasonable accommodations for those with disabilities. Any employer who hires someone with a disability is expected to accommodate the disability unless undue hardship is the result. These accommodations include providing auxiliary aids for those with vision or hearing disabilities and making sure that physical barriers are removed if possible. If barriers cannot be removed, employers must provide alternatives.

The National Organization on Disability (NOD) is a great place to start if you want to find out more about disability issues. On its Web site (www.nod.org) you can find Frequently Asked Questions, a summary of the Americans with Disabilities Act (ADA), findings of the NOD/Harris Survey on Americans with Disabilities, links to other sites, and more. Or contact the organization for information: National Organization on Disability, 910 Sixteenth St. NW, Ste. 600, Washington, DC 20006.

If you own a business, make every effort to hire workers with disabilities and to implement Americans with Disabilities Act (ADA) requirements (www.usdoj.gov). You may be surprised how little it costs to fully accommodate a worker with a disability, and what a tremendous contribution that worker can make to your company. Make the effort to court clients who are disabled as well; doing so makes good business sense. A good resource is W. C. Duke and Associates (www.wcduke.com), which offers industry-specific "Opening Doors" seminars and video programs on disability etiquette and ADA compliance.

Really, these legal requirements are no more than what common courtesy dictates. If you hire someone who uses a wheelchair but have no way for that person to enter and exit the building, you haven't considered his comfort.

Using considerate language

A good place to start treating those with disabilities with respect is the language you use. Your choice of words and the way you say them have an enormous impact on the way you interact with others. Many disability groups consider terms such as "physically challenged" patronizing:

- ✔ **Avoid using words such as "handicapped," "crippled," and "invalid" to refer to those with disabilities.** Saying "Tom has epilepsy" is preferable to saying "The epileptic guy? His name is Tom."

- ✔ **Avoid using words such as "healthy" and "normal" to refer to those without disabilities.** Many people with disabilities are in excellent health.

- ✔ **Don't refer to someone as "wheelchair-bound" or "confined to a wheelchair."** The chair, in fact, is a freedom machine, affording independence and mobility.

- ✔ **Use people-first terminology.** A general rule is to acknowledge the disability but always place the person first. Simple as it may sound, if you use the term "person with a disability" rather than "disabled person," you're off to a good start. For example, the preferred term for a person who can't speak is "without speech" — not "mute" and never "dumb."

- ✔ **Talk to everyone in a medium tone of voice.** Don't talk too loudly to anyone with a disability.

- ✔ **Avoid getting overly concerned about figures of speech in the presence of people with disabilities.** You can say "I see what you mean!" to someone who has a visual impairment, for example, and you can invite someone who uses a wheelchair to go for a walk.

Acting properly

If you are interviewing or employing a person with a disability, certain rules of etiquette can help you deal with that person appropriately:

- ✔ **As an employer, train your staff to anticipate and accommodate those with disabilities:** Know where the accessible parking facilities, elevators, restrooms, and drinking fountains are in your building. Be prepared to give clear directions to those with visual impairments.

- ✔ **Educate yourself about the assistance technologies people with disabilities are using:** These devices include wheelchairs, hearing aids, enhanced and auditory computer screens, transcription devices, walking aids, and guide animals. Find out about the assistive technologies that your coworkers use, and adapt your presentations and communications to accommodate them. People with vision impairments use scanners to move text from page to computer and screen-reading software to synthesize the words on the screen. People with hearing impairments use telecommunications devices for the deaf (TDDs) or similar tools. High-tech devices of all kinds are available to individuals with limited mobility. For an interesting primer on available assistive innovative products, check out Apple's Web site at `www.apple.com/accessibility/`.

Section 508 was enacted to eliminate barriers in information technology, to make available new opportunities for people with disabilities, and to encourage development of technologies that will help achieve these goals. Visit `www.section508.gov/` for resources and tools that are provided as a service to help implement Section 508.

- ✔ **Offer to shake hands when you meet someone with a disability for the first time:** If the other person extends the left hand, shake the left hand using your right hand, not your left. If shaking hands isn't possible, a nod of the head is fine. In the United States, a light touch on the shoulder or forearm to acknowledge the person is also appropriate. For example, Senator Bob Dole is disabled in his right arm. He will extend his left hand to you for the handshake and your response should be to extend your right hand, turning it over to meet his left hand to complete a proper handshake.

- ✔ **Avoid staring at someone with a disability or averting your gaze:** Staring and averting your gaze are equally hurtful to a person with a disability. If someone stares at you, it makes you wonder what's so strange. But it may actually be worse if people avert their gaze, which can make you feel that you're so hideous that other people can't stand to look at you. Either way, you feel awful. Not surprisingly, then, my advice is simple: Look everyone in the eye.

- ✔ **"Helping" someone who has a disability is discouraged unless the person has given you permission to do so:** People who have disabilities aren't incompetent. Just as you would be offended by others who routinely offered to carry your briefcase because you're so small or volunteered to make your phone calls for you because your voice sounds like a bullhorn, people with disabilities are offended by patronizing offers of assistance. Refraining from helping someone can be painful sometimes. As painful as watching someone struggle may be, however, a decision to decline your assistance must be respected.

If you're asked to help, ask for specific instructions, and follow them carefully. Otherwise, assume that the person is no less able to care for himself than you are.

Dealing with specific disabilities

Some rules of disability etiquette are firm; others aren't. You should never feed a guide animal, but whether you should help those who have visual impairments cross the street depends on their interest in having your assistance. In the following sections, I explain how to interact with folks who have hearing, visual, and mobility impairments.

Hearing impairments

Hearing disabilities range from the mild to the severe; they're usually hidden and often hard to detect. If you're having difficulty getting a response from someone you are speaking to, he may have a hearing disability. He probably isn't being rude.

If someone is hearing impaired, the best way to get his attention is to move so that he can see you or to touch him lightly on the shoulder or forearm.

If the person with a hearing disability would like to use American Sign Language (ASL), and you know it, by all means use it. If you don't know how to sign, admit it; then either find someone who does know or use writing. Although some people would love to teach you a new language, insisting that a person with a hearing impairment teach you ASL is rude. If you want to learn it, go buy a book or take a class.

If the person has an interpreter, here are a few tips:

- ✔ **The interpreter sits or stands next to you, facing the person with the hearing disability:** An interpreter does not say and use every word you say. Interpreters often explain and paraphrase the meaning of your words, versus a translator, who must, to the best of his ability, use the exact words you have chosen to use, in the translated language. In this situation the translator may fall behind, so pause occasionally to allow him to catch up.

- ✔ **Always talk to the person, not to the interpreter:** In a business situation, never consult the interpreter. The interpreter's job is to facilitate conversation, not to make business decisions. If there are specific industry words the interpreter should learn, make every effort to provide the interpreter with a list or hold a brief meeting ahead of time.

Although interpreters are common in some workplace circles, particularly political and diplomatic ones, they're not universal. Those with hearing impairments often use sign language or read lips. If the person you're talking to can read lips, here are some tips:

- ✔ **Face your conversation partner:** Don't walk around.
- ✔ **Speak clearly and slowly, but naturally:** Exaggerating your lip movement only makes lip-reading harder.
- ✔ **Don't eat or smoke while talking, and don't talk with your hands near your mouth:** These activities may make it difficult for the person who's trying to read your lips.

Avoid these embarrassing mistakes at all costs:

- ✔ **Never shout:** Shouting won't do any good, even if the person has only partial hearing loss.

- ✔ **Never simplify what you say:** You're talking to an adult, not a child.

Visual impairments

Like hearing impairment, vision impairment comes in a wide variety of kinds and degrees. Visual impairments include tunnel vision, in which one sees only a small, central part of the visual field; partial vision, in which one sees a portion of the visual field, usually one side; and total vision impairment, in which one sees nothing.

Always use words with someone who has a visual impairment. Here are some tips to keep in mind:

- ✔ Announce yourself and whoever is with you to the person with a visual disability. Say something like this: "Hi, Juan; it's Sally. I have Wanda Lee with me as well."

- ✔ Say "Hello" and "Goodbye," and tell the person when you're moving around the room.

- ✔ In meetings, use names with exchanges between people to help the person with the visual impairment follow the conversation: "Valerie? John here. Can you give us the latest on the Lohman account?"

- ✔ Offer to read instructions or other printed material aloud.

- ✔ Where danger looms, voice your concerns politely. Say, for example, "Ben, there's a chair directly in front of you. Would you like me to move it?"

You can really inconvenience someone if you make the following blunders:

- ✔ Never touch or move anything in the office of a person with a visual impairment.

- ✔ Never move furniture elsewhere in the office without informing someone with a visual impairment.

People with visual impairments often use a variety of technologies to navigate through the world. Some carry canes, and some are accompanied by guide dogs. Offering assistance to someone with a visual impairment is always appropriate, but if he refuses the offer, accept it politely. And keep the following pointers in mind:

- ✔ **If you're asked to guide, offer your elbow.** Describe your route, announcing upcoming transitions and changes. When you reach your destination, avoid leaving the person in empty space. Find a chair, table, or a wall. Place the person's hand on the back of the chair, on the table, or on the wall for orientation.

> ✔ **At meals, describe the location of the food on the plate by using clock time, such as "Shrimp at 7 o'clock; peas at 3."** Offer to help cut food.
>
> ✔ **When exchanging money, place bills in separate stacks, and present each stack.** Say, for example, "Your change is $47.54. Here are two twenties, one five, and two ones. And here are the 54 cents."
>
> ✔ **When signing documents, offer to guide the person's hand to the correct position, and offer a straight edge (such as a ruler) for alignment.**

When dealing with guide animals, never touch a guide or service animal unless the handler gives you permission, and never call out a guide animal's name. Committing these faux pas is dangerous, not only to the animal and its handler, but also potentially to you. If you touch a guide animal, you may inadvertently be giving it a signal to do something that its handler doesn't want it to do. Also, calling out a guide animal's name can divert its attention from assisting its handler.

Mobility impairments

Mobility impairments vary from walking with difficulty to walking with a cane to using a wheelchair. As always, treat those with mobility impairments with respect.

People with mobility impairments often cannot go where people without those impairments can. Be gracious in picking out routes to destinations, taking the impairment into account.

If someone uses a motorized wheelchair, wait until the wheelchair is powered down to shake hands. When having a conversation with someone in a wheelchair, move so that the two of you are at the same eye level.

Don't let yourself make the following gaffes:

> ✔ While you put a client's coat in the closet, never move mobility aids out of reach.
>
> ✔ Never "try out" another person's mobility aids; they're part of his personal space.
>
> ✔ Never push a person in a wheelchair without permission.
>
> ✔ Never lean or hang on a person's wheelchair.

Going the extra mile

If you have a disability, taking the initiative yourself is perfectly acceptable. At the workplace, you may say, "Jim, I don't know whether you've ever worked with a person with a mobility impairment before. Here are a couple things that will make working together easier for us."

As a colleague or an employer, educate yourself about the assistance technologies that your coworkers use, and adapt your presentations and communications to accommodate them. For example:

- People with hearing impairments use TDDs or similar tools.

- People with visual impairments can use scanners to move text from hard copy pages to computer screen-reading software to synthesize the words on the screen. They include options for magnifying the screen or specific objects on screen, or adjusting the display characteristics to make it easier to read.

- High-tech devices of all kinds are available to individuals with limited mobility.

Respecting Racial and Ethnic Differences

Along with the cultural diversity inherent in the global marketplace comes confusion about how to behave. People don't always know how to interact with others from different ethnic and racial backgrounds. In fact, people don't even know whether their behavior should be different.

Race and ethnicity are less important than your beliefs and attitudes about these things. Don't typecast or stereotype because of physical or cultural features. The paramount rule of etiquette — respect for others — rules out such behavior. Nevertheless, differences do exist, and you need to know how to respect them. You also need to know the etiquette of particular situations and how to adjust your verbal and nonverbal behavior for those situations.

Over time, a standard code has emerged to allow people to get along with one another in business and to know what to expect from each other. Standard American English is the international language of business, and standard Western manners are the official protocol in the United States.

For better or worse, if you don't speak or behave according to these standards, you immediately set yourself up for criticism. But by the same token, if you don't recognize and respect those who follow other traditions, you may get yourself in a jam.

A paradox lurks here. The standards of business etiquette in the United States require Standard American English and Western manners. But Standard American English may not be your native language, and you may be a member of a tradition whose codes of manners are different from Western manners. Luckily, you have a way out: When you're in the United States, do as the Americans do.

You don't have to adopt American business etiquette around the clock, of course. At times, U.S. business etiquette is entirely inappropriate, and your role as a professional need not consume your life entirely. U.S. business etiquette applies when you're doing business in the United States. When you're not doing business, or when you're not doing business in the United States, other codes of etiquette may apply. This is code change.

In addition, knowing more than one language helps almost everyone in the business world. Learning even a few words and phrases can be a real plus. In certain businesses — the music industry, for example — slang and jargon are useful. But in almost all other situations, speaking and writing clearly and grammatically are paramount (see Part II for communication tips).

Now that you can communicate, how do you behave? Respect dictates that you take it upon yourself to learn about other cultures. If your business regularly takes you to other parts of the world, take a course in protocol, or read about those parts of the world. Flip to Part V to find out how to do business on a global scale.

Respecting Gender and Sexual Differences

Dealing with gender and sex in the workplace can be a mess. In the same way that business is color blind, it is sex blind.

The way to get along is to assume that everyone has a sex life — and then forget about it! I don't mean that everyone has to act the same way or that you can't express your individuality. But what people do in their private lives is exactly that: private. Don't assume that everyone is heterosexual; don't assume that everyone is gay. Assume that other people are interested in love and sex but that the details are none of your business. Never make jokes or snide remarks about gender or sexual preference.

Business is gender blind. What matters are rank and status, not gender. You may be completely stumped when it comes to working with members of the opposite gender, however. If you're a woman, do you open the door for others? Do you wait for your male boss to open the door for you?

To prevent crashes, here's the rule: In business, the first person to the door opens the door for everyone else, regardless of gender. Full arms exempt you from door duty, however.

Like all good rules, this one has an exception: You always open the door for your client or customer.

Use the following common-sense tips as a guide to intergender relations:

- ✔ Offer to help an overburdened colleague, regardless of gender. If your colleague has an armful of books and papers, for example, offer to take some of them.

- ✔ The host pays for a business lunch, regardless of gender.

- ✔ Help others if they're having a difficult time with a coat, regardless of gender.

- ✔ Men and women stand to greet someone, regardless of the other person's gender.

- ✔ Women shake hands in business, as men do.

Chapter 4

Look Sharp! Creating Professional Style and Presence

∙ ∙

In This Chapter
▶ Beginning with wardrobe basics
▶ Putting together workplace attire for women and men
▶ Grooming yourself properly
▶ Minding your body language

∙ ∙

*L*ike it or not, most people believe that what you see is what you get. What they usually see first is your clothes. Clothes are a nonverbal code of communication. What you wear signals your image to others. What signals do you want to send?

In business, creativity in ideas is often more important than creativity in dress. Derived from the military dress code, the idea here is that if everyone dresses in a relatively similar manner, the playing field isn't so bumpy. Some restraint is appropriate, because you want to emphasize the product or service of your company, not your wacky sense of personal style (which is why you have days off). You are the vehicle for the product or the service, not the center of attention.

Then you have to consider your body language. Comporting yourself with ease and dignity signals to others that you care enough about them, and enough about yourself, to pay attention to your physical presence. This chapter helps you be aware of what your clothes and your body are saying.

The basic etiquette principle of not calling too much attention to yourself applies to clothes, too.

The Essentials of Building an Appropriate Work Wardrobe

No doubt about it — clothes are a source of anxiety in the business world. So many styles are appropriate in today's business world that getting dressed in the morning can be baffling.

The solution? KISS — Keep It Simple and Sophisticated. You want your confidence to come from your professional abilities, not to be manufactured in Italy. Still, your clothes are important; if you dress with your next position in mind, you're more likely to get there.

In this section, I describe the staples of any work wardrobe, explain how to deal with formal dress codes and casual work environments, and show you how to take inventory of what you own before you start shopping.

Sticking to basic colors and pieces

Memorize these colors:

- ✔ Navy blue
- ✔ Charcoal gray
- ✔ Black
- ✔ Khaki
- ✔ White

These hues are the staple colors of every business wardrobe. Regardless of how formal or casual you are or whether you're male or female, these colors are the ones you start with. Don't get me wrong; color can look great. A bright-colored shirt, for example, can punch up a dark gray suit for both men and women. But in general, you are better off starting with the neutrals I just listed and adding color, rather than starting with color and trying to find something appropriate to match. You can add a mango shirt, tie, or scarf to a charcoal suit more easily than you can accessorize a mango suit.

Here are some guidelines for both men and women to keep in mind:

- ✔ **In the suit world, start with the basics:** A navy blue wool suit and a charcoal wool suit, white shirts, black shoes, black belt, and black leather briefcase/notebook computer case.

- ✔ **In the casual world, start with the basics:** Khaki pants or skirts, white shirts, black or brown shoes and belt, and a black or brown leather or ballistic nylon briefcase/notebook computer case.

> ✔ **Add your own touches in keeping with your company's dress code and style.**

This system is rigid, of course, and you certainly don't have to follow it exactly. But starting with a good foundation of high-quality, neutral-tone clothing allows you to build a wardrobe that minimizes your anxiety and maximizes your investment. Remember to buy the best quality you can afford. Your wardrobe is an investment in your profession; treat it accordingly. With some discipline, you can create a wardrobe that stays current and looks smart without breaking your paycheck.

You shouldn't feel uncomfortable or present an image that is not you, but you *should* present the best you that you possibly can.

Dealing with dress codes

A wrinkle in business clothes is that different businesses and professions have different dress codes. If you're in a traditional profession like law or banking and you're calling on clients or having business lunches, you want to dress within the basic guidelines for that profession. In this case, that would be more on the conservative side — business suits and ties for men; business suits, skirts, slacks, and jackets for women. In some cases, depending on the style, a dress is appropriate. The most current dress style to own for work is a classic sheath.

If you work in a more informal environment or the hi-tech industry, a less conservative or business-casual attire is appropriate. (Read on for more on the business-casual dilemma.)

Most companies today have a dress code, which may be articulated in an official document available from the human resources department. If so, get a copy of it and read it. More frequently, the dress code is unstated but enforced by practice. In these cases, you simply have to watch and learn. Watch the people around you, especially your boss. Whether your boss is a man or a woman, notice the style. How formal is it? Plan your wardrobe in a similar style. If your boss always wears suits, you should buy a suit or two. But you don't have to match exactly; use your own personal style.

You don't need a millionaire's budget to be perceived as confident and self-assured. Being *consistently* well groomed, tidy, and dressed in attire that fits you properly is far more important than the designer label or cost of your clothing. Wear clothing that is appropriate, of the best quality you can afford, and in good taste. Your clothing should reflect your positive attitude toward yourself, your work, and others.

If you work in retail or advertising, you usually have many more clothing options. Within the limits of what is considered good taste (and assuming you're young enough), you can add a little flair by wearing the latest trends and fads — many times your employer encourages this.

Defining "business casual" and "casual"

The casual look has invaded business in a big way. Dressing casually for business takes a great deal of thought, however. Casual may allow for something other than a suit, but it doesn't mean that you should go to work in a skimpy top and Birkenstocks (unless you work at a surf shop). Business casual isn't the same as other kinds of casual.

Business-casual wear is its own category and has caused a lot of confusion in the business world. Before business casual was in existence, the terms used were *formal business* wear, *informal business* wear, and *casual* wear. (These terms are still used today as well.)

Business-casual wear is a growing trend and an accepted dress code that started in white-collar companies in the late 1980s and early 1990s, particularly in the information technology businesses in Silicon Valley, California. (Just to add to the confusion, business casual is also referred to as *smart casual.*) In some parts of the United States (and other countries), this style of dress or work attire has taken the place of formal business wear or international standard business attire (suits, neckties, and dress shoes).

Just to make everything even more confusing, business casual and *Friday* casual are different:

- Business casual (or casual) for men generally means khaki pants, dress slacks in linen or wool, Dockers, or corduroys with a sports jacket, button-down shirt, or sweater, and a casual loafer or Dr. Martens shoes.

- *Friday* casual includes all the preceding items but adds jeans, tennis shoes, and, in some workplaces, T-shirts. This doesn't include inappropriate items, such as shorts, revealing tops, or soiled or ragged clothing.

Taking stock of what you have

Begin by thinking about your profession and your place of work, and your leisure time. If the two are very different, separate your work wardrobe from your leisure or casual wardrobe. Before you pull out the credit card and head for the mall, take inventory of what you currently own by following these steps:

1. **Take everything out of your closets, drawers, boxes, and laundry baskets.**

2. **Divide your clothes, shoes, and accessories into piles.** The rule to remember is that if you haven't worn the item in six months, get rid of

it! Please be environmentally conscious and try your best to toss out as little as possible. Take into consideration whether the item of clothing can be donated or used for another purpose. Leather shoes can take up to 40 years to decompose.

- Everything with holes, stains, or rips goes into the "fix or toss" pile.

- Everything that doesn't fit right now goes into the "donate" or "sell" pile.

- Separate clothing that you consider as wearable, yet casual, non-work clothing.

- Separate everything that may qualify as business attire.

3. **Look carefully at all items that qualify as business attire, including formal and informal (business casual).**

   Do they really fit? Try them on to be sure. If they don't, move them to the donate or sell stack. Are they worn out or hopelessly out-of-date? If so (be honest), they go to the donate or sell pile.

4. **Divide the clothes in the "fix or toss" pile into those items that can be repaired and those that cannot.**

   If clothes can be repaired, take them to a good tailor or to Goodwill. Try to recycle items whenever possible.

Now you should have examined your entire wardrobe and accessories enough to know what you own.

Casual Workplace Wear for Women

Casual business attire (or business casual) for women requires some thought because women have so many choices. Keep to the KISS principle — Keep It Simple and Sophisticated — even with casual clothes. Dark colors convey authority; bright colors convey friendliness. Light colors, such as taupe and khaki, generally are more casual than black, gray, and navy.

Because all casual clothing is not suitable for the office, the following guidelines can help you determine what is appropriate to wear to work. Here are a few tips to get you started:

✔ Start with the following items:

- A dark jacket and several high-quality cotton shirts and plain white blouses.

- Dark skirts or pants (boot-cut or straight leg) and one or two dresses (sheath style). Select colors in a dark neutral shade such as black, brown, navy blue, or gray.

- Three to four pairs of high-quality leather shoes (in brown, black, and navy).

✔ Twin sets or other sweaters (cardigans) — which can be a great place to add color — provide more finish than just a shirt or blouse but are less formal than a jacket.

✔ Ensembles are casual variations on the traditional suit. Many items come in coordinated fabrics that you can mix and match. Pair them with a crisp white or colored blouse or a light sweater and/or jacket, an A-line or straight (pencil) skirt, and slacks or pants. You may wear matching jackets, pants, and skirts together for a more formal look or as separates for a more casual look.

✔ Dark colors are a good first choice for jackets, pants, and skirts because they wear well. Add blouses and shirts, scarves, belts, shoes, and jewelry in interesting colors and textures.

TIP

✔ Consider having your colors analyzed by a color expert. By knowing what color looks best (and worst) on you, you can choose items to buy and wear that will always enhance your appearance. Even without having your colors done professionally, you can normally tell what colors look best on you. Take a moment to see how the color makes you feel. If you're shopping, ask a salesperson's opinion. Also, take notice of the color you're wearing when you receive compliments like "Gee, that color looks great on you!" Eventually, you'll figure it out.

FAUX PAS

A number of small things can kill a positive impression. Try to avoid these image and fashion mistakes:

✔ Excessive use of bright color and wild patterns

✔ Excessive jewelry or jewelry that signals your arrival with tiny clinking sounds

✔ Shoes that always "match" your blouse

✔ Any sheer fabrics that show your undergarments

✔ Undergarment straps showing and visible panty lines

✔ Wrinkled or stained clothing

✔ Loose hems

✔ Spiky, strappy sandals in metallic colors or with rhinestones, or open-toed shoes (not appropriate for most businesses)

✔ Missing buttons

✔ Dirty or overly bleached or colored hair or obvious roots

✔ Chipped nail polish

✔ Chewing gum

Business-casual dress codes have been established to allow employees to work comfortably in the workplace while still projecting a professional image on the job, with customers or clients.

Formal Business Clothes for Women

You're well advised to stay conservative at a formal workplace until it's blazingly obvious that you don't have to. You'll want to have some suits and appropriate, conservative coordinates in your business wardrobe.

Suits

The keys to suits (either skirt suits or pantsuits) are fabric, fit, and comfort:

- ✔ For autumn, winter, and spring, wool is still the best choice. For summer, cotton, gabardines, and linen are good choices, especially if blended with a small amount of polyester and other stretchy fabrics. Tropic weight wool and other wool blends are another good option. (I explain these types of fabrics in the later section about men's suits.)

  If you work in an office, you can occasionally wear leather effectively, but the key to doing so is keeping it understated and tailored. Any hints of the motorcycle world or other dark regions are off-limits.

- ✔ Have the suit professionally fitted if you have problems with off-the-rack clothes. Choose suits with jackets and skirts that are appropriate for your body type. Long jackets that cover the hips can be flattering to some women, yet many of the short styles today also look professional. Buy clothes that you can wear now rather than clothes you may be able to wear someday, if only. . . .

- ✔ Comfortable clothing is essential not only because it's distracting to be constantly tugging, pulling, or adjusting an item, but also because clothes that are either too loose, too tight, too long, or too short look unprofessional.

Navy blue, black, charcoal gray, taupe, white, burgundy, and forest green are acceptable business colors. Although dark colors typically are worn in winter, winter white is also making a fashion statement. Light colors are worn in the spring and summer. This rule really is no longer hard and fast. Some women can wear red, but oranges, yellows, bright purples, and other loud colors are best used in small amounts.

Skirts

The most important things to concern yourself with here are fit and length:

- ✔ Don't make your skirt too tight, and don't make it too short. Sit down in front of a mirror. If you're concerned about the view in any way, the skirt is too short. Likewise, if you must walk like a geisha, the skirt is too tight.

- ✔ If you appear to have just arrived from Queen Victoria's court, the skirt is too long. Straight skirts are preferred over full or pleated skirts, all other things being equal. But all other things are rarely equal, so if you wear full or pleated skirts, make them longer than straight skirts. Business skirts typically are hemmed just around the knee.

Pantsuits

You find pantsuits, which are flattering for most women, in almost every venue of the contemporary business world. Keep the colors muted: blue, black, charcoal, taupe, burgundy, and some greens are good choices. And make sure that your pantsuit is fitted properly.

Blouses and shirts

What you wear with your suit is as important as the suit itself. Blouses made of transparent material are inappropriate. High-quality cotton and silk are good choices, as are high-quality microfiber blends. Collars on women's blouses and shirts are much more varied than those on men's shirts. Have fun, but avoid the Tinker Bell look. Choose opaque materials for business shirts, and coordinate your blouse color with your suit color. Whatever you do, avoid wearing tank tops or any low-cut top. What about today's trend of wearing lingerie as outerwear? Some of these slip style of tops can be worn under jackets; however, it doesn't come across as professional, so save them for evenings.

Any attire that reveals too much cleavage, skin, your midriff, or your undergarments is not appropriate for the workplace, even in a casual business setting.

Stockings and pantyhose

Pantyhose and stockings are both acceptable in the workplace, so long as they're matched to your other clothes, aren't heavily patterned, and don't suggest anything other than a commitment to work. Currently, very sheer skin-toned stockings are the standard, although some people prefer black or gray with dark skirts. During warm months, or if you feel comfortable doing so, going without pantyhose is fine (though wearing underwear is *always* advisable).

Shoes

Even if you've never bothered to visit the cobbler, in business, I strongly advise you to take care of your shoes. Keep them functional, attractive, clean, and shined.

Have you found a scuff on your favorite pair of black pumps? Keep a black marker with you to touch up scuffed shoes.

Most women find that low-heeled pumps or flats are suitable for the vast majority of business situations. They're good-looking, comfortable, and available in sufficient variety to coordinate with anything you may be wearing. Make sure that you have at least one or two pairs of good-quality black shoes to wear year-round.

Never wear white shoes (except sneakers) before Memorial Day or after Labor Day — unless you're a bride.

Heels can be as high as, say, 1½ or 2 inches, but heels much higher than that look unprofessional. Keep the higher heels for your skirts; 2-inch heels with a pantsuit are too dressy for day.

Open-toed sandals or shoes and mules are popular but inappropriate in conservative establishments. Hiking boots, clogs, running shoes, spike heels, and platforms are appropriate for specialty businesses only.

Accessories

Welcome to the bottomless pit of accessories! What if you don't know 397 ways to tie a scarf? What if you don't know anything about jewelry or handbags? Don't worry; you can still save your wardrobe by keeping it simple and sophisticated.

Handbags

Handbags should be large enough to carry a few items of makeup and whatever technology you use to plan your week, but no larger. Your handbag shouldn't be able to carry your weekly groceries or your dry cleaning.

Don't skimp on quality; buy the best handbag you can afford. Dark leather is by far the best choice; save the bright colors for social occasions. Though they are quite fashionable, avoid spangles, sparkles, and jewels on handbags unless you work at the local retro fashion shop.

Briefcases

You still find briefcases at the end of most businesspeople's arms. Some women carry a briefcase in lieu of a handbag, which is much neater. If you must carry an additional handbag, keep it small.

Increasingly, the briefcase and notebook computer bag are merging into one article. Briefcases traditionally are made of black or brown leather, and again, black is the dressier of the two. Don't skimp on quality. For a more professional look, coordinate your handbag color with your briefcase color. If you choose a separate notebook computer bag in addition to a briefcase and handbag, make sure that they all coordinate.

In some professions, canvas or ballistic-nylon bags are de rigueur. Watch those around you to see whether this alternative is common in your business.

Belts

Belts should be leather and ½ to ¾ inch thick, though if they're worn properly, some of the wider belts, worn lower on the hips, can look stylish. Coordinate their color with your outfit. Avoid metallic belts, belts covered with studs, bejeweled belts, and belts made of plastic or fur. Buckles should be subdued and smallish, made of metal or leather.

Proper attire dictates that when a garment (such as pants) has belt loops, you are supposed to wear a belt to be fully and properly dressed.

Scarves

Scarves are readily acceptable in all but the stuffiest workplaces. They should be made of silk, wool, cashmere, or a blend of these fabrics. Cotton scarves rarely hang properly for long.

Some part of the scarf should match some color in your outfit. Although you can wear a scarf in different ways — under a jacket, draped over the shoulder, as an ascot, in your hair — always make sure that it looks as though it's meant to be there, rather than as though you forgot to put your towel back on the rack after your shower. Avoid really loud scarves, metallic scarves, and scarves with obvious topography.

Jewelry

Some women are nuts about jewelry — the more, the better. But in business, this enthusiasm is best replaced with another maxim: Less is more. Keep your jewelry simple and understated.

Very delicate jewelry looks best on small-boned women. Clunky jewelry is best on big-boned gals. Here are a few additional jewelry tips:

- **Earrings can be of precious metal, such as silver or gold, and can contain diamonds or pearls.** Hollow hoops, so long as they are smallish, are acceptable as well. Match your earrings' size, shape, and color to your necklace (if you're wearing one), and make sure that any color coordinates with your garment colors. Even if larger earrings are in vogue, save the enormous or jangly ones for social occasions, especially if your job requires you to make presentations. You don't want the audience to be distracted by your jewelry.

- **Necklaces can be of precious metal, such as silver or gold, or of pearls.** Match your necklace shape to the collar shape of your blouse or other garment. A V-shaped necklace with a round collar doesn't cut it.

- **Watches can be either analog or digital.** All things considered, analog watches (those with faces and hands) are still better than digital watches. A large digital or sports watch that boasts an altimeter and a computer isn't appropriate, even if you did wear it on your last trip to Mount Everest.

  Choose your watch band carefully. Make sure that it complements your other jewelry and garments. Leather (black or brown) and matte metal bands are acceptable, with a slight edge going to black leather. Also, avoid joke watches, cartoon watches, and watches that are hard to read or require a professional maintenance team.

- **Brooches and pins should be worn only when you don't wear a necklace.** Make sure that the brooch is large enough not to be lost but not so large as to draw attention to itself or look like a *Star Trek* communications badge. Brooch shape is best coordinated with suit style: edgy with blunt-cut jackets and V-necked and square-necked blouses; rounded with round-necked blouses.

- **Rings should be simple and few.** Big sparklers are not appropriate at the office unless they're part of your engagement ring. Your best bet is to limit rings to a wedding ring/engagement ring/anniversary ring set. If you must, you may add a small class ring or family heirloom on the ring finger of your right hand.

Eyeglasses

A person who wears glasses has the greatest responsibility to choose a pair that fits their face and personality. Eyeglasses frame your face and either bring out your best features or, if they're the wrong style, detract from your features. For most people, finding the right look and fit for your face is the absolute toughest thing to achieve. There are just too many choices out there from which to choose! As with other fashion, be sure the style fits your profession. If you work in a law firm, you may not want to wear glasses with bright red frames.

At one time, large bright-colored or metallic glasses were thought to bring authority to women in business. Those days are gone, and so are all the tired facial muscles that went along with these glasses.

Today's look in eyeglasses is small and stylish. Glasses are among the few areas in business dress where you're allowed to assert your individuality even in conservative environments. Like ties, glasses are a small enough part of the overall look to accommodate creativity without ruining the outfit. With this choice, of course, comes the responsibility to assert yourself with care. You can certainly wear your red glasses with the pineapple inlays on the temples, but you may also want to have a more subdued pair on hand if you're meeting with old Mr. Fuddyduddy to discuss his annuity portfolio.

Never wear tinted glasses in the office; they make you look shady! Lenses that change color with available light are acceptable, however.

Casual Workplace Wear for Men

Business casual can be a tough assignment for some men. While most men understand formal or business dress (suit, white shirt, tie, polished dress shoes), they have difficulty when the occasion calls for attire that falls somewhere between formal business dress and casual dress. One of the biggest reasons that men struggle with sharp casual clothing is there is some gray area with company policies and the guidelines of business casual.

As I explained in the earlier section "Defining 'business casual' and 'casual,'" business casual and Friday casual are distinct from one another:

- ✔ Business casual generally means khaki pants, a plain polo shirt or a long-sleeved casual button-down oxford shirt, a V-neck sweater, sometimes a sports coat or blazer, and brown leather shoes. Loafers are a good choice, and you should wear socks.

- ✔ Friday casual includes all the above, and in some companies can include jeans, T-shirts, and tennis shoes, but this does not mean ratty or torn jeans, and it never means cutoffs or an old T-shirt with something offensive written on it.

Don't forget these general guidelines:

- ✔ A short-sleeved shirt is, by definition, always a casual shirt.

- ✔ Khaki and flannel pants are casual for most businesses.

- ✔ Tank tops, shorts, and sandals are weekend wear, not business wear.

- ✔ Advertising, artist, and fashion types can wear leather jackets.

- ✔ Plain shirts are best in general; shirts with ads on them are for fishing.

- ✔ Button-down oxford shirts are casual; T-shirts are for musicians and computer types (and for mowing the lawn).

- ✔ Loafers and dark walking shoes are casual; clean sneakers, running shoes, and hiking boots are for play but can make occasional appearances on Fridays.

- ✔ Blazers and sports coats are casual for some businesses and dressy for others.

Formal Business Clothes for Men

Men don't have as many options as women do. Formal means a suit of some sort, but dressing well means much more than just slapping on a suit, as I explain in the following sections.

Suits

If you're a professional, you probably own at least a few suits: two or three made of wool and other blends for autumn and winter and one made of cotton or tropic weight wool and microfibers for spring and summer. When choosing a suit, look first for fabric, fit, and comfort; look second for style.

Fabrics include wool, cotton, linen, and various microfibers. Wool is easily the most versatile fabric, coming in summer or tropic weight and winter weight and in a variety of fabric styles. Worsted wool is composed of tightly twisted fibers; gabardine and crepe are worsted wools. Various woolen fabrics, such as tweed and flannel, are more loosely twisted. Wool blends are fabrics in which wool is woven with microfibers such as nylon or polyester. Although wool-blend suits aren't as traditional as worsted wools or tweed, they are strong and durable, and they feel good.

Cotton and linen suits are also available. One classic cotton suit is the seersucker, a vertically striped affair rarely found off the East Coast or out of the Deep South. Linen suits are popular in some quarters because they're comfortable in extreme heat and high humidity. But be forewarned: Linen wrinkles immediately. Although these two fabrics have their adherents, tropic-weight wool is still by far the most popular choice for a summer suit.

Your suit fabric should never shine or change colors in different lighting.

You can choose among three basic suit styles (and their multiple variations):

- ✔ **American cut:** These suits can have two or three buttons. They have center-vented jackets with natural shoulders, and pants with a straight line.

- ✔ **Italian cut:** These suits have unvented jackets with padded shoulders, and pants that are fuller than those in American-cut suits.

- ✔ **British cut:** These suits have side-vented or unvented jackets with square shoulders and a tapered waist, and pants that are narrower than those in both American-cut and Italian-cut suits.

When standing or walking, button the top button of a two-button jacket; button the middle button of a three-button jacket. Unbutton your jacket when sitting down. If you button all the buttons on a suit, you'll look like you did when you were a 4-year-old ring bearer at your Aunt Ellie's wedding.

Double-breasted suits rarely look as good as you think they will.

The only rule about fit is that you have the suit professionally tailored. Purchasing a $1,500 suit off the rack is absolutely pointless if it won't be tailored to fit you. As I mention earlier in this chapter, regardless of the price tag of the garment, if it doesn't fit properly, it ruins the entire image. Normally clothing that is more expensive is well-made and fits better, so buying high quality can pay off in the long run. Most good men's clothing stores and department stores have tailors, and many times alterations are a complimentary service. Even if you think the suit looks great and fits properly, get the opinion of a good tailor first. Long sleeves, long jackets, long pants, and shoulders that are too large destroy the overall appearance.

If the back of the collar of the suit has a gap, it does not fit well. The collar should always be sitting on the back of your neck, even when you move about. That shows it is a well-fitted suit.

As for color, navy blue, black, charcoal gray, and dark brown are the standard colors for business suits. Navy blue and charcoal gray wool are excellent choices for first suits. Conservative pinstriped suits are acceptable in some businesses, as are some patterned suits. Khaki and tan make appearances in late spring and summer only. An exception: You can wear the camel-hair sports coat year-round.

Brush off your jackets and pants at the end of each day and before you leave the house in the morning. If you don't have a clothing brush, you can use masking tape or a pet tape roller.

Pants

Traditional dress slacks or more casual khakis, corduroys, and wool and linen pants are appropriate, either with or without a jacket or blazer, though a sports jacket can pull the look together. No matter what style of pant you wear, always make sure they are ironed neatly and fit properly.

Shirts

Buy five long-sleeved white shirts and five long-sleeved light blue shirts. (There's no such thing as a short-sleeved dress shirt.) If you work in a conservative environment, you've just finished your shirt shopping!

Collar styles come and go. Currently, spread collars, point collars of various extremes, and button-down collars all have their purposes:

- ✔ Spread collars are considered to be dressiest because you can't wear them without a tie.
- ✔ Point collars are the best compromise collars because they look good with or without a tie.
- ✔ Hidden button-downs are increasingly popular. Button-down collars are still quite popular for certain professions (such as academia and publishing) and for casual-wear days.

Socks

Socks are simple: Like shoes, socks should be at least as dark as your suit or pants when it comes to formal and business-casual attire. Wear dark socks coordinated with the color of your suit. Wear khaki or dark brown socks with khakis. Patterns are permissible so long as they're not ostentatious. Socks should be cotton, wool, or silk. Polyester socks will create problems I'd rather not discuss here. Socks should be mid-calf or full calf in length to prevent your untanned shins from blinding others.

White socks are unacceptable in business. And in case the thought crosses your mind, wearing no socks is equally unacceptable.

Shoes

Match your footwear to your clothing and the occasion. Wearing wing tips with a casual pant or khaki is too dressy; wearing an informal loafer style is best. Laced shoes are more appropriate with a formal suit. Well-shined shoes show you care about detail. Like socks, shoes are relatively simple: Plain- and cap-toed oxfords, wingtips, and plain or tasseled loafers are the extent of your choices for dress business shoes. There are suede styles that can be worn for a more casual look.

Your shoes should be at least as dark as your suit. Coordinate your shoe color with your suit color: black shoes with charcoal gray, black, and navy blue suits, and brown shoes with brown and tan suits.

To prolong the life of your shoes, keep shoetrees in your closet and use them to retain your shoes' shape and size. Also, keep a shoeshine kit in your closet and polish your shoes at least once a week or wipe them down the day you wear them. And, if heels get worn down, have them replaced.

Keep a black marker with you to touch up scuffed shoes.

Accessories

You're probably thinking, "Real men don't accessorize!" Think again. The little things are what matter most.

Briefcases

Briefcases traditionally are black or brown leather. Don't skimp on quality. If you choose a notebook computer bag instead, hold it to the same high-quality standards you would a briefcase.

The debate of the ages: Do you wear black or brown shoes with navy blue?

There are two trains of thought when it comes to the color of shoe you wear with navy blue (for both men and women). There are some rules of fashion that state all shades of blue are incompatible with any shades of brown, and black shoes always will be de rigueur with navy blue suits. (Take notice of military uniforms.) Then there are those who believe brown is seen as more sophisticated than black and that a brown shoe can look elegant. However, this only applies if the shoes are a dark hue of brown, not light brown or tan. If your brown shoes are of a darkness approaching black, you're in good shape.

Belts

Belts should match or closely match the color and texture of your shoes. Your socks should match your pants. Brown shoes, brown belt; black shoes, black belt; and so on.

Ties

Ah, the tie! Do you use it to express your individuality or your bank balance? Or do you think that attempting to express your inner soul through your tie is lame? Either way, follow these simple rules with ties:

- ✔ Ties should be silk.
- ✔ Ties should be understated.
- ✔ Ties should be coordinated with the suit and shirt.
- ✔ Ties should end at the top of your belt.

Play it safe. If you're partial to the unusual, keep an extra clean white shirt and a couple of plain or understated ties in your office, just in case your conservative client pays a surprise visit. Don't wear Mickey Mouse ties unless other people in your office wear Bugs Bunny or Dilbert.

The bow tie is a special case. If you work in a think tank or at an Ivy League university, bow ties are acceptable. But outside the tradition-obsessed halls of academia and jurisprudence, the bow tie is often (perhaps unfairly) treated with suspicion. So be careful: If you love yourself in a bow tie and think that there aren't enough bow-tied men in the world, go for it.

Watches

If you go for status symbols, buy an expensive watch. Otherwise, a medium-range watch with a leather or metal band is the way to go.

Eyeglasses

As with women, a man who wears glasses should select a pair that fits his face and personality. Choose a pair that is flattering. Try to update the style of your glasses every three to four years. Wearing styles that went out of style years ago can age a person. Take the time to see what's new. Looking through a men's fashion magazine can be helpful.

Hats

Forty years ago, fedoras were the hats of choice. Today, the only hat of choice, it seems, is the baseball cap. Let these rules suffice: Make sure that baseball caps are insignia free, and don't wear them indoors at any time. Other hats — especially winter hats that offer varying degrees of arctic protection — are acceptable out in the elements but not in the building.

You Clean Up Well! Personal Hygiene and Grooming

Wearing the right clothes does no good if you haven't bathed or your nails are dirty. Bathe or shower every day, and use a deodorant or antiperspirant; then use the specific guidelines in the following sections.

Hands

Everyone should follow these guidelines for hands:

- ✔ Keep your hands and fingernails scrupulously clean and well cared for.
- ✔ Don't bite your nails or cuticles.
- ✔ Keep your cuticles pushed back.
- ✔ Get an occasional professional manicure. Both men and women benefit from this treatment.

Women should follow these guidelines for nails:

- ✔ **Clear nail polish is easy to maintain.** If you wear colored nail polish, stick to red or pink, and get a professional manicure weekly. Do your best to never go out with chipped nail polish. Keep a color handy at work for the occasional accident.
- ✔ **Nails should be no longer than half an inch beyond the end of your fingers.** If you can't pick up a dime with your fingertips, your nails are too long.

Men, your rules are simple: Nails should be clean, short, buffed, and filed.

Hair

Hair should be clean, well-combed, and trimmed. Eliminate dandruff with a good shampoo. Other than that, almost anything goes. (Everyone looks bad in a mullet, of course.)

Ladies, keep your hair out of your eyes. If your hair is long, consider pulling it back, but avoid looking like a schoolgirl. Barrettes and other ornamentation should be simple.

Men, keep your hair trimmed and orderly. Long hair is acceptable in some companies but not in others. If yours is too long for the company where you've been hired, you'll be told so. If you aren't told, ask. If your hair is long, consider pulling it back in a ponytail. If you have a beard or other facial hair, keep it trimmed and free of crumbs. If necessary, shave your neck and upper chest to below your T-shirt line. Eyebrows, nostrils, and ears should be free of stragglers at all times. Shave every day and before leaving the office, if necessary, if you have an evening appointment.

Face

Wash your face daily. If you have acne, consult a dermatologist; many excellent treatments are available.

Also, you should brush your teeth after every meal. Equip your office with a toothbrush, toothpaste, breath mints, and mouthwash.

A woman's makeup should enhance her natural features, not create new ones. A foundation that matches her skin tone, lipstick, mascara, and a light dusting of powder are often enough. Heavy eyeliner, metallic or bright-colored eye shadow, and thick rouge are only for the stage.

Scents

Use perfume or aftershave/cologne sparingly so that it neither precedes you nor lingers after you.

Piercings and tattoos

Tattoos shouldn't be visible during the business day. In more conservative business settings, remove your piercing ornaments during the day.

Sending All the Right Signals: Body Language and Comportment

Clothes may make the person, but body language may make or break the deal. How you carry yourself when engaged in conversation is often as important as what you say. Body language is nonverbal, but it communicates volumes about you nonetheless. Paying attention to your body language communicates to others that you pay attention to detail.

Body language is an interpretive affair. Like most human behavior, your physical behavior is symbolic. Take some simple examples:

✔ **Failure to maintain eye contact during conversations is a sign of evasiveness and cowardice to some people.** In some cultures, however, avoiding eye contact is polite behavior.

✔ **Stroking your chin while thinking is supposed by some people to indicate reflection and deep thought.** But sometimes, your chin just itches.

The truth is that practically any behavior you engage in can be freighted with significance. You may scratch your ear one evening in a bar and, unknown to you, signal the man with the newspaper that the diamonds are in the umbrella stand.

With almost infinite symbolic interpretations for body language, no wonder people are nervous about it! Your best bet is to know about some of the body-language pits you can fall into and how to avoid them.

Standing

When you stand, you want to stand with your back straight, middle section in alignment with your back, shoulders back, and head up. This posture connotes comfort with yourself and ease in the situation.

Slouching, sticking your belly out, stuffing your hands in your pockets, and folding your arms defensively all suggest aggressive unease. Winding yourself up like a corkscrew, with your ankles crossed and your arms holding themselves, is the very picture of insecurity and nervousness.

Sitting

Take care in the way you sit, for no other position connotes so much on its own. Think of the diversity of sitting positions that you've seen in business meetings, from practically horizontal to alert and upright. Sit with a straight back and with your legs together in front of you or crossed, either at the knee or at the ankle. Normally, women don't cross their legs, but men are allowed.

Given male and female physiology, the position of your legs while sitting can send some primeval signals to those around you. Take care that the signals you send are neither overtly nor covertly aggressive or sexual:

✔ **Jiggling your knee is a sign of nervousness.**

✔ **Leaning forward can suggest aggressiveness at times, so do so with care.**

✔ **Leaning back with your hands behind your head and your pelvis lifted is an unseemly display for a man.** So is sitting with your legs open if no desk shields your conversation partner from you. Avoid sitting with one ankle over the other knee in all but the most casual settings.

✔ **Leaning back with your legs crossed and one side off the seat of the chair is an unseemly display for a woman.** So is sitting like a sexy starlet on a late-night talk show.

Hands

Some people talk with their hands; others stand there with their hands glued to their sides. Most people haven't the foggiest notion what their hands are doing when they talk.

Using your hands can be effective sometimes, aggressive sometimes, and irrelevant most of the time. Using your index finger can be effective in emphasizing a point. But plenty of chest-pointing bosses use their hands in a barely controlled way to assert their power over you.

Controlling your hands takes effort and willpower. Monitor your hand movements. Avoid making sweeping, cappuccino-clearing gestures during meetings. If you have to, sit on your hands.

Head movements

Head movements communicate important information. Nodding in agreement can be immensely helpful to others, but too much nodding makes you look like one of those bobbing dogs in the back window of a car. Shaking your head can signal disagreement or disapproval, but avoid shaking your head too much.

Facial expressions

Facial expressions are crucial in your repertoire of body language. No other part of your body can convey the immense richness of nonverbal communication that your face does. For example:

✔ You already know that smiles are important signals of generosity and nonaggression. But forced smiles are neither: They're signals that you can barely tolerate the other person. And incessant smiles are signals of servility or foolishness.

✔ Likewise, frowns signal disagreement, disapproval, and sometimes anger. But they can also suggest hard thinking and focused concentration.

These facial expressions are the most obvious ones, but hundreds of others exist: an arched eyebrow, pursed lips, flared nostrils, squinting eyes, a wrinkled nose, a bitten lip, a tongue out of the mouth, a grimace, widely opened eyes . . . and on and on. Every one of them has a culturally agreed-on set of meanings.

Take a day to monitor your most frequently used facial expressions, and when the inventory is complete, assess their appropriateness and their effectiveness. You'll probably be surprised by the kinds of things you weren't even aware that you do!

You can learn to control all these emotions and develop a poker face, of course. Some people think that a poker face is a great thing to have in business.

Eyes

Maintain eye contact when talking with others. Do not study your hands or clean your fingernails while others are talking. When talking in a group, make eye contact with everyone; don't focus on only one person.

Part II
Building Better Communication Skills

The 5th Wave   By Rich Tennant

BUSINESS LETTERS TO AVOID

Scented letters

Origami letters

Frivolous letters

Confusing letters

In this part . . .

I help you get started by tackling one of your most common challenges: meeting and greeting other people. Many of us get tripped up on introductions, so I set you on the right path about who to introduce to whom, how to use titles, and how to give the all-important firm hand-shake. Then I give you tips on making sparkling business conversation that everyone will want to be part of.

Speaking on the telephone is another situation in which manners seem to slide, so you discover how to speak and listen considerately on the phone. You explore new tactics for handling voice mail, cell phones, and more. You also look at the written word and ways to sharpen your writing skills.

I close this part with brand-new advice on navigating cyberspace, handling e-mail, and being mannerly when using all sorts of high-tech gadgets.

Chapter 5

The Art of Meeting and Greeting

*I*n today's fast-paced, high-tech world, people tend to forget the importance of simple human contact and kindness — remembering people's names, trying to make a good first impression, and greeting people with a firm handshake. I'm asked many business etiquette questions; invariably, I find that many of them center on introductions. Rightly so. Even though people may have loosened up somewhat in their use of titles, you still find a very distinct pecking order in who is introduced to whom in the business world.

Being able to introduce people and explain who they are makes everyone feel comfortable in a new situation and is one of the most useful skills you can acquire in the business world. The ability to introduce yourself or others confidently demonstrates that you are at ease and in control — and by extension, you set others at ease too. In this chapter, I introduce you to the proper techniques for meeting and greeting people that will make you look — and be — completely at ease in public.

Making Introductions with Ease

The goal for making introductions is to provide information about each other in order to give you a common ground to carry on a conversation. How many times have you been at a business event where you were the one in a group not introduced to anyone? Or the person doing the introduction forgot your name? How did that make you feel? Not so good, right? Knowing how to make a graceful introduction will not only allow you to concentrate on making a positive impression but it will also empower you. The following section provides general guidelines on how to make a proper introduction in various business situations.

Deciding who makes the introductions

The rules of who makes introductions depend on the situation:

- ✔ In formal business situations, your host (generally, the most senior executive from the company that planned the event) meets, greets, and introduces you to other guests. If your company is hosting the event, and you're the only or most senior representative of your company in a group, your job is to assume the role of host and make introductions.

- ✔ In less-formal situations, you don the role of host for your immediate circle and facilitate introductions.

- ✔ If you enter a group in which introductions have already been made, introducing yourself is always appropriate and in most instances expected.

Understanding the pecking order

Who goes first? Traditionally, in social situations a man is introduced to a woman.

The most common mistake made in introductions is the failure to keep all honorifics equal. If you use Ms Hughes, you must use Mr. Cunningham. You could use Karen Hughes and John Cunningham, although this would make it a less formal introduction. Of utmost importance to keep in mind is never to use first names only.

Introducing someone junior to someone senior

In business, introductions are based on a person's rank and position in a company. Whether that person is a man or a woman, young or old, makes no difference. You always introduce, or present, a "lesser" person to a more-senior person. You name the senior person first and the person who is being introduced, or presented, last.

If you're introducing a junior account executive named Alex Goldberg to the vice president of your division, Joanne Michaels, the proper form is "Joanne Michaels, I'd like to introduce Alex Goldberg. He is an account executive with Jones & Co. and Joanne Michaels is our division's vice president."

If someone uses her first and last names when introducing herself, the proper response is to still use her proper honorific or title and her last name: "Hello, my name is Janice Jones." Response: "Hello, Ms Jones" or "How do you do, Ms Jones." Don't use her first name unless she invites you to do so. If the person is of equal rank, you can feel comfortable using both his first and last names, if that's how the person introduces himself. I discuss titles and forms of address in more detail later in this chapter.

Introducing your boss to a client

It must be noted a client always takes precedence over your boss or the owner or president of your company. You introduce the president of your company, Chris Rosati, to the vice-president of your client's company, Myra Pay, as follows: "Ms Pay, I'd like to introduce Mr. Rosati, the president of Acme Graphics." You use "Ms Pay" if you normally address her this way. If you normally address your client as "Myra," then the introduction should be "Myra Pay, I'd like to introduce Chris Rosati, the president of Acme Graphics. Ms Pay will say, "How do you do, Mr. Rosati." Mr. Rosati will reply, "How do you do, Ms Pay." They may both say, "Please call me Myra/Chris."

"How do you do" is not really a question. The correct response is "How do you do" or "Hello," but never "Hi."

Introducing two people of equal rank

When you're introducing two people of equal rank in the corporate hierarchy, introduce the person who is not in your company to the person in your company. If you and Mike Hirschman are both vice presidents in your company's Chicago office and you see Valerie Martinez, a vice president in the Los Angeles office, you say, "Valerie Martinez, I'd like to introduce Mike Hirschman. Valerie is vice president of our Los Angeles office, and Mike works here with me in our Chicago office." Because everyone is of equal rank, the key in this example is to honor the guest from another office over your pal in the same office. As a result, her name is said first. If you happen to introduce peers to one another, a simple, "Carol, this is Karen Miller, Karen, meet Carol Andre; Carol works in our marketing department" will do.

Introducing people in a group

In a large group, introduce several people to one person at a time, following the hierarchy by using the "important" person's name first. Depending on the rank of the people in the group, the "important" person's name is first; the person or persons being introduced, or presented to the important person, is named last.

"Mr. Rogers, I'd like to present Lauren Lundsten and Michele Swanberg. They're summer interns from USC working for our firm for the next three months. Lauren and Michele, this is Mr. Andrew Rogers, the senior partner of our law firm."

If you're in a group and making many introductions, it's helpful to give people a little information about one another to help them start a conversation. You don't want to make an introduction without offering something about each other's company or position and how they may relate to each other. You might say, "Mr. Raymond Godfrey, I would like to present Mr. Dwight Schaffer, who is the president of our company. Mr. Godfrey is the president of Express Shipping, and also serves on the International Shipping Council."

Introducing yourself

You often have to introduce yourself in business situations. If you're waiting in a conference room for a meeting to begin, and someone new to you arrives, you stand, offer your hand, and introduce yourself and your role: "Hi, I'm Mike Perez. I'm chair of the Echelon Promotion Board." At that point, the other person can introduce herself to you: "How do you do, Mr. Perez. I'm Linda Pollack, and I'm going to be handling PR for the new communications campaign." Be sure to always use both your first and last name, not just your first name.

Never leave people guessing about your name. To save someone the possible embarrassment of forgetting your name, always offer a handshake and state both your first and last name. "Hello, I'm Allison Pay." Now the person can easily introduce you around. Even if the person remembers your name and says, "Of course, Allison; how could I forget you!" everyone will be comfortable and happy, and you'll have smoothed over a potentially awkward moment simply by saying your name right away.

Applying titles and forms of address

What's in a title? A whole heck of a lot. In a business situation, titles are crucial in introductions, because they put the people being introduced into context for others. Is he a marketing person, a salesperson, an engineer, an accountant? This information is critical to making sure that everyone is comfortable with one another (and immediately opens the door to conversation that can ease initial awkwardness). People want to know to whom they are speaking so that they can make appropriate comments.

Never assume that you can automatically call someone by a first name. You should use a person's proper honorific until he invites you to use the first name. Stick with Mr., Ms, Doctor, General — whatever is right. In the case of a woman, if you're not sure which variation she prefers — Mrs. or Ms — just ask her. If you know that the woman is a physician, a PhD, or a military officer, use the appropriate title.

In contemporary society, a grown woman is never a "Miss." Only young girls under 18 are addressed as Miss.

If someone has been an ambassador, a governor, a senator, or a judge, he remains so all his life. Always use the title in front of the person's family name.

Americans tend to jump to the first name very quickly, as any recent phone solicitation will convince you. This trend is an epidemic; regrettably, hosts and superiors often set the wrong example. When in doubt, err on the side of formality.

Remembering names (and behaving properly if you forget)

Everyone has problems remembering names, at least now and then (and sometimes more often). What's the best way to handle this embarrassment? First, try to recall and share something — anything — you do remember about the person, such as, "I know we met last month at the fund-raising event." Say, "I'm so sorry, sometimes I can't even remember my own name!" In some situations you can feel comfortable using humor, but you do not want to make a joke of the circumstances because in some cultures it's considered an insult to forget someone's name. It's best to simply apologize and move on.

If — horrors! — you forget someone's name when you're about to make an introduction, don't make a scene. It's not the end of the world. Simply say, "I've momentarily forgotten your name." The person should jump in and say, "It's Rex Martin." You can say, "Of course, Rex, I'd like to introduce Linda Thornhill." It's a big deal only if you make it a big deal. Admit your mistake and move on.

The ability to remember names and titles, especially in a large group, makes a lasting impression. If you can master this new form of professional polish, you will present yourself with confidence and authority — and outclass the competition. Remembering names is a skill, and one that you can acquire:

1. **Repeat the person's name a few times to yourself after you're introduced.**

2. **Use the person's name immediately in the conversation after an introduction.**

3. **Immediately introduce that new person to someone else you know.**

   If you don't have an opportunity to speak up immediately, you may want to try finding a word association with the person's name, such as "Bob — B — Brown shoes."

4. **Jot down the person's name, if you happen to have a pad and pencil.**

5. **Listen, listen, listen.**

   Good listening skills and concentration are the real keys to recalling a name. If you heard the name but didn't understand it, simply ask the person to repeat the name. You also can ask for a business card; just be sure to read it as soon as you receive it (see "Exchanging business cards," later in this chapter).

Correcting others' introductions

If someone mispronounces your name or gets it completely wrong, just smile and say something like this: "Thank you, but my name is actually Karen Miller, not Morton." Should you mispronounce someone's name, simply apologize, ask for the correct pronunciation, repeat the name aloud, and continue with your introduction.

If you happen to have a name that's easily mispronounced, you may jump in and help the person making the introduction. Many people find it helpful to find something your name rhymes with or something people can visualize ("It's Sue Fox, like the animal").

Never walk up to someone and ask, "Remember me?" Doing so is cruel! Always stop and reintroduce yourself politely. If you see someone you've met but can't remember the name, simply say something along the lines of this: "I remember meeting you recently. Was it at corporate headquarters?" Usually, the other person is flattered that you remember having met him or her, even if you've forgotten the name. And if you've been introduced to someone previously, allow yourself to be reintroduced if you're not recognized. Don't make this situation an issue.

Exchanging business cards

The biggest mistake you can make when you receive someone's business card is to glance at it and then slide it into a pocket. This treatment shows little respect for the other person, regardless of their position and rank. When you're handed a business card, read it thoroughly. You may want to repeat the person's name for pronunciation and acknowledge the person's company as being well respected, or ask something about the company or his position. Finally, express your gratitude for being given this information.

Handling the Handshake

Does a handshake really matter? Think back to the last time you got a limp handshake or a bone-crusher. What impression did it make on you? Was it distracting? Disgusting? Shocking? Whatever your reaction, you probably weren't feeling positive about the other person.

What a sloppy handshake says about the person behind the hand is that he just doesn't have things together. And if you're the sloppy shaker, you're telling the client, boss, or interviewer that you have problems. That conclusion can lead him to make a subconscious decision that he doesn't want to do business with you — or that you won't make a good representative of his company.

The handshake is the physical greeting that accompanies a verbal greeting. Because the handshake is used universally in business, knowing when to shake hands and how to shake hands confidently is vital.

Not shaking hands is a very clear form of rejection and is extremely insulting to the other person.

Using the perfect form

What is a proper handshake? The act seems so simple, yet people get confused about how to do it.

In the United States, you're expected to offer a firm handshake and make eye contact at the same time. A firm handshake with good eye contact communicates self-confidence. In U.S. etiquette, an appropriate handshake begins with the introduction:

1. **Extend your hand and grip the other person's hand in such a way that both are pushed all the way in to meet web-to-web and your thumbs are facing straight up. (See Figure 5-1.)**

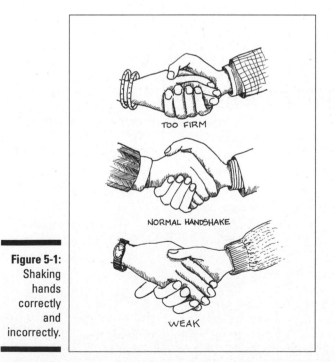

Figure 5-1:
Shaking hands correctly and incorrectly.

TOO FIRM

NORMAL HANDSHAKE

WEAK

2. **Shake just a couple of times in a vertical up-and-down motion.**

    The range of motion is 2 or 3 inches. The motion is extended from the shoulder, through the elbow, and straight through to your hand.

3. **End the handshake cleanly, before the introduction is over.**

    If you want to count, a good handshake is held for 3 or 4 seconds.

Handshaking is a form of nonverbal communication that says a lot about a person. For example, an overpowering handshake can indicate dominance or control. A weak handshake can indicate insecurity, disinterest, shyness, and aloofness. An awkward handshake indicates nervousness or a lack of social skills, which in turn reflects on credibility.

Understanding some rules of protocol

When someone makes an introduction, *always* remember to stand (if you're seated at the time) so that you can shake hands on an even level. That rule goes for women as well. If you happen to be seated at a table where reaching the other person is difficult or awkward, however, you don't have to stand. In this situation, mention how regretful you are that you cannot stand to meet them properly. By doing this it shows your savvy of correct business etiquette.

If you're wearing a name tag, place it on your right shoulder, because that's where a person's eye naturally wanders when shaking hands.

Shaking hands can be awkward in some situations. Should you be introduced to someone when your hands are full, carrying files or other packages, don't try to rearrange everything. Simply nod your head in a cordial greeting, state how, unfortunately, you are unable to shake their hand, and respond to the introduction.

When holding a cocktail at a stand-up reception, hold your drink in your left hand. You don't want to offer someone a wet or cold hand to shake. Except for opera-length gloves, when wearing gloves as part of formal attire, always remove them before shaking hands (the same goes for wearing sunglasses or gloves outdoors — you should always take them off, unless the temperature is bitterly cold or the sun is overly glaring).

Knowing when to shake hands

The answer is, all the time. When in doubt, offer your hand. Shaking hands is appropriate when you're

- Renewing an acquaintance
- Acknowledging someone who enters your office, cubicle, or home
- Greeting a client, new coworker, host, or others you know or are meeting for the first time
- Meeting someone you already know outside work or home
- Concluding a transaction
- Leaving a business or social event

In fact, because you should shake hands more often than not, the real question is, when don't you shake hands? Mainly, you should avoid shaking hands when the other person has his hands full, and putting everything down to shake your hand would be a big inconvenience, or when the person is of a certain culture or religion (see Chapter 22 for details). The final exception may be when the person you want to greet is someone much higher ranked than you and with whom you really have nothing in common. In this case, rushing up to shake his hand and introducing yourself may appear overly pushy.

Avoiding the clammy-hand dilemma

If you tend to have cold hands, stick your right hand in your pocket to warm it up as you approach a situation in which you'll have to shake hands. And if you have perennially clammy hands, try the high-school prom-date approach: Quickly swipe your right hand on your skirt or trousers so that when you present your hand, it's dry. You can do so quickly and gracefully, and no one will be aware that you made the gesture. If you are prone to sweaty palms, try rubbing a sanitizer with alcohol or antiperspirant (nonsticky and unscented!) on your hand before leaving the house and meeting someone.

Chapter 6

Making Polite Conversation

Few skills are more appreciated than the ability to make conversation. The person who is able to draw people into conversations, introduce interesting topics, and make everyone comfortable is valued in all situations, business and social. Conversation is an art as well as a skill.

In this chapter, I introduce you to some techniques for improving your conversational skills. You discover that good speaking and listening skills require practice. I also show you how to keep the channels of communication open in the office, how to mingle at social gatherings, and how to avoid making some common conversational mistakes.

Speaking Wisely and Listening Well

Those people who have been able to cultivate the skill of conversation have a leg up on others who are stuck behind a computer or buried under a stack of paper. To become an interesting conversationalist, first keep in mind these three principles:

✔ Always try to put the other person at ease.

✔ Engage in a genuine exchange of information.

✔ Show that you care about what's on the other person's mind.

Good conversationalists also share these abilities:

- ✔ They know how to give and accept compliments gracefully.
- ✔ They can talk about many subjects and are able to maneuver through conversations pertaining to things they know little about without difficulty.
- ✔ They can quickly discern potential topics of interest to any given group and steer the conversation in that direction.
- ✔ They don't repeat gossip.
- ✔ They never correct another person's vocabulary or grammar.
- ✔ They know when to discuss business and when not to.
- ✔ They involve everyone in the group in conversation, not just one person.
- ✔ They know how to step in to fill in an embarrassing void in conversation.
- ✔ They have a good sense of humor and are able to relate stories well.
- ✔ They can sense when other people are bored.

Keep in mind, though, that engaging in polite conversation involves a lot more than just talking about appropriate topics; it also requires sharp listening skills and the use of tact, as you find out in the following sections.

Sparking a conversation

There's no one way to spark a conversation. The best conversationalists know that the topic depends on the group and the context of the situation. If you happen to be shy or feel uneasy about chatting with coworkers or those you've just met, you may need to work a little harder. In conversation, as with other skills, practice makes perfect.

Good conversation starters involve everyone in your group in a lively discussion. For example, introducing the topic of baseball and then going on and on about statistics with one other person in the circle who is a fan is not a good idea. If you're in a group of people and you need to raise a conversation, try one of the following topics:

- ✔ **Nationally prominent sports (so everyone can participate):** Examples include the Super Bowl and the Olympics.
- ✔ **Current events:** Make sure to read a newspaper, a newsmagazine, or Internet news on the day of the event. Appropriate current events include business news, personal-interest stories, stories about nature, and stories about local civic accomplishments.
- ✔ **Positive items of interest to everyone in the company:** Potential topics include the new advertising campaign, company blogs, and the redesigned corporate cafeteria, for example.

✔ **Best-selling books, cultural events, or a recent film:** Talking about the latest film, play, musical performance, or art show interests almost everyone.

✔ **A compliment about the event, host, food, wine, or venue:** Providing positive comments always gets the conversation rolling on a pleasant note.

Try to include everyone in the group in the conversation by asking various people questions and drawing out their opinions. Commenting on why you're attending the event, asking other people why they're attending, or asking others to tell you something about themselves are various ways to start a conversation.

Asking a question is also a good way to break the ice. It all begins with a resolution on your part to say something when you find yourself making eye contact with another person. For example: "I'm currently working in the marketing department on the Delta project. You've probably seen my name copied in some of your e-mails — Jon Kenton. Aren't you working on the budget for our new Internet marketing campaign?"

The other party's duty is to respond with a reasonable answer. A simple yes or no turns off the whole conversation and leaves an awkward silence.

The power of question-and-answer dialogue will keep the conversational ball rolling. Be prepared to listen to the answer and try not to be thinking ahead about what you want to say.

To stay out of hot water conversationally, follow these guidelines:

✔ Avoid asking very personal questions (about someone's impending divorce or broken engagement, for example).

✔ Stay away from religion, politics, sex, and money. If you raise one of these topics, even in a joking manner, you're walking on thin ice, as you never know whether you're offending other people's sensibilities.

✔ Avoid using inappropriate language, such as slurs or curse words, and never tell a joke that you think may be even slightly off-color. (If you think the joke may be off-color, it probably is.)

✔ Recognize when you've been speaking with someone for more than 5 or 10 minutes. This elapsed period is your cue to move on to another conversation. People appreciate the conversationalist who stays away from talking nitty-gritty business at a company event. No one wants to get into a long-winded discussion of the outcome of your latest personal-injury case as you detail everything your client did to make life difficult for you. Save this conversation for Monday morning in the office.

If you notice you've hit on an uncomfortable topic someone isn't interested in, as awkward as it may be, try to turn the conversation to another subject — even simple small talk will do. Watch for physical communication signals as well as verbal ones.

Listening politely

The wisest people seem to listen more than they speak. As a well-mannered person, you want to emulate that behavior. (By doing so, you train yourself to listen better, and other people will also listen very carefully to the words you do speak.)

When you listen well, you remember all the conversation's major points, including any actions that are your responsibility. You can ask intelligent questions at the end of the conversation, and you may even learn something!

If you find that you've been monopolizing the conversation, simply apologize and throw the ball in the other person's court without drawing too much attention to your faux pas. You can easily do this by asking a question.

Listening well means more than just sitting quietly. Your body language also shows that you're attentive:

- ✔ **Neither slump down in your chair nor sit rigidly without moving.** Keep both your feet flat on the floor, or cross your feet only at the ankles. Don't cross your legs at the knees, and don't prop your feet up on chair rungs. Keep your hands and arms relaxed, resting on the arms of the chair, or sitting in your lap. Don't fold your arms across your chest.

- ✔ **Watch the speaker, and don't let your eyes wander all over the room.**

- ✔ **Sit comfortably, without shifting every few minutes.** Crossing and uncrossing your legs or arms signals boredom. For more on body language, see Chapter 4.

- ✔ **Acknowledge and confirm that you're listening by using periodic oral sounds, such as "ah-hah," "yes," "I see," and the like.**

When receiving instructions from bosses or clients, repeat what you think you hear them saying to clarify everyone's understanding of the issues at hand.

Using tact in any situation

A tactful person is also a diplomatic person, which means she gently conveys difficult information so that it's acceptable to the receiving party. Flatly issuing commands and loudly mouthing opinions are great ways to show complete ignorance of the use of tact. If a client or coworker is sharing a new idea or strategy, be quiet and listen; then come up with a suitable response, such as, "That's an interesting concept, can you give us the details?"

The untactful thing to do would be to blurt out your first thought about a disagreeable idea or strategy ("Are you out of your mind?!?" or worse, "We've tried that before and it didn't work!"). This reaction may not achieve your objective of steering the client from that horrifyingly bad idea. What may work better? "That's an interesting idea. Why don't we take it back to the team and review our research on consumer response? I'll give you a call tomorrow morning to let you know what we find."

Ending a conversation gracefully

All things must come to an end (no matter how good or bad), and conversations are no exception. No rule says you have to remain trapped in a conversation you'd rather end. A pleasant ending to a conversation can go a long way, so take time and thought to end on a positive note. People remember what they hear *last* the longest.

The ideal way to end a conversation is to smile, shake hands, thank the other person for his time (though it isn't always that simple), and close by saying "It was nice talking to you." How you extricate yourself is another measure of your mastery of good manners. For example, a polite exit line can be: "I didn't know about all the fascinating projects you've been working on. Perhaps we can meet for lunch soon so you can tell me more."

You should never be dishonest when coming up with an exit line. Make sure your reason for ending the conversation is legitimate so you don't risk making the person feel bad.

Handling Office Conversations

You can't avoid communicating with others you work with. And whether you're small-talking with a coworker or meeting privately with your boss, each mode of communication has its own set of etiquette guidelines.

Not only is clear communication one of the best ways to ensure that your career advances, but it also ensures that your work environment is a pleasant one and that everyone functions efficiently. Office conversations that take etiquette rules into account will help avoid unintentional errors that miscommunication engenders. Read on to discover how to communicate politely with your coworkers, make your point concisely with a group or an individual, and speak to your boss respectfully.

Developing cubicle courtesy

The cubicle is a curious invention, giving the illusion of privacy without actually providing privacy. Although you can't see your coworkers, you can certainly hear them. Engrain that fact in your mind. Loud telephone conversations or group social chats centered on your cubicle can annoy people working nearby. Although everyone expects and accepts the occasional social call, receiving multiple calls (don't fool yourself into thinking that your next-door neighbor won't be listening) and getting lots of visits from coworkers who want to chat will annoy everyone around you. Keep chatting to a minimum, or, if possible, make your personal calls away from your cubicle while you're on a break or at lunch, or make them while the people around you are in meetings.

Chatting politely with coworkers

You'll likely spend more time chatting with colleagues than with your boss (although I give you some pointers for chatting with the boss in the next section). Here are some tips for talking to your coworkers:

- ✔ **Be careful in the language you use with coworkers.** Although slang may be all right among your friends, your coworkers may have sensitivities you're not aware of. Too much slang or use of foul language can turn off coworkers.

- ✔ **Keep in mind that you want to be friendly but you don't want to monopolize others' time.** Never bother someone by talking when that person is obviously trying to concentrate on making a deadline.

- ✔ **Keep secrets.** Any new information is your personal property, and you shouldn't share it with others.

- ✔ **Keep personal discussions of your love life and your spouse to a minimum.** Close social friends can discuss almost anything, but people you work with are not entitled to deeply personal details of your life. Moreover, there's a chance that something you say may be repeated, or — worse — turn into office gossip.

- ✔ **Make sure that the tone of your conversations is positive.** The person who goes from cubicle to cubicle complaining and putting down other people won't go far.

- ✔ **Don't brag or boast to coworkers or other colleagues.** It's considered rude to discuss details about achievements or things your boss said to you privately, brag about your paid vacation, or succumb to conversation faux pas by dropping names.

✔ **Always weigh your words carefully.** Whether you're chatting with a coworker or participating in a meeting, always think before you speak. Do your best not to repeat gossip, talk about other employees, or say anything that could be offensive or confidential.

✔ **Be gracious and considerate to others you work with.** When a colleague has had bad news, such as a sick child or a project that didn't go well, stopping by to show your concern is perfectly acceptable. By all means express how sad you are and offer your assistance. If a colleague is feeling discouraged, offering some words of encouragement is compassionate. Even if you're in the middle of making a tight deadline, take a few minutes to help the other person. Someday, you may be the person needing help.

In business, as in social situations, people appreciate someone who knows how to make a conversation flow pleasantly. Take the initiative in starting conversations, and always remember to be friendly, upbeat, and enthusiastic!

Getting some face time with the boss

Part of the reason you were hired is because your boss liked your personality and thought you'd fit in and become a valuable addition to the team. Keeping cordial relations with your boss is important, as is conveying that you enjoy her company as a person as well as your superior, so stop by for some friendly small talk.

Friendly chitchat is appropriate if your boss's office door is open and if another member of the team is already there having a chat. On the other hand, if your boss's door is closed, or if he's working quietly in his office typing intently on the computer, he's likely trying hard to get some serious work done and won't welcome a frivolous interruption. Likewise, if your boss is on the phone or has a scowl on his face, you should probably wait for another time.

Respecting ethnic, cultural, and gender differences

Inadvertently insulting someone with a racial or ethnic slur is one of the fastest ways to embarrass yourself and hurt others. As a well-mannered person, you should have no problem avoiding this pitfall, because you're alert to your coworkers' sensitivities and needs! As people from different ethnic, cultural, religious, and national origins unite, you need a tolerant and inclusive attitude, which means watching your language and your actions. Here are some guidelines:

- ✔ **Learn the currently accepted terms for the ethnic groups, religions, and nationalities of those with whom you work.** Get rid of all those slang terms that you may have heard in the past.

- ✔ **Don't identify or refer to others by race or ethnic identity.** People are people.

- ✔ **Use names and titles, and avoid other labels.** Sexist terms are strictly taboo. A person is a sales representative, not a salesman or saleslady. An administrative assistant is not a secretary, and an information-systems specialist is not a computer jockey.

- ✔ **Be alert to a person's special needs.** If one of your colleagues must be absent for a religious observance, offer to cover his responsibilities for the day.

- ✔ **Always make a conscious effort to speak inclusively.** Don't let sexist terms creep into your vocabulary, and listen to the words that slip out of your mouth.

See Chapter 3 for more information on respecting everyone's differences in the workplace.

Offering your opinion gently

Never interrupt or correct someone while she's speaking. If you want to offer a different opinion, don't say, "Linda, you're wrong. If you took time to read the report, you'd understand." It's better to avoid a confrontation and harsh words by not using the accusatory "you" and by gently providing another point of view. You might say, "Linda's point about our on-time delivery record is interesting. I was reviewing last year's customer-service survey yesterday, and it pointed out a different reason why our delivery record may not be up to par."

Meetings are the place to show that you're a team player. Use *we* when you're referring to work done by your team. Acknowledge your coworkers' contributions by using *we* instead of *I* and *our* instead of *my.* Try to avoid saying things like "I launched the new fund-raising campaign." Instead, say, "Our team worked together to launch the new fund-raising campaign." See Chapter 10 for more information on meeting manners.

Branching Out and Getting Noticed with Effective Mingling

Nowhere is the art of mingling more important to your career than at a company party. You should be mixing with as many people as possible — not just those in your department whom you know well. Believe it or not, mingling is a vitally important business skill. Mingling well demonstrates that you're a friendly, open, and engaged person who is interested in other people. Mingling poorly shows others that you're either unsure of yourself or so egotistical that you can't listen to others.

Make the rounds at the party. Don't spend all your time talking to one person; you want to circulate. Many other people will be anxious about mingling and will welcome your efforts to make conversation. The following tips show you how to make the most out of an event and be a good representative for your company:

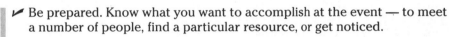

- ✔ Be prepared. Know what you want to accomplish at the event — to meet a number of people, find a particular resource, or get noticed.

- ✔ Remember to carry business cards and exchange them when appropriate.

- ✔ As you circulate, make sure you politely excuse yourself from the conversation. To say nothing as you exit is considered rude.

- ✔ Hold your drink in your left hand so that if you are introduced to someone, you don't extend a cold, wet hand to shake.

- ✔ Be well-informed on current events and company news so you'll have small-talk options and various ways to start a conversation.

- ✔ Always avoid making negative comments. You don't have to lie, but never slander your employer or coworkers. Even if you think the company is mismanaged, keep it to yourself.

- ✔ Don't overindulge at work events. Your behavior is a reflection of your company, and staying sober can keep you from saying things you will regret later.

- ✔ Introduce yourself and others properly. If possible, learn the names of the attendees and the appropriate way of making an introduction beforehand. If name tags are available, wear one on your right shoulder. For more about meeting, greeting, and introducing people, see Chapter 5.

Make good eye contact, give solid handshakes, and try to speak to people you haven't met before. You never know what doors may open for you simply because you made the effort to greet your colleagues in another department. Follow the preceding guidelines and you'll be set!

Mingle! The definition of the word is "to socialize," "come together," and "blend." Don't let fear stop you from approaching someone you've never met. With a bit of practice and planning before the event, you'll soon be conversing with confidence.

While making small talk with a new group of people, the worst thing you can do is keep glancing around for someone better to engage in conversation. You can't find a faster way to make someone feel unimportant. When you're speaking with someone, she should receive your full attention — no wandering eyes!

Cocktail parties and other mingling events usually are noisy and punctuated with interruptions. They're not ideal venues for serious business conversations, so people will appreciate your keeping the conversation light. If you see the potential for a fruitful business discussion, hand the other person your business card, and say you will call her to make an appointment to continue the conversation.

Dealing with Common Conversational Faux Pas

Many people are scared to death about conversing with others, particularly groups of people, mostly out of fear of making mistakes. Never fear. Making mistakes happens to everyone, and with a bit of practice and planning, you can converse confidently.

If you've made a social faux pas, the worst thing you can do is slink off into a corner and vow to move out of town, assume an alias, and never see that group of people again as long as you live. Yes, that reaction is a normal human reaction to embarrassment. You should fight it, however. You're much better off taking a deep breath, staying put, and facing the consequences with a little humor. You're much better off taking responsibility for your blunder than blaming it on someone or something else. Keep that in mind as you read about some common conversation mistakes in the following sections.

Saying something awkward

Relating your grandmother's mysterious bladder problem to your client in the hospital system's marketing department may seem just fine to you, but it may well cause the vice president of marketing to feel squeamish. If your conversation partner begins moving away from you for no apparent reason or looks disturbed, you know that you've hit on an uncomfortable subject.

Religion, politics, how much things cost, salaries, gossip, and office secrets are off-limits as conversation topics. Turn the conversation to current events, food, positive news about colleagues, hobbies, industry talk, current trends, or sports; all these topics make for good small talk. (See the earlier section "Sparking a conversation" for more information.)

Cutting in on a conversation

Wanting to add your two cents to a conversation is only natural. If, however, you feel the urge to cut in on someone else's sentence with a fascinating tidbit of information that you think makes you look witty and erudite, sit back and wait a second. If a pause occurs, use it as your cue to talk. If a pause doesn't occur, or if the conversation changes course, be content with the thought that although you may have missed a chance to contribute your wisdom about the latest theory regarding the effect of debt on earnings per share, at least you look composed and cool. Surveys show that the most annoying thing people do when communicating is interrupting when others are speaking.

Talking too loudly

Speaking loudly in public, especially in restaurants, is common nowadays. It's not the loudest person who impresses his companions; it's the person with quiet confidence and good manners. Always try to use low, intimate tones.

If you're speaking loudly in a restaurant because you're talking on a cell phone, shame on you. Cell phones should be turned off before entering a restaurant. Even if you don't mind interrupting a business dinner with a call, others in the restaurant may appreciate having their meals in peace. See Chapter 7 for more details on improving your phone manners.

Drawing a blank on what to say

If you come upon a pause in the conversation and have no idea what to say, depending on the length of the pause, it may be just fine. Relax. There is no need to feel you have to fill every second with conversation. Yet, the good conversationalist can get the other person to talk about herself. You might mention an article you read and ask the person's opinion: "I've been reading everything I can about the XYZ Company merger plans, but I still wonder whether it makes sense. What do you think about their plans?" Or you may ask about the person's recent travels. If all else fails, you can always compliment something about the event you are attending, whether it's the food, interesting guests, or a table setting.

Chapter 7

Improving Your Telephone Manners

You're one of the new breed; you go everywhere outfitted with the latest wireless technology. At your office, your phone system has more gizmos than a starship: voice mail, call waiting, call forwarding, caller ID, speakerphones, and a headset. You are always in touch, whether you're at a business lunch, on your way to the dry cleaner, or in the backyard with your kids.

Funny thing — even with all your technologies at hand, you're still not pleasing everyone. People seem annoyed when you fiddle with your cell phone during a meeting. Your kids groan every time your cell phone rings. Other drivers send daggers your way when they see you chatting away in the car as you weave your way in and out of six lanes of traffic at 70 miles an hour (which in some states is illegal).

The problem isn't the technologies; it's the way they're being used and abused. One telling symptom of the need for new etiquette rules is the fact that newspapers, magazines, the Internet, and business conversations are liberally dosed with the latest funny story or outrageous thing someone has done with the new technology. Think about the past few months: How many times has someone told you about something hilarious someone else did with a cell phone? How many articles and letters to the editor have you read describing the outrage someone feels when a cell phone starts to ring at the worst time or the impossibility of finding your way out of an automated answering system?

Pretty clearly, a lot of us need some help with telephone etiquette. So this chapter gives you the scoop on how to talk and listen on the phone, how to use various phone technologies, how to use your phone with a minimum of intrusion into others' space, and how to conduct conference calls and video-conferences with grace.

Speaking and Listening on the Phone

Some people just don't know how to speak on the phone. You can hear every breath they're taking and the crunch-crunch of their afternoon corn chips, or they have the receiver so far away from their mouths that they sound like they're talking to you from the slopes of Mount Kilimanjaro. Some people also don't know how to listen on the phone. They respond "Uh-huh" to whatever you say while you hear the clicking of their busy fingers on the keyboard in the background, or they talk so much that you can't get a word in edgewise.

These typical scenarios are common, but shouldn't be this way! If you use the information in the following sections, you'll be a polite speaker and listener on the phone in no time.

Practicing the basics

The basic facts of communication are these: One person is a speaker, and the other is a listener. In most circumstances, the speaker's job is to be as clear as he can be and to speak in a polite, even tone. The listener's job is . . . well, to listen to what the speaker says and then respond appropriately.

Sounds simple, doesn't it? But messing the process up is amazingly easy. Usually, people just forget. As speakers, we mumble, shout, whisper, or speak with food in our mouths. As listeners, we do other things when we're supposed to be listening, listen without hearing anything the other person says, or respond to another person's question from left field — with an entirely different topic.

Everyone gets overworked and distracted, and no doubt you have those moments when someone calls you at exactly the wrong time. But it's crucial that you pay attention to what you say, how you say it, and how you listen and respond to others on the phone. Studies have shown that the top reasons why customers do not become repeat customers are employees' indifference and rudeness on the phone.

So what can you do? Practice speaking and listening with someone you trust by using these guidelines:

- **Speak clearly, and pay attention to your conversational partner.** Find the correct distance from your mouth to hold the receiver so that your voice doesn't sound like part of the ambient background or like a hectoring protester speaking into a bullhorn.

- **Practice listening, too.** When you get a phone call, make a point of turning off other noisemaking equipment, including the radio. Turn away from your computer if you have to so that you can avoid the temptation to fiddle with the document on your screen. Excuse yourself from any conversations you are currently having so as to give your telephone conversational partner your undivided attention.

Calling on the phone

So many people work in front of a computer screen all day that it's easy to forget the usual social graces — which include things they learned as children, such as how to answer and place a call. Every time you make or receive a telephone call at work, you're representing your company. And, many times, the first contact a person has with a company is over the phone, so the impression you make on the phone may be a lasting one. Therefore, you want to sound professional. Now for some basic telephone manners:

- **Prepare for the phone call before you make it.** Have some idea of what you're going to talk about. Have a pen and paper handy.

- **Make notes if necessary, especially if you're forgetful.** Planning is better than having to make a second call.

When you call someone, introduce yourself the right way:

1. **Say, "Hello."**

2. **Identify yourself and your affiliation.**

3. **Ask for the person to whom you would like to speak.**

Here's an example:

> "Hello. This is Tom Canon from Canon Technologies, calling for Ms Hillander concerning next spring's conference. Is she available?"

Always state the reason for your call. Don't feel put off if you're asked to state the purpose of your business.

If Ms Hillander is available, you will be transferred to her. When she answers, repeat your name and affiliation, state your business, and give an estimate of the time you think the call will take, as in this example:

> "Hello, Ms Hillander. This is Tom Canon from Canon Technologies, calling about next spring's conference in San Francisco. Do you have ten minutes to talk about marketing strategy?"

That's all you need. You've said who you are and what you want to talk about. Now you pass the ball into the other person's court and let her respond.

If the person you are calling is not available, whether you're leaving a voice mail or a message with a real person, give your name, your company's name, your telephone number, a time you can be reached, and a brief message. Refrain from leaving a monologue to replace the conversation you would have had. If you're leaving a voice mail, repeat your phone number and speak slowly.

When your conversation is finished, end it cordially and quickly. A business call is not a social call, so you don't need to drag the conversation out beyond the business at hand. If you know the other person well, however, you may end the conversation with a few questions about something personal, such as "I was glad to hear your mother is back from the hospital" or "How did Sarah's soccer game go?"

Keep the following guidelines in mind during a phone conversation:

- ✔ Answer as promptly as possible.
- ✔ Exercise patience on the phone, and let other people finish their sentences.
- ✔ Focus on listening.
- ✔ Speak so as not to be misunderstood.
- ✔ Listen to what the other person is saying.
- ✔ Don't interrupt and speak over and while the other person is speaking.
- ✔ Confirm you're listening with periodic oral sounds, such as "ah-hah," "yes," and the like.
- ✔ Don't chime in to interject you own comments and opinions.
- ✔ Be sure to speak directly into the mouthpiece, slowly and clearly. Articulate properly, for example, "yes" instead of "yeah."

- ✔ Your posture when you speak on the phone strongly affects how you sound to the person on the other end and the energy that comes across on the telephone. Don't slump in your chair; sit up straight. Also, smiling while you speak can actually make the tone of your voice more pleasant.

- ✔ If you dial an incorrect number, apologize before you hang up. This is also considerate if you get someone's voice mail.

Be helpful! If a caller has reached the wrong person, assist him in getting to the right party. If you can't find the person, or they have no voice mail, offer to take and deliver a message.

Watch out for these mistakes:

- ✔ Never sneeze, belch, blow your nose, snort, or cough into a phone. Of course this can be unavoidable, so always turn your head away from the phone and offer an apology.

- ✔ Never use phone calls as an opportunity to get caught up with paper-shuffling.

- ✔ Never eat, drink, or chew gum while you're on the phone.

- ✔ Never answer the phone abruptly by simply saying "yes." Never use slang terms or words that are inappropriate in business, such as "honey," "dear," and "sweetheart."

Answering the phone

The majority of phones today seem to be answered by voice mail. Getting an actual voice on the other end of the line is a pleasant surprise! Companies have lots of protocols for answering the phones. Most companies use an automated voice-mail system with a variety of menus. If well constructed, these answering systems can be helpful and efficient. If poorly constructed, they can be a confusing and frustrating experience.

The first contact a potential client or customer typically has with your company is when someone answers your company's phone. Make sure that it's answered well. When you answer the phone, speak clearly, identify your company, and ask the caller how you may direct the call or how you may help. Answer any questions, if you can. If you can't, direct the call to the appropriate person.

Many greetings are acceptable, but they all contain the following information: your company name and your name. Here's a greeting that gets it right:

"Good morning. Holistic Health, Inc. James Moody speaking."

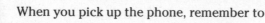

This greeting is simple, succinct, and informative. If you say it with the right inflection in your voice — that is, upbeat and engaged — you set the right tone for the rest of the conversation immediately.

When you pick up the phone, remember to

- ✔ Stop whatever else you are doing.
- ✔ Speak clearly into the receiver.
- ✔ Be upbeat. Try smiling while you're speaking; it works!

Putting a caller on hold is frustrating to the caller, so refrain from doing it unless you absolutely have to. If you have to, remember that the process is easier on the caller if you say "Will you please hold for a moment? I'll go get that information" than if you command the caller to "Hold!" and push the button. Try your hardest to remember that people are on hold when you put them there. Update the caller every half-minute or so on the progress you're making in putting his call through.

If you need to connect a caller to someone else, tell him the name of the person you are directing the call to, and provide that person's extension number. If the call then gets disconnected, the caller will appreciate having the name and the extension when he returns the call.

Screening calls for other people is a delicate matter. Not only may the caller feel slighted when an administrative assistant tells him that Mr. Bigshot is not available, but also, he may resent telling an administrative assistant about the call and having the assistant determine its importance. Tact is necessary. Good bosses provide their receptionists and administrative assistants the protocols they want to use for screening and the language to be used with callers. If your boss doesn't set the criteria for screening or the language to be used, ask him to do so.

Making the Most of Telephone Technology

Cell phones, speakerphones, voice mail, answering machines, caller ID, and call waiting — these communications technologies are much more prevalent now than they once were, and they are undeniably helpful. Still, they have to be used with care, lest you use them as an opportunity to exercise your frustrations or inadvertently make your caller annoyed . . . or (worse) mad.

Cell phones

Cell phones have a place in today's business world. But that place is when you are alone — such as while you're walking or riding in a cab. If you're using your cell phone anywhere in public, such as on a train or in a mall, find a secluded corner to converse away from others. Respect other people's right not to hear your conversation.

Public phones have been around for a long time, usually in phone booths that protect the callers from noise and passersby from the details of the calls. Keep the same principle in mind when using your cell phone. Try to construct a virtual phone booth around yourself for the duration of the conversation.

That trick isn't always possible, however, and when it isn't, you should be exceedingly sparing in your cell-phone use. Cell phones have no place in restaurants; at the theater, movies, or symphony; in churches or classrooms; or in meetings. You are in these places to do something other than talk on the phone. Whenever you go into one of these settings, have the courtesy to turn your wireless phone off.

The more available you make yourself, the more available everyone expects you to be. People will begin to get upset if you are not instantly and constantly available! Ask yourself, do you really want to be connected 24/7/365, and is it absolutely necessary?

Think before you speak! A number of recent studies have concluded that motorists who use cell phones while driving are four times as likely to get into accidents. Most everyone agrees that handheld cell phones while driving can constitute a hazardous distraction. Also, the theory that hands-free sets are any safer has been challenged by the findings of a number of studies. Researchers at the University of Utah, published in the summer 2006 issue of *Human Factors,* the quarterly journal of the Human Factors and Ergonomics Society, conclude that talking on a cell phone while driving is as dangerous as driving drunk, even if the phone is a hands-free model.

If you inadvertently forgot to turn the phone off and it starts to ring, hasten to quiet it, even if that means turning it off without answering it, and apologize to those around you, as appropriate and convenient. Sometimes just silencing your phone is all that is necessary.

Never answer a cell phone or begin a cell-phone conversation while you're in a bathroom. The potential for embarrassment is high.

Now that you know when it's appropriate to have a cell-phone conversation, you should be aware that some cell phones create problems during conversations:

- Cell phones have a habit of clipping off the beginnings of words and sentences. When you're talking to someone on a cell phone, the give and take of the conversation can lead you into a black hole of clipped queries.

    To get out of the black hole, I recommend that you treat cell-phone conversations with the same courtesy you use for landline phone conversations — plus some. Remind yourself never to talk over your telephone partner's voice and to wait patiently to speak until he has finished talking.

- Another quirk of wireless phones is their occasional tendency to drop calls. You can't do much to avoid embarrassment and frustration when you realize that the last two minutes of the review of the Steven Spielberg flick you've been dictating to your editor drifted off into cyberspace. Take a deep breath, and try again.

Speakerphones

Speakerphones are appropriate to use when you want to have a group meeting with someone on the phone, but rarely otherwise. If you put people on speakerphone, by all means tell them that you are doing it, and tell them who else is in the room. Don't make the mistake of thinking that the person on the other end of the phone can't tell when you put them on the speakerphone. The additional echo of a speakerphone is instantly identifiable.

Suppose your caller is conferencing with three people in your office. First, introduce your colleagues to the caller. Second, when talking, be especially careful to identify yourselves to the caller at the beginning of your input to the meeting. Having no visual means to connect voices to people, the caller may be at a complete loss about who is talking without repeated identification. (I give more details on conducting conference calls later in this chapter.)

Speakerphones are loud. If you're using one, close the door to your office.

Voice mail and answering machines

Voice-mail systems allow people to leave a message for you when you are away from your office or on another line.

When you record a greeting for your voice-mail system, remember that you are at work and not at home. Messages such as "Hello, I'm Johnny Cash, and I'm not here" aren't helpful, and messages such as "I'm chillin' — leave me your 411!" will be indecipherable to most business callers. It's preferable to say something like the following:

> "This is Georgette Johnson in the billing department at MacIntosh Marketing. Please leave me a message, and I'll return your call as soon as possible. Thank you."

Some people record messages on a daily basis or direct callers to others in the office who may be able to assist the caller. Most people change their message when they are out of town on vacation or away on business for more than a day. It is appropriate to record a message informing the caller when you will be out of the office and saying that you will return the call when you get back. You may also leave the name and number of someone else in the office who can help the caller if he cannot wait until you return.

When you leave a message on someone else's voice-mail system, the first thing to do — before leaving the message — is give your name, your company affiliation, your telephone number, and the date and time of your call. The next thing to do is leave a short message that is direct and to the point. Message machines are no substitute for talking one on one, so don't think that the person listening to your message needs to hear all the gory details. At the end of the message, repeat your name and your phone number, slowly.

When you get a message on your own voice-mail system, remember to return the call the same day, if possible, or the next morning.

All of what I've said about voice mail applies to answering machines as well. But one little issue concerning answering machines requires separate treatment: Never admit to using your answering machine as a screening device. If you want to take the call, pick up and say something like this: "Hi. Sorry; I was in the other room." This technique keeps your paranoid callers from feeling screened ("Well, I made it through this time, but what about next time?").

Caller ID

Caller ID has legitimate uses, and it's becoming more and more popular. At times, knowing who is on the other end of the phone is a tremendous advantage. The four or five extra seconds you have to concoct your latest explanation about why you haven't completed the new company marketing strategy can, on occasion, save your hide.

You should avoid a couple of behaviors with caller ID:

- ✔ Just because you were "suddenly" out of the office when Mr. Drummond called doesn't mean that you shouldn't return the message he leaves on your voice-mail system. Having elected not to answer the phone doesn't relieve you of your obligation to return the call.

- ✔ It's better to avoid saying "Hello, Jim" when you recognize the number. This sort of greeting is a little unnerving to the caller, who may wonder whether you have ESP.

Call waiting

Fortunately, call waiting is losing out in popularity to voice-mail systems, especially in business. Soon, it could be gone completely.

If you find yourself using a phone equipped with call waiting, the best thing to do is ignore the clicks. Remember that your current conversation takes precedence unless special circumstances apply. If you absolutely need to answer the second call, you should alert the caller you're speaking with as soon as you answer. Let him know that you may have to take another call that you're expecting. If the call is short, you can ask him to hold; if you expect the call to be longer than a minute or two, apologize and ask him if you can call him back.

Conducting Conference Calls and Videoconferences with Care

Conference calls are increasingly popular, largely because the technology has improved so much in the past ten years. In the not-too-distant future, real-time videoconferencing will be affordable for most businesses via computers; it is a reality now for many businesses.

Perhaps surprisingly, videoconferences are helping reintroduce people to meeting manners. The explanation is straightforward: The camera has the unfortunate ability to focus on one person at a time. Any flaws in a person's body language — slouching in the chair, for example — become glaringly obvious on camera. Being part of a videoconference is a little like seeing yourself on video for the first time: All those tics and quirks that you thought you'd mastered years ago suddenly slap you in the face!

Conference calls and video (or Web) conferences are wonderful tools when used properly. A few moments of real conversation over the phone or through video can be worth a thousand e-mailed words. As with all meetings, however, these electronic get-togethers require attention to etiquette. (Flip to Chapter 10 for general information on in-person meetings.)

Conference calls

Some conference calls, usually for smaller groups, consist of several people calling in to one participant's office. The central person conferences everyone together by pressing the conference button for each addition. Other types of calls are monitored, meaning that all participants call a central number and are placed in the conference by speaking to an operator or by entering a password.

You should always identify yourself when you join a call, but do so with caution. On a monitored call, you may not be able to hear other speakers for a few seconds, so don't announce yourself immediately; if you do, you may step on another speaker. If you join the call late, other callers usually hear a beep of some kind. Don't announce yourself immediately. When a break in the action occurs, the host will probably say something like "Who just joined the call?" Then you can announce your name and apologize profusely for your tardiness.

Don't ever sit in complete silence on a call without announcing yourself. The other callers deserve to know everyone who is listening to them. Not announcing your presence is akin to hiding behind the curtains in the boardroom.

Try to identify yourself each time you speak during a conference call. That way, you can compensate for the lack of visual clues. And remember to be especially considerate about other people's contributions to the conference. Give each person enough time to finish what he is saying before you reply.

Most teleconferencing systems today have mute features. However, if the conference call is open to everyone, remember that every additional person on a phone call adds an extra layer of background noise. When you're on a conference call, put your phone on mute unless you're actually speaking. Don't forget to take yourself off mute when you have something to say. This rule is amazingly hard to remember.

Videoconferencing

Given the growing trends of outsourcing and teams working together as well as the increasing cost of air travel, the need for conferences between groups of people at opposite ends of the country — or the world, for that matter — has never been greater.

Many companies today are using affordable Web and videoconferencing software for Internet meetings. Some companies still use old-style videoconferencing, though more of it is being done on the Internet and then projected onto a large screen.

The following Web sites offer products that make Web or videoconferencing simple to use:

- ✔ www.ivci.com
- ✔ www.megameeting.com

When you are scheduled for a videoconference, begin your preparation for it well in advance. Train those who are unfamiliar with the format by staging mock meetings and videotaping them. Show everyone the tapes, and make suggestions if necessary. Have an agreed-upon agenda for the meeting in place, if you can. Make sure that everyone whose input is required during the videoconference can make it at the scheduled time.

During the actual meeting, take care to sit properly, listen attentively, speak clearly, and be patient. Be aware that some long-distance audio can introduce slight delays in the conversation (although the technology has improved greatly), and compensate for those delays.

Some people appear to think that because they aren't in the same physical space as their videoconferencing colleagues, they're free to do things that they would never dream of doing were they in the same room. But this opinion is an error in judgment. Your videoconferencing setup may not allow you to view everyone, but that doesn't mean they can't see all the people on your end, and it doesn't mean that a camera won't find you just as you're counting holes in the ceiling tiles. It's best to always be aware of your body language and facial expressions during a videoconference.

Chapter 8

Sharpening Your Written Communication Skills

*W*ith all the spell-check, grammar-check, and letter-writing programs on computers, you may think you no longer need to know how to write well. Think again. Writing is still an essential skill for the professional, as you may have discovered the day your boss returned one of your letters sprinkled with her red editing marks.

Think about how many letters, e-mails, memoranda, and reports you get every week. Even if you're not a grammar expert, you can tell that some of them are more effective than others. Some are so disorganized that you can't find the point. Others are so brusque as to be a little offensive. With still others, you look in vain for a paragraph that doesn't have a misspelled word. By contrast, an effective letter or report is grammatically correct and contains no spelling errors; its tone is appropriate to its content; it's direct without being curt; and it gets to the point quickly and stays there.

In this chapter, I show you how to compose various types of business correspondence. You also find out how to avoid some basic grammatical, stylistic, and spelling errors; how to write in a consistent and well-organized manner; what to have in your stationery drawer; and how to address business envelopes. By the end of the chapter, you'll no longer be intimidated by business writing. You may even have enough knowledge to become the office expert!

Communicating with Clarity and Courtesy

Perhaps you don't have a strong background in grammar. Maybe you avoided every university class that had a heavy writing component. You're the best technician in your division, but now you're expected to write memoranda and letters to all kinds of people, and you don't have an administrative assistant. Result? Your trash can is full of rejected drafts, and your temperature rises to the boiling point every time you have to write a memo.

For all but the luckiest of us, clear writing is a skill that must be learned. Sure, naturally great writers exist, but for the rest of us, practice — and lots of it — is required. The trouble is that you don't have time to practice. So you do it on the fly, with each piece of correspondence that you write.

I have two suggestions for you. The first is to read this section carefully. The second is to buy a dictionary, a thesaurus, and a copy of Strunk and White's *The Elements of Style*. This little book (fewer than 100 pages) is recognized as the best primer on writing ever composed. Other good writing books are available (and plenty of business-writing books too), but Strunk and White provide more about writing in less space than in any other book.

With that said, it's time for your crash course on clear and courteous business writing. I assume that you learned elementary grammar and know the difference between a noun and a verb, a subject and a predicate, a proper noun and a common noun. If you don't, consult your Strunk and White.

Writing well

Clear business writing requires a good grasp of grammar and spelling, a good vocabulary, the desire to not be misunderstood, and ruthless self-editing. Business writing also requires a touch of grace.

Brushing up on the basics

You're probably starting with a good grasp of basic grammar and spelling. You acquire a good vocabulary in only one way: by reading. To paraphrase, "You are what you read." Business executives around the world recommend that you read a lot of difficult material in diverse fields. This recommendation is twofold: You learn new perspectives and information; and you learn new words. Both types of learning help your writing. The intention is to be as clear as you can be and to avoid all avoidable ambiguity. Writing requires an attention to detail that is not needed in conversation.

Editing is perhaps the most difficult thing to do with your own writing. After all, you wrote it, so you don't want to change it. But you should, because even trained writers can always find changes to make.

Edit, edit, edit — at least three times. Before anyone else gets the chance to hack away at your work, be your own worst critic. Eliminate the grammatical mistakes, spelling errors, and poor style. Read the letter out loud. Can that sentence be clearer? Make it so. Reread the letter out loud. Perhaps that word is too aggressive. Change it. Reread the letter. This paragraph isn't as clear as it should be. Rework it. Reread the letter. It looks good? Give it to someone else, and have her read it. When she can find no fault, reread it once more. Then print it, sign it, and send it!

Adding grace

Business writing, like all professional writing, is bound by the code that performance — not the person — is the subject of criticism. Focus on the topic at hand, rather than on the person who is talking about it, even if the person is a rude so-and-so. Here are the mistakes to avoid:

- ✔ Never swear in business correspondence.
- ✔ Never call people names in business correspondence.
- ✔ Never make off-color remarks in business correspondence.

Courteous writing requires that your tone be moderate. Tone is a function of word choice and sentence style. Choosing your words carefully demands a vocabulary rich enough to have words to choose from.

Speak softly, whether in person or in writing, even to your enemies. Your lawyers are carrying the big sticks.

Avoiding writing errors

Writing clearly requires that you eliminate the mistakes that threaten clarity. The first mistake is thinking that writing is no more than transcribed speech. It isn't. When you're talking in person or on the telephone, you can rely on the context of conversation to fill in gaps and to compensate for being ungrammatical. That context is absent in writing, so a good writer makes sure that her writing is clear, grammatically correct, and to the point.

When you acknowledge that writing is different from talking, the next important task is to eliminate the errors to which every writer is prone, which I discuss in the following sections.

Spelling errors

Believe it or not, spelling errors can doom business relations. You may find it hard to believe, but clients notice when your letters aren't proofread.

Many spelling errors are easily remedied by running your document through your computer's spell-check program. But beware — spell-checkers don't catch all the errors that can creep into a document. A trained eye is still better than a spell-check program. Remember to always double-check the spelling of the person's name to whom you are writing.

Grammatical errors

Most people are bored to tears by grammar, and for good reason: It's boring to most people! Grammar is a necessary skill for composing effective business letters, e-mails, and memoranda, however. Repeatedly making grammatical errors instantly brands you as being poorly educated and careless. Bad grammar leaves a bad impression.

So you slept through your grade-school grammar classes; your major in college required that you take only multiple-choice exams; and in graduate school, everyone was wowed by your fabulous technical expertise. Now you sweat bullets every time you have to compose a letter. Not to worry! The following sections note some of the most common grammatical errors and how to correct them.

Subject/verb agreement

If the subject of the sentence is singular, so is the verb; if the subject is plural, so is the verb. This rule applies even if other words intervene between the subject and the verb.

Mistake: The job description — a full-time shipper in a variety of small-business settings — are not detailed enough.

Better: The job description — a full-time shipper in a variety of small-business settings — is not detailed enough.

The subject is the job description, not the business settings.

Subjects such as *everyone, everybody, neither, nobody,* and *someone* should be treated as singular.

Mistake: Everyone has their own idea.

Better: Everyone has his or her own idea. Everyone has an idea. We all have our own ideas.

Sentence fragments

A sentence is a complete thought that must have a subject and a predicate phrase, including a verb. Sentences that lack subjects or predicates are sentence fragments.

Mistake: We are unwilling to take action. While we acknowledge your concerns.

Better: We are unwilling to take action, even though we acknowledge your concerns.

Run-on sentences

Run-on sentences include too much for a single sentence. Breaking one long sentence into several shorter sentences is a quick and easy fix.

Mistake: Mr. Weaver informed us that his Tonka truck was irreparable but that he didn't want to trade it for a similar toy, instead he wanted to get a cash refund so that he could buy his son a different toy which we disagreed with and so refused his suggestion.

Better: Mr. Weaver informed us that his Tonka truck was irreparable. However, he didn't want to trade it for a similar toy, preferring to get a cash refund so that he could buy his son a different toy. We disagreed with Mr. Weaver and refused to comply with his demand.

Dangling modifiers

Modifiers are sentence clauses that modify or affect the subject of the sentence. Modifiers dangle when what they modify is unclear. The results are often quite funny. The following was written by a man describing an ad campaign being considered by his company:

Mistake: Numerous times, I sat in my living room and watched June Cleaver vacuum and dust while wearing a dress, high heels, and pearls.

The clause "while wearing a dress, high heels, and pearls" is meant to modify "June Cleaver." However, it actually modifies the author!

Better: Numerous times, I sat in my living room and watched June Cleaver vacuum and dust while she wore a dress, high heels, and pearls.

Punctuation errors

Punctuation errors are among the most common writing errors. They make your correspondence look unprofessional. Here, then, is a brief refresher course on punctuation.

Commas

The comma marks a pause, sets off parenthetical material, separates main clauses in a compound sentence, or follows introductory expressions.

Mistake: If you're going to buy a camera you should get a flash.

Better: If you are going to buy a camera, you should get a flash.

Periods

The period ends a sentence.

Mistake: Please consider our proposal, we think you will agree that our service has overwhelming advantages.

Better: Please consider our proposal. We think you will agree that our service has overwhelming advantages.

Semicolons

The semicolon marks the end of a thought to which the next thought is intimately linked, or punctuates lists that are longer than three items.

Mistake: When using our product, care is required, without proper care, all warranties are null and void.

Better: When using our product, care is required; without proper care, all warranties are null and void.

Colons

The colon marks the break between a sentence and a list that follows. The colon is not used in lieu of a period, a comma, or a semicolon.

Dashes

The dash takes the place of a comma (when offsetting a parenthetical remark), period (when the succeeding sentence has the same subject), or colon (when the material following the dash expands on something before the dash). The dash is more informal than any of the punctuation marks it replaces. When used sparingly, it can be an effective tool.

Mistake: Tom who never said a mean thing about anyone admitted to thinking that Terry was vicious.

Better: Tom — who never said a mean thing about anyone — admitted to thinking that Terry was vicious.

Disorganization

Because words are organized into sentences, sentences into paragraphs, and paragraphs into the finished product, start with your sentences. Make sure that they are grammatically correct and that they say what you want them to say — and don't say anything that you don't want them to say.

Paragraphs composed of nothing but grammatically correct sentences are a good start. But your paragraphs also need to be organized. Typically, the most important sentence is the topic sentence, in which you identify what will be discussed in that paragraph. The balance of the paragraph is devoted to articulating, defending, explaining, or describing what you announce in your topic sentence.

Mistake: There is a golf course nearby and the pumps were plugged in at the time of the house inspection. Mr. Olson informs me that he did not mislead you about the need for sump pumps on the property. We are not really sure what this litigation is about. Mr. Olson put the pumps in after spring rains one year and did not conceal this fact during the inspection.

Better: We are not sure what this litigation concerns. First, Mr. Olson did not mislead you about the need for sump pumps on the property. Mr. Olson put the pumps in and disclosed this at the time of the house inspection. Moreover, they were running at the time of the inspection. Furthermore, the golf course is clearly visible from the property.

The first paragraph meanders through events that are not obviously connected. The second paragraph starts with a topic sentence that tells you exactly what the issue is. The other sentences defend the claim made in the topic sentence.

Passive voice

Passive voice is easy to diagnose: When the subject of the sentence is no longer the actor who does things, you have passive voice. Look at the difference between these two sentences, which "say" the same thing:

Mistake: We were told by the director that our scene would not be shot because we were likely to be hit with rain before the afternoon was through.

Better: The director told us that the forecast for rain would probably scuttle our shoot.

The first sentence is in passive voice; the second is in active voice. The first sentence implies that no one is responsible, because things just happen.

Excess verbiage

Bad writers use more words than are needed. Good writers don't; they know what words will convey their message efficiently. You improve your writing immediately by eliminating verbiage. Verbiage is like a jungle: Too much lushness means you can't see the sky.

Mistake: Due to the fact that any and all persons who had relations in connection with the reorganization of the hospital have experienced the move that human resources has had to make to the west wing owing to their downsizing, it is perhaps to be expected that some procedures have suffered.

Better: Human resources' move to the west wing has caused some procedural problems.

Chop! Chop! Chop! Out of the suffocating verbal vines emerges one clear sentence.

Surveying Corporate and Executive Stationery

Every corporate and executive office has a variety of stationery in its drawers. Each type has its function. But all types should share some characteristics:

- ✔ First, the paper should be of high quality. Paper for business letters should contain some rag-cotton content — typically, about 25 percent. When you're at the paper store, you can determine the rag content by looking at the box the paper comes in. You also want paper that is watermarked. You can determine whether paper has a watermark by holding a piece of it up to the light; you will be able to see the watermark embossed on the paper.

- ✔ Second, the stationery should be uniform in color, weight, and letterhead across sizes. Your company needs an identity, and one way to establish identity is through stationery. Having one font for your letterhead and another for your monarch sheets makes your corporate identity look uncertain.

Here are a few more guidelines:

- ✔ Don't skimp! Stationery is an essential part of your corporate identity.
- ✔ Quality usually trumps gimmicky color, shape, and design.

The following sections explain what goes in the stationery drawer.

Corporate letterhead

Letterhead should be 8½ x 11 inches, with high rag content and with the following relevant information printed on it:

- Business name
- Business address
- Business telephone number
- Business fax number
- Business e-mail address or Web page, if appropriate

Businesses that are partnerships, such as law firms and group medical practices, typically list all the partners or members on the letterhead.

Envelopes are printed with the company name and address.

Plain sheets of paper

Plain sheets should be 8½ x 11 inches and of the same quality as corporate letterhead. This paper is for letters longer than one page. (Second and subsequent pages are not presented on letterhead.)

Monarch paper

This type of paper should be 7¼ x 10½ inches, with high rag content. The sheets are used for personal business letters and have the following information printed on them:

- Person's name, but not the company's name
- Business address

If monarch sheets are used as corporate letterhead (as consultants, physicians, and attorneys sometimes do), include the business name.

Envelopes are printed with the person's name and business address.

Correspondence cards

These small (typically, 4½-x-6½-inch), nonfoldable cards are used for personal messages, announcements, and thank-you notes. They have the following information only:

- ✔ Person's name, not business name
- ✔ Business address

Envelopes are printed with the person's name and business address.

You may also use a fold-over card of the same size. These cards are sometimes called *informal* and may have a logo on the front.

Business cards

Business cards generally are 3½ x 2 inches, although other sizes are increasingly used in certain businesses. You present the business card to other people at business functions. The card should contain the following information:

- ✔ Person's name and title
- ✔ Business name
- ✔ Business address
- ✔ Business telephone number
- ✔ Business e-mail address
- ✔ Business fax number
- ✔ Business Web-page address

Your company logo may be incorporated into the design of the business card. You may also include a brief description or motto of your business.

Although some people prefer to leave the back of the card blank, you may print additional information about your company on the reverse side.

Writing Common Types of Business Correspondence

A letter is still the single most important form of communication in business. It is less ambiguous than a meeting simply because no one has to rely on memory to know what occurred; there, in black and white, is what you said.

For that reason, important business decisions are formalized in letters. In the following sections, I explain how to write a proper business letter and another common kind of correspondence: the memorandum.

Business letters

Most business letters are written with the intention of getting the reader to respond in some way. Given that goal, your writing should be efficient, clear, error-free, friendly, and pertinent.

When composing business letters, keep the following pointers in mind:

- ✔ Use high-quality paper with at least 25 percent cotton rag content. (I describe different types of business stationery earlier in this chapter.)

- ✔ Never send a letter written in anger unless you've waited 24 hours to review it.

- ✔ Plan your correspondence before writing it. Know what you want to say and in what order you want to say it.

- ✔ Compose your correspondence after planning it. Use direct, active language; vary your sentence structure; adopt a moderate, friendly tone; and give clear directions.

- ✔ Revise the letter to include any new information.

- ✔ Edit the letter for spelling, grammar, style, tone, and content.

- ✔ Edit again.

Each time you reread the letter, it is recommended that you focus on one aspect. Do not attempt to look for more than one or two elements when you reread letters. Instead, reread letters several times, focusing first only on grammar, then on spelling and missing or incorrect words (that a spell-checker won't catch), and finally on tone, content, and style.

The form of a business letter is standardized. All business letters have the following elements:

- ✔ **Dateline:** Three to six lines beneath the letterhead, flush left or right. The dateline contains the month (fully spelled out), day, and year.

- ✔ **Reference line:** One or two lines below the dateline, flush left, and repeated on each additional page. The reference line contains case or file numbers or policy numbers.

- ✔ **Recipient address:** Three to six lines below the dateline, flush left. The recipient address is composed of:

  - **Addressee's courtesy title and full name:** Courtesy titles in business are *Mr., Ms,* and *Dr.* Spell names out completely.

- **Addressee's business title:** The title appears on the line below the name.

- **Business name:** This text appears on the line below the business title. Spell it exactly as it appears on the company's letterhead. If the letterhead abbreviates *Company* as *Co.*, you do too.

- **Street address:** This address appears on the line below the business name. Spelling numbers out isn't necessary unless confusion would result otherwise; using "1745 26th Street" is just fine.

- **City, State, Zip:** When typing the state name on letterhead, the entire word is to be spelled out, such as California or Pennsylvania. It is not technically correct to use the U.S. Postal Service two-letter code — for example, CA or PA — on the letterhead. It is properly used on the envelope to expedite the processing of your letter for mailing.

✔ **Greeting or salutation:** One or two lines below the last line of the recipient's address. Usually, the salutation is "Dear Ms (Mr., Dr.)," followed by a colon. If you use first names in person, you may do so in your salutation.

✔ **Body:** Starts one line below the greeting. The body of the letter contains whatever you have to say. Be polite and courteous, but don't be a windbag. (Pay attention to the tips I provide earlier in this chapter.)

✔ **Complimentary close and signature:** Two lines below the last line of the body of the letter, flush left or centered. All the following closes are appropriate in business letters when you don't know the addressee: Yours truly, Very truly yours, Yours very truly, Sincerely, Yours sincerely, Sincerely yours.

If you know the addressee by her first name, you can use any of the following: All the best, Best wishes, All best wishes, Regards, Best regards, Kindest regards

Immediately below your complimentary close, you hand-write your signature. Use your full name if you don't know the addressee; use your first name only if you're on a first-name basis with that person.

Immediately below your handwritten signature, you type your signature, along with whatever complimentary and academic/professional degrees and ratings you like to see following your name.

✔ **Final notations:** Two lines below your typed signature. If, for example, the letter is typed by someone other than you, that person's initials appear here. If you are enclosing something with the letter, you may type the notation *enclosure* or *encl.* If you are sending copies of the letter to other people, you may type *cc:*, followed by the alphabetically listed names of those receiving the letter.

Check out an example of an appropriate business letter in Figure 8-1.

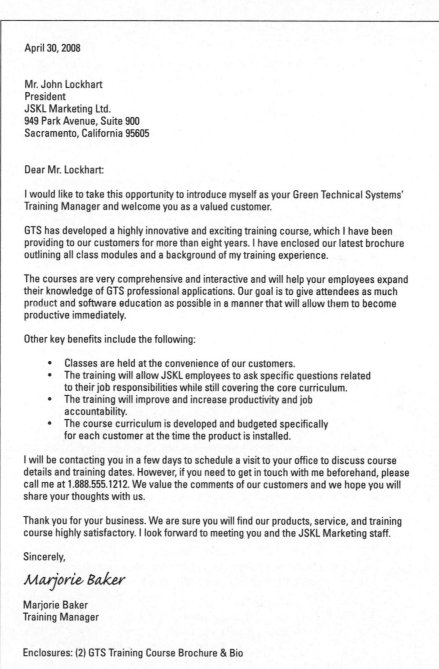

April 30, 2008

Mr. John Lockhart
President
JSKL Marketing Ltd.
949 Park Avenue, Suite 900
Sacramento, California 95605

Dear Mr. Lockhart:

I would like to take this opportunity to introduce myself as your Green Technical Systems' Training Manager and welcome you as a valued customer.

GTS has developed a highly innovative and exciting training course, which I have been providing to our customers for more than eight years. I have enclosed our latest brochure outlining all class modules and a background of my training experience.

The courses are very comprehensive and interactive and will help your employees expand their knowledge of GTS professional applications. Our goal is to give attendees as much product and software education as possible in a manner that will allow them to become productive immediately.

Other key benefits include the following:

- Classes are held at the convenience of our customers.
- The training will allow JSKL employees to ask specific questions related to their job responsibilities while still covering the core curriculum.
- The training will improve and increase productivity and job accountability.
- The course curriculum is developed and budgeted specifically for each customer at the time the product is installed.

I will be contacting you in a few days to schedule a visit to your office to discuss course details and training dates. However, if you need to get in touch with me beforehand, please call me at 1.888.555.1212. We value the comments of our customers and we hope you will share your thoughts with us.

Thank you for your business. We are sure you will find our products, service, and training course highly satisfactory. I look forward to meeting you and the JSKL Marketing staff.

Sincerely,

Marjorie Baker

Marjorie Baker
Training Manager

Enclosures: (2) GTS Training Course Brochure & Bio

Figure 8-1:
A proper
business
letter.

Memoranda

Memorandum is singular; *memoranda* is plural. If your Latin is weak, try using *memo* or *memos.* Memos are written communications within companies or within units of companies. Memos typically make announcements, discuss procedures, report on company activities, and disseminate employee information. They're informal and public. If you have something confidential to communicate, don't do it in a memo.

The tone of memos usually is informal and friendly. Although you don't need to be curt, officious, or patronizing, a certain succinctness is acceptable. Structure the memo so that the most important information comes in the first paragraph and that subsequent paragraphs spell out what is discussed in the first paragraph.

All memos are structured similarly. They have the following elements:

- ✔ **An addressee:** Flush left, in capital letters, near the top of the page
- ✔ **The sender:** Flush left, in caps, immediately below the addressee
- ✔ **Date:** Flush left, in caps, immediately below the sender's name
- ✔ **Subject:** Flush left, in caps, immediately below the date
- ✔ **Suitable paper:** White bond, either note size or standard to fit most desk in-baskets.

Figure 8-2 is an example of a properly structured memo.

Some people appear to think that the world can never have enough memos, and they stuff others' mailboxes to overflowing with them. Remember that everyone is busy and has a job to do. Other people appear to think that memos, because they are public, are effective management tools. Although memos are effective for direction and suggestion, criticism and praise are best given in person. If you must use a memo to criticize, make sure that the criticism is not of the person, but of the performance.

Even though the majority of information today is conveyed via e-mail, it's important that the style of using an attached memo (document) is still an important style of writing in 21st-century business. Sending hard copy memos may be a thing of the past, but it's still important to use the correct style when sending a memo in the body of an e-mail. When you're conveying larger amounts of information, it is better to send the information as a properly formatted memo attachment than to send it all via an e-mail blast. This way the message can contain the correct headings, numbered items, and other formatted information that an e-mail does not allow as easily.

Memorandum

TO: GTS Sales Staff

FROM: Karen Moore

CC: Mr. John Sakazaki

DATE: April 18, 2008

SUBJECT: Customer Presentation

The JSKL Marketing presentation you prepared last week to showcase our new product line was exceptional!

Your enthusiasm, sales strategy, and product knowledge were impressive and certainly sealed the deal with Mr. Lockhart!

Thank you for your outstanding work and dedication. Bonus checks will be distributed next week.

My sincere congratulations to all of you!

Figure 8-2:
A proper memo.

Handling Formal Correspondence

At some point, you will have the opportunity to host social business events, respond to an invitation, thank a colleague for a gift or an event, or announce something for the business.

Business and social invitations

Include every bit of information that is required for the invitee to decide whether to accept or decline the invitation. Make sure that everyone who should be invited is invited, which requires consulting all the department heads and other relevant people about their guest lists.

Although casual invitations are often extended by telephone, more formal or larger events call for written invitations. Whether your invitation is in person or in writing, here's a checklist to guarantee that you include what you need to (see Figure 8-3 for an example):

✔ **Who is the function's host?** Having an executive name herself as host gives the invitee a person to contact and thank.

✔ **What is the function?** The nature of the event should be explicit.

✔ **Where is the function?** The place where the function will be held and the phone number of the host are listed near the bottom of the invitation.

✔ **When is the function?** The time when the function will begin is listed. If the event is a cocktail party, the time when the party will end is also listed.

✔ **Will food be provided?** If the event is a sit-down dinner, the invitation should say *dinner*. *Cocktails* in an invitation means that hors d'oeuvres will be provided, but no more. *Buffet supper* means that the event will feature something more substantial than hors d'oeuvres but less substantial than dinner. *Cocktail buffet* means that the event will feature something more substantial than hors d'oeuvres but less substantial than a buffet supper.

✔ **Will dancing be involved?** If the event will include dancing, say so.

✔ **Will sports be involved?** If the event will feature volleyball, basketball, swimming, hang-gliding, or golf, say so.

✔ **What is the expected dress?** The style of dress should be specified. *Formal* or *Black Tie* means tuxedos for men, while women have a couple of options: either a long gown or a short, dressy cocktail dress. *Evening Formal* means a dark suit, a white shirt, and a tie for men; women can wear a short cocktail dress or a dressy pantsuit. *Business Dress* means a regular suit and tie for men, while women can wear a dress, a skirt with a blouse, or nice slacks with a top or a sweater. *Informal* means blue blazer and tie; and *Casual Dress* means business casual attire, such as a nice colored shirt and slacks for men, and a nice dress or pants outfit for women.

✔ **How should invitees reply?** The host determines how you should respond — by e-mail, telephone, or by return reply card. If a reply is requested, the letters *RSVP* usually occur near the bottom of the invitation. If you see *Regrets Only,* that means that you do not have to respond if you are going, but do have to respond if you are not going. The most important thing to remember is to reply by whatever due date was set by the host.

Thank-you notes

Thank-you notes are sent to the host within a day or two after the function. These notes are short, gracious, and to the point. Two to three lines is a perfectly acceptable length; you don't need to write several paragraphs. Thank-you notes are not for discussing business or bringing the host up to speed about your family life.

In honor of

Mr. John William Sakazaki

The Officers and Directors of Green Technical Systems

request the pleasure of your company

at a retirement dinner

Saturday, the fifteenth of March

Six o'clock to nine o'clock

Restaurant Sent Sovi
19956 State Street
Sacramento

RSVP   Business Dress
Ms. Carol Connor
19500 Capital Avenue
Sacramento, California 95605
916.555.1212

Figure 8-3:
An invitation
to a
business
event.

Thanking people for something usually follows the form in which the invitation was extended. If you receive a telephone invitation, a telephone thank-you is appropriate, although a thank-you note is a nice touch. If you receive a written invitation, you should write a thank-you note.

Thank-you notes are not reserved for parties and dinners. The general rule is this: If someone goes the extra mile for you, a thank-you note is appropriate; if the thank-you is just for day-to-day business, a verbal "Thank you" is good enough. Thank-you notes are always appropriate for gifts you've received. Use white, cream, or gray paper for a professional look; texture and weight aren't as important. Note cards or fold-over notes (informal) in white, cream, or gray can also be used. You can have these engraved, embossed, or printed with your name or monogrammed in the center of the card's front.

When you write a thank-you note, be sure to do the following (see Figure 8-4 for a sample):

- Thank the person for the gift.
- Recognize the effort that went into giving the gift.
- Tell the person how you will use the gift.

If you're feeling at a loss for words in starting a thank-you note, try writing these words: "What a [wonderful luncheon, fantastic evening at the theater, thoughtful gift]." The rest of the note should flow from there. Try not to start with "Thank you"; mention the event or gift, or make a general comment, first.

Announcements

Businesses on occasion make public announcements of important events, such as a move, a significant new hire or promotion, a meeting, or a significant death. If you are asked to compose such an announcement (like the one in Figure 8-5), keep three things in mind:

- Keep it simple.
- Get to the point immediately.
- Print it on correspondence cards, not letterhead.

April 18, 2008

Mr. John Lockhart
President
JSKL Marketing Ltd.
949 Park Avenue, Suite 900
Sacramento, California 95605

Dear Mr. Lockhart:

It was a pleasure speaking with you last week about our new computer product line. I would like to thank you for your order and faith in our company.

Green Technical Systems is dedicated to providing high-quality products and unsurpassed service, and we hope that you will allow us to continue to serve your business in a way that is mutually beneficial.

Ms. Patricia Parker, the sales representative in your area, will be handling your account. She will be contacting you this week to schedule a follow-up visit to familiarize you and the JSKL Marketing staff with our product line.

If you have any further questions, please feel free to call us at our toll-free number.

Thank you again for your purchase.

Sincerely,

Karen Moore

Karen Moore
President

cc: Ms. Patricia Parker

Figure 8-4: A thank-you note.

GREEN TECHNICAL SYSTEMS
is pleased to announce
KAREN MOORE
has been named Chief Executive Officer
following the retirement of John Sakazaki.

Ms. Moore will assume this position effective May 1, 2008.

Figure 8-5: A business announcement.

Addressing Envelopes for Business

First impressions are lasting impressions — especially with business correspondence. Letters are mirrors that reflect your taste and character (or those of your company). You should use printed envelopes that match your company letterhead with a printed return address. The recipient's address should be typed or printed by a software program.

Printed labels affixed to an envelope are not professional. Your letter could get set aside or thrown away because the envelope looks like junk mail.

Keep these additional points in mind when you're addressing an envelope for a business letter or a business social event:

- ✔ **Include your complete return address.** If you are not using printed envelopes that match your company stationery, print your name and company name and return address legibly in the top-left corner of the envelope. It's also acceptable to write the return address on the envelope flap, although the U.S. Postal Service prefers to have it on the front. A complete address comes in handy if your recipient wants to post a reply.

    Keep the lines aligned on the left. Write the street address and suite number (if any) on one line. Start a new line for the city, state, and zip code. Use numerals instead of writing out numbers, and make sure that you use the postal code abbreviation for your state — that is, NY for New York, IL for Illinois, AZ for Arizona, and so on.

- ✔ **List the recipient's formal title and address.** Regardless of the informality of the letter itself, the address on the envelope should be complete. The recipient's name and title should go on the first line. The second line is the street address, and the third line is the city, state (use the postal code abbreviation with no periods), and zip code.

- ✔ **Neatness counts!** If you address the envelope by hand, write legibly. Take a deep breath just before you begin. If you mess up somewhere along the line, start over on a fresh envelope. Strikeovers, ink blots, messy erasures, and the like are signals that you don't really care, but of course, you do care.

You can find more valuable information about addressing business envelopes on the U.S. Postal Service Web site: www.usps.com/businessmail101/addressing/deliveryAddress.htm.

Chapter 9

Keeping Up with Electronic Etiquette

- -

In This Chapter

▶ Guarding information

▶ Communicating around the clock

▶ Displaying great etiquette on the Internet and via e-mail

▶ Understanding the rules for high-tech gadgets

▶ Using laptops and office equipment courteously

- -

*N*ew technology has turned business on its ear and created a whole new set of etiquette conundrums. Yes, all this new technology saves time, but it also contributes to the ever-more-hectic pace of life and work. In this environment, in which everyone is trying to fit more activity into less time, misunderstandings about etiquette are bound to arise. But the problem isn't technology; it's the way technology is being used and abused.

You can easily forget good etiquette when you're using the latest technology, yet it isn't too late to change your behavior by being aware of it and by being sensible and considerate of others. (Emily Post didn't know anything about e-mail, but she did know that the essence of etiquette is putting other people at ease.)

Although the information in this chapter may not be new to you, knowing the rationale behind it is smart. No matter what, you must know how to present yourself as a considerate professional when you're using the latest technology. (Be sure to review Chapter 7 for information on improving your phone manners as well.)

Keeping Your Information Secure

Technology has made communication easier for you and me. It has also made communication easier for the bad guys — those who want to steal your company's proprietary technology, employee Social Security numbers, or other confidential information. Yes, all this new technology sounds a little like *Mission: Impossible,* but information security is part of business etiquette. After all, what could be more impolite than letting your company's secrets fall into the wrong hands?

Because the character of the Internet keeps changing, and the lingo can be confusing, the rules of common courtesy may be hard to grasp initially. Add the fact that an online faux pas has the potential to reach millions of people who have access to the Internet, and you may be a bit nervous about how to act online.

Some companies ask new employees to sign a confidentiality agreement, which states something to the effect that the employee will not share any information he learns at the company to help another company succeed. These agreements aren't just formalities; they're important, legally binding contracts that dictate how you should conduct yourself. If you sign one, keep a copy of it, and understand what it says.

Many large companies have specific guidelines about information storage and security, document retention, and so on. If you're not sure about your company's guidelines, ask. And don't leave any hard drives behind the copier or coffee machine!

Here are a few more guidelines:

- If you work with vendors, don't reveal more about internal projects than they need to know to complete the job. (Don't share lists of employee names and phone numbers, for example.)

- When you leave your desk for more than a minute, turn on your screen saver, and set a password to lock it. If you're not sure how to do this, check with the person who set up your computer.

- When you leave at night, lock up your disks and documents. Make sure that all confidential information is inside your locked cabinet and that any piles on the floor are just magazines and unopened mail.

- If you travel with a laptop computer, don't leave it in an unlocked conference room or sitting out in plain sight in your hotel room.

For complete details on security alerts, activities, reports, and updates, check out the National Cyber Alert System: www.us-cert.gov. Also, the Federal

Trade Commission has created a Web site for consumers and businesses as a source of information about computer security and safeguarding personal information. You can find further information by visiting the Web site: www.ftc.gov.

Handling 'Round-the-Clock Communications

In the old days, workers in the vast majority of professions had predictable work hours. Most professionals worked from 8 or 9 in the morning until 5 or 6 in the afternoon, and any incomplete work waited until the next day. People took lunch breaks every day. When Mr. Threemartini was out for the afternoon, generally no one could reach him unless the situation was urgent. He would return calls the next morning, when he arrived at the office to find a stack of pink phone-message slips.

How things have changed! Now, with all the new technology — cell phones, personal digital assistants (PDAs), and text-messaging devices, to mention just a few — people are connected 24 hours a day!

In such an environment, everyone has to be a bit flexible in understanding the needs and priorities of colleagues. If you're the boss, don't expect your 3 a.m. e-mail to have been read before the 8 a.m. staff meeting. If you're the employee, be aware of your boss's idiosyncrasies, and learn to anticipate them (even if you'll never love them). If you're in either position, don't call or text-message someone after hours unless an emergency arises or you have discussed the contact in advance ("Please contact me when you get those numbers, Bob, and I'll call you from the prime minister's dinner party.").

Here are a few additional guidelines:

- ✔ If you're seized by a fit of creativity in the middle of the night, read your e-mails again the next morning before sending them. Your idea (not to mention your level of coherence) may look different in the light of day.

- ✔ Don't practice voice-mail avoidance by returning all your calls at odd hours. If someone has left a message for you, requesting specific information, leaving a specific answer late at night is fine. If someone needs to talk to you, however, don't return the call at 10 p.m. and then insist smugly that you have done your part. You're not fooling anyone.

- ✔ If you send an e-mail that needs an immediate response, call to alert the recipient.

Practicing Civility on the Internet

Some observers believe that the Internet has been a great democratizer because it has made great volumes of information available to everyone who has access to a computer and modem. People who have never left their hometowns can take virtual tours of the Louvre or travel anywhere in the world by using Google Earth. But the world is made up of two kinds of people: those who know how to use the Internet with élan and those who don't.

Be sure to keep these rules in mind:

- First and foremost, a business Internet account is for business. Even if everyone else seems to be doing it, resist the temptation to shop for shoes online during that interminable conference call. Some companies may allow you to use your Internet account for personal use during breaks or lunch hours, but ask first.

- Unless your job description requires you to participate in company blogs and online chatting, you shouldn't be doing these activities on company time. If your job requires that you manage or respond to blogs and chat rooms, make sure you use the appropriate etiquette. Most blogs and chat rooms have rules and guidelines, so follow them! A few general tips: Use the spell-checker, be accurate and honest, and stay on topic.

- Be aware that many employers monitor employee Internet use. Find out whether your company has an official policy on Internet use, and be sure to follow it carefully. Wouldn't it be embarrassing to explain that you were fired because you were updating your MySpace page or writing comments in an inappropriate blog on company time?

- If it's necessary in your job to navigate the Internet or intranet sites at work, it's important to remember that your communication is coming from your work e-mail address. You're bound to run into problems with obsolete links, error messages, or outdated information. Some sites solicit your information via Contact Us or Feedback links. Your feedback is important, but remember that a real person will read your e-mail. Send feedback such as "As a frequent user of your site, I find this problem frustrating" rather than slacker-like feedback such as "Your site is lame, and your company blows!" The ruder and less rational your feedback is, the more likely the Webmaster will be to dismiss it as the raving of a lunatic shut-in.

- You have no excuse for viewing adult Web sites at the office, even if you do so after hours, when you're the only person around. Despite the uproar about children discovering inappropriate Web content, happening upon dirty pictures by accident isn't easy. And with the current legal climate around sexual harassment in the workplace, most employers have a zero-tolerance policy for this kind of behavior.

> ✔ Some Internet service providers have rules and policies about online behavior. If you're at work and discover anything online that is inappropriate, that makes you feel uncomfortable, or that you believe is harassment, contact your company's IT department or the company's Internet service provider immediately.

Take the time to understand online lingo. Many Web sites list Internet terms and acronyms. Knowing some of the key vocabulary will not only help you communicate clearly, but also show that you are a savvy Internet user. For the lowdown on Internet vocabulary, check out *The Internet For Dummies,* 11th Edition, by John R. Levine, Margaret Levine Young, and Carol Baroudi (Wiley).

Figuring Out E-Mail Etiquette

A couple of years ago, e-mail surpassed postal mail as the highest-volume carrier of messages. Its popularity has been booming ever since and shows no signs of stopping. Though volumes have been written about the etiquette of communicating through this new medium, many of the worst offenders don't seem to be listening. Are you one of them? The following sections explain how to avoid some of the pitfalls of instantaneous communication.

Communicate clearly

The best feature of e-mail is also the worst: Communication with one or many people, across the hall or across the world, can happen immediately. That immediacy can be a tremendous asset when you need that kind of power. It can also be a real problem when you use it as a substitute for thoughtful, meaningful communication.

One problem with overusing e-mail is that your tone can easily be misunderstood. In person or on the phone, listeners can get visual or verbal cues, and pick up emotions and nuances, particularly sarcasm. Even in the age of irony, and even if you use the ubiquitous smiley, readers may miss your point. "I heard Thursday's staff meeting went really well!" has a completely different meaning when it's spoken in a sarcastic tone (the meeting didn't go well at all) than it does when it's spoken in a happy, direct tone. Chances are good that your readers will misunderstand this statement in an e-mail.

In a conversation, people often ask clarifying questions, as in this example:

"Did you send that report to Steve?"

"Steve Ferrill?"

"No, Steve Peterson. He wanted me to add some information about SLAs."

"Well, I sent it to Steve Ferrill. What's an SLA?"

You can easily see how, in an e-mail about Steve and SLAs, both parties could end up confused. Always reread your e-mail message for clarity before you send it, and follow up with a phone call if you don't get a prompt response.

Write with style

Here are a few stylistic mistakes that people make when using e-mail:

- **Forgetting the rules of spelling and grammar:** Perhaps because of the sheer volume of e-mails that people send, e-mail tends to be a very informal medium. *Informal,* however, should not mean *sloppy.* Watch for problems such as sentence fragments and spelling errors. If you're not sure about the rules of grammar, read Chapter 8, and purchase a style manual such as *The Elements of Style* by William Strunk Jr. and E. B. White.

- **Being unprofessional:** Just because you're sending an e-mail instead of a memo or telephone call doesn't mean you can let your professional standards relax. Although a touch of humor in the tone of an e-mail can be fine, make sure you preserve your professionalism. Although smileys may be helpful in social e-mails, try to avoid using them in business.

- **Omitting a greeting and/or closing:** Even worse is using "Hey" as a greeting. Is it really that hard to type "Hi Charlene" or "Best wishes, Biff"?

- **Using ALL CAPITALS:** Capitals are harder to read than regular text. In addition, many people view their use as the e-mail equivalent of yelling, so if you wouldn't scream something in the conference room, don't type it in all capitals.

- **Using all lowercase letters:** Are you e.e. cummings? If not, capitalize proper nouns, names, and the first letter of each sentence.

- **Using offensive language:** Though you should watch your language at work in general, spoken expletives float away into the air. Written ones sit there on the computer screen, maybe for longer than you want them to.

Think before you send

Some other e-mail annoyances are simply the result of taking too little time to think. They include

- **Sending a message to too many people:** Does everyone on your project team need to see the details about setting up a conference room for next Thursday? No. After you have completed the legwork with the person or people who are really affected, you can notify others with a single message.

- ✔ **Using Reply All or a similar function instead of Reply to Sender:** If your manager sends out a message thanking everyone on the team for great work on the project, don't respond to the entire group, telling him that it was your pleasure and that he's a great leader.

- ✔ **Not double-checking the list of recipients,** especially if the message says something potentially negative: A public-relations executive received a particularly irritating e-mail from a despised colleague. The executive forwarded the note and her sarcastic commentary on it to a friend — or so she thought. In fact, she had clicked the Reply button and sent the e-mail right back to her nemesis. Imagine her humiliation when she had to apologize!

- ✔ **E-mailing someone who sits across the aisle from you:** If you're recapping a meeting, e-mailing is fine. But if you have a question for discussion, try the old-fashioned approach of speaking to each other.

- ✔ **Sending and receiving personal e-mail at work:** The equipment and Internet time belong to your company, so using them for personal purposes probably violates company policy. And although I know you would never send anything potentially offensive or harassing from work, it could be equally damaging to receive such material at work from a friend.

Avoid venting

E-mail is a great tool for venting your spleen. Unfortunately, you shouldn't do it at work. Observe the following rules:

- ✔ Don't use e-mail to lambaste a colleague, and especially don't copy others on the message. That's tantamount to chewing someone out in front of a room full of his peers. Disagreements or discipline are best handled in person or at least over the phone.

- ✔ If you receive a scathing e-mail, resist the urge to write a similarly scathing message in return. Take the high road. Offer the olive branch, or at the very least, distract the other person by making him wonder why you haven't responded.

- ✔ Never, ever write something in an e-mail that you wouldn't want published in the newspaper. Even if you send them to people you trust, e-mails that contain sensitive, mean, or potentially embarrassing information have a way of being forwarded beyond your original audience.

E-mail should not be a substitute for face-to-face discussions and telephone time, and e-mailing should not go on too long. After two back-and-forth exchanges on the same issue, it's time to pick up the phone.

Be aware that managers in e-mail-intensive companies may get 200 or more messages *per day!* Take pity on them; be brief, and if you don't get a response when you need one, follow up by phone.

You should also return e-mail messages promptly, even if only to say, "I received your message but won't be able to give it my full attention until next week." If your e-mail program supports this feature, you should also set a vacation auto-reply when you will be out of touch for more than a day or two. The e-mail program will respond automatically to correspondents (usually, only once to each person) to let them know that you're away and not reading e-mail.

Always remember to add the subject in the Subject line. This not only helps the person quickly locate the e-mail at a later time, but it is also the polite thing to do. One of the worst offenses in e-mail etiquette is how people use the Subject line to send their entire message, leaving the text area totally blank . . . not even an auto-signature. Although the sender may think it is only one sentence, it is often an extremely long sentence. Regardless, it is not correct and is a sign of laziness. Subject lines are meant to be a quick reference to what is written in the body of the e-mail.

Being Mannerly with High-Tech Gadgets

Today, many people seem to be more focused on their fancy gadgets than on other people. Face-to-face meetings have become a low priority because they're constantly being interrupted by technology, and many people can't figure out what to do. What's more important: the gadget or the person you're with?

If you don't want to be seen as a rude person, consider the advice in the following sections when you use high-tech tools.

The same etiquette rules that apply to handheld devices apply to cell-phone use. See Chapter 7 for more on this topic.

Managing text-messaging on PDAs

Be with the one you're with! Social norms say that the person you are conversing with takes precedence over text-messaging on your personal digital assistant (more commonly known as a PDA). This rule applies in business as well. Most businesses prefer employees not make personal calls and send personal e-mails on company time. The same rule applies to text-messaging. If the text message isn't related to work, don't do it. Or wait to respond during your break, lunch, or after work. It is not only rude but also distracting to check or send text messages in the presence of other people, whether socially or for business.

Follow these additional rules for proper text-messaging:

✔ Before using any handheld device, consider your location. Sending text messages is acceptable in semiprivate situations, such as in the airport, in a cab or a train, alone in a café, or waiting in line. Just don't hold up the line by asking the person at the counter to wait until you finish sending or reading a message. When dining out with others, keep your electronic gadgets neatly tucked away at mealtime — never left sitting on the table.

✔ If you receive an urgent or important message in the presence of someone else, excuse yourself, and find a secluded corner where you can communicate.

Listening to audio files on MP3 players

It's best to check company policy first, however, most businesses allow their employees to use MP3 players or other devices as long as they use a headset or earpiece so the music or program does not disturb coworkers. Normally this is fine in an office environment or if you work in a cubicle, or if your job requires you to cover some background noise, such as that of a warehouse worker. Just remember to keep the volume low. An exception applies to those who work in the public eye, such as sales clerks or receptionists. In these instances, listening to private selections is clearly inappropriate.

Shooting pictures and videos on cell phones

No longer a novelty, the camera phone has become ubiquitous. When it comes to business, however, you should steer clear of certain things. A picture may be worth a thousands words, for example, but think twice before you use your cell phone to take covert shots of fellow employees or unreleased products without approval.

Photographing or videotaping people you work with without their knowledge or approval is not professional. Respect others' privacy. Always ask permission before taking a photo or video of someone and never post photos to any Internet sites unless you have a signed agreement.

Using laptop computers appropriately

What possible etiquette pitfalls could surround laptop computers? Here are some:

- ✔ Some keyboards are quieter than others, but loud typing during a meeting can be very distracting to your colleagues. If you're getting the look of death from the person sitting next to you, switch to a pen and paper.

- ✔ The same rule applies to conference calls; ambient noise can drown out speakers. Set your phone on mute unless you're speaking so that others won't hear you typing.

Using Office Equipment Appropriately

The key to using and sharing office equipment is remembering that it belongs to everyone. Here are a few tips:

- ✔ If you notice that the fax machine or copier is out of paper, put in more paper.

- ✔ If the fax machine or copier is broken, either fix it (if you know how to do so without making the problem worse) or call someone who can fix it. Then put a sign on the equipment to let other users know the problem has been called in.

- ✔ If you need to make lots of copies, and someone else needs to make only a few, let him go first.

- ✔ Have respect for the IT folks and other people who fix your office equipment and maintain computers, phones, and other office equipment by keeping it clean. Think of how much more pleasant your job is because of them!

Part III

Behaving in the Boardroom and Beyond

The 5th Wave   By Rich Tennant

al Fundraising Dinner

"Does the check writing pen go above the dessert spoon or next to the salad fork?"

In this part . . .

I put you through a real etiquette workout, reviewing everything from meeting manners to gift-giving. I help you shine in the boardroom by outlining proper seating arrangements and give you details on chairing a meeting properly. I hit the potential highs and lows of company events and help you figure out the office-party minefield.

This part covers practical guidelines for business meals and the importance of dining etiquette. It also talks about the importance of taking part in company off-site activities and the etiquette challenges surrounding them.

I give you words of wisdom on surviving trade shows and conferences, as well as tips on mingling and networking and on the significance of representing yourself and your company. I show you what to do if the responsibility for planning a special event falls to you. I close with the best ways to mark milestones with colleagues, clients, and bosses, and appropriate gift-giving associated with those events.

Chapter 10

Minding Your Meeting Manners

If you've been in the work world very long, you know that meetings are the butt of frequent jokes, and, in many cases, the bad reputation that meetings have is well-deserved. Conducting efficient and effective meetings is possible, however.

If you can master the art of the meeting, you will be a powerful asset to your organization. And even if you're not planning the meeting, you still need to know the proper etiquette for your role as a participant.

Planning a Meeting

Planning a meeting can be a thankless job. Your work often goes unrecognized unless something goes wrong, in which case you become the object of intense scrutiny. If you're lucky, though, your boss recognizes and appreciates your skill. In the following sections, I provide some handy tips for figuring out the purpose of a meeting, putting together an agenda, and scheduling an agreeable time.

Determining the purpose

Perhaps the single most important element of a good meeting is purpose. You must know why you're holding the meeting and what you hope to accomplish. If you're initiating the meeting yourself, spend a few moments clarifying the purpose in your mind. If you're asked to plan a meeting for your boss, ask her to take the time to explain her expectations.

A clear purpose is essential for a successful meeting. Ask yourself or your boss these questions: "What goal (or goals) do we hope to accomplish? How will a meeting help accomplish this goal?"

After you've determined your purpose, make sure that a meeting will help you achieve your goal. A meeting can be a good way to disseminate information to several people at the same time. Although e-mail or other means of communication can be effective, a meeting allows for eye contact, body language, and opportunities to ask questions so as to clarify the information. On the other hand, a meeting may not be a good idea if the information is unlikely to generate discussion.

Drawing up an agenda

After you figure out the purpose of your meeting, put together an agenda outlining what the meeting will cover. An agenda helps participants prepare for the meeting, which minimizes choruses of the always-popular "I'll have to get back to you on that." Ask participants to review the agenda and to come prepared. No one likes to look disorganized and incompetent in front of a room full of people. If you provide your coworkers an opportunity to prepare, they'll take advantage of it.

Be aware that if you don't set an agenda, participants may arrive at the meeting with their own hidden agendas — possibly ones you don't like. A written agenda puts you in the driver's seat.

A complete agenda includes a list of topics to be covered, assignments of who should be prepared to cover each topic, time estimates for discussion of each topic, and start and end times. Be sure to leave a little more time than you think you'll need. You find out later in this chapter how to control the musings of those long-winded bores in your office, but you should still build in plenty of time for discussion. Your agenda also should include the meeting location and a list of attendees so that they can discuss items before the meeting if necessary (or gird themselves for verbal battle).

Including all this information means you'll have to hold off on your meeting announcement until you have all the details. Resist the temptation to shoot out an e-mail prematurely; otherwise, you'll end up having to send two or three messages, and people will start to think of you as unorganized.

If you're new to the company or organization, consider consulting another coworker or your manager to review your agenda. Nothing is more painful than sitting in a meeting with exactly the same agenda items or strategies that have been covered or tried previously. Otherwise, the attitude of the attendees usually is "Been there, done that."

Scheduling the meeting

Scheduling a meeting can be tough, and it gets more complicated with every added participant. In some cases, you have to schedule a time that's convenient for the most important players and ask the other participants to rearrange their schedules.

One strategy is to come up with three meeting times on different days and at different times of day, and then propose those times and ask people to respond with their availability. E-mail and calendar-sharing software programs are excellent tools for this task.

In many corporate situations, a meeting is actually part of a larger event. Large corporations with employees in several locations often host combination meeting/social events to get managers or employees together in one place. If you're in charge of putting together an awards banquet/golf outing/Cajun cookout/all-night dance party, read the section in Chapter 13 on planning special events. With any luck, you can get help from a consultant or another employee who can show you the ropes.

Taking a Seat

At a company that makes a point of minimizing hierarchy, seating arrangements probably are no big deal. Even in many larger companies, seating arrangements often are inconsequential at internal meetings that do not include vendors or clients. In more formal sessions, however, you may need to be aware of possible seating rules that affect where you should sit after you've confidently strolled into the meeting.

Many people have theories about the psychology of seating arrangements: that you should sit directly across from the most important attendee so as to be noticed (or sit behind a large person if you don't want to be noticed); that you should sit at the right hand of the important person; that the right hand of the important person is less impressive than the left hand; and on and on. Probably some people even recommend sitting in the lotus position with your fingertips pressed together for greater meeting harmony.

In fact, you need to follow just a few basic guidelines:

✔ Don't sit where the host or most important attendee plans to sit, which usually is at the head of the table — an easy task if that person is already seated. If not, you can remain standing until she arrives or, depending on the situation, take a seat that you know the boss won't desire.

- ✔ If the host or the most important attendee has an assistant coming to the meeting, the assistant probably will want to sit directly to the right of the boss.

- ✔ If you start to suspect that you have chosen the wrong seat — for example, if your boss is suddenly giving you that look — say something like "Would you like to sit here?", and make getting-up motions. This strategy is far preferable to having your boss ask you to move.

- ✔ Always be flexible. If the room is small, for example, and the last arrival will have to navigate around you to get to the last available seat, you might offer to move.

If you are the meeting planner, you may give polite direction to attendees about where to sit. You could say "Sebastian, why don't you sit at this end?" or "Miss Barker and Dr. Cooper, please be seated at the head of the table."

Being an Effective Chair or Participant

Meetings may masquerade as a chance to update the status of a project or catch up on industry developments, but they're really used as a way to learn about and measure participants. Whether you're running the meeting or are a participant, meetings provide you with an opportunity to shine in front of your peers and superiors. That's why communicating by using all the right verbal and nonverbal signals is important. The following sections tell you what those signals are and how to use them to be an effective chair or participant.

When you're running the meeting

When you're the host, your job is to take charge and make sure that the meeting runs smoothly. Meetings aren't football games, so not every meeting requires formal rules. Knowing the rules can be helpful, however, in politely corralling boorish (or simply inexperienced) colleagues and letting them know that they are out of line.

Starting the meeting

Your first job is arriving at all meetings a little early. If you're in charge, your next job is beginning the meeting promptly. Part of civility in the workplace is respecting the value of everyone's time. Those who sit around waiting for latecomers to show up are understandably annoyed. Their schedules are also full, and they don't deserve this kind of treatment. If you develop a reputation as a person who starts meetings on time, people will be more likely to arrive on time to your meetings. Conversely, if you develop a reputation as someone who always starts late, people will start showing up late, and the situation will spiral downward.

In some cases, you may need to bend your starting-on-time rule if the boss or some other very important attendee is late. Even so, you probably shouldn't delay for more than about 5 minutes. This person may exercise her prerogative to have you repeat the part of the meeting that she missed. If you're lucky, she will call in advance to warn you, apologize profusely upon arrival, and not make this behavior a habit. Most people are late once in a while, but frequent lateness is a subtle way of telling others that they're not important — not a good management strategy!

Adhering to the agenda with Robert's Rules of Order

Another important job for the meeting host is sticking to the agenda. Though you sent the agenda to all participants in advance, you may want to bring along copies to distribute, ensuring that everyone knows what's about to happen. Then you should keep an eye on your watch so that you can hold up your end of the bargain: Participants arrive at your meeting on time, and you do your best to get them out on time.

To run a meeting effectively, you should be at least somewhat familiar with Robert's Rules of Order, a system of parliamentary procedures first published in 1876. Although the system sounds daunting, Robert's Rules are simply a system for agreeing on how meetings should be run. Some of the rules are extremely detailed, but knowing all of them isn't necessary. You should, however, be familiar with the basic concepts of procedure.

Not all meetings are formal enough to require Robert's Rules. Many of the meetings you'll run will be entirely informal affairs in which people get together to hash things out. Yet even for these meetings, some procedure must be followed. Everybody can't talk at the same time, and you'll have to agree on some method for discussing the options, reaching a decision, and implementing it. Knowing the basic steps of procedure, as Robert's Rules spells them out, can help:

- The moderator — usually, the same person as the host — is in charge of keeping the meeting on track and preventing participants from interrupting one another. At the beginning of the meeting, the moderator should make it clear what rules are being used, such as not interrupting while someone is speaking and avoiding confrontations.

- Participants generally raise their hands when they want to speak, and the moderator recognizes a speaker. If the meeting is a small one, you don't have to raise your hand above your head; a small hand gesture will do the trick. Even a particularly earnest look may get across your desire to speak.

✔ When a participant is recognized, she is said to have the floor, meaning that she can speak for a reasonable amount of time about her suggestion or point of view. If someone attempts to interrupt, the moderator has the right to remind that person — politely — that someone else has the floor at the moment. You can say something like, "Thank you John, however, you'll have an opportunity to take the floor shortly. Let's let Carol finish." The moderator should eventually recognize everyone who wants to speak, of course.

Some organizations have been known to have an object of some kind that is passed from speaker to speaker. Although this method makes it patently obvious who has the floor, it also has the disadvantage of reminding people of the humiliating potty pass from grade school.

✔ In addition to preventing interruptions, the moderator should prevent speakers from repeating themselves or blathering on too long. An appropriate comment might be "Gene, I think we have heard enough to understand your position. I'd like to recognize Jezebel now and hear what she has to say."

✔ The speaker should voluntarily yield the floor when she's finished speaking by sitting down (if she is standing) or simply saying, "I'm finished."

In some cases, a meeting includes voting. Meeting formality can depend on the culture of the company. If the environment is more on the conservative or formal side, the following steps are normally followed:

1. **After ideas have been discussed, a participant makes a *motion* (an idea to be voted on).**

   The participant makes the motion by saying something like "I move that the water cooler be filled with sparkling wine." Although you, as the moderator, usually don't make a motion, you can start the process after you feel that adequate discussion has taken place by saying something like "Do I have a motion to fill the water cooler with sparkling wine?" At that point, someone who advocates that position should jump in and make the motion.

2. **Another participant should second the motion.**

3. **You, acting as the moderator, ask whether further discussion is needed.**

4. **Say "All in favor, say 'Aye'" and count the votes; then say "All opposed, say 'Nay,'" and count those votes if necessary.**

If the discussion starts wandering far from the central topic, the moderator or host should suggest that the new topic be tabled for another meeting. Most participants will acknowledge the need to stay on track and finish the meeting on time, even if they are very concerned about the new topic.

If you are the chairman of an organization or find yourself leading meetings frequently, you may want to pick up a guide to Robert's Rules for easy reference. Even if no one else knows them, your familiarity will help you run an efficient meeting. I highly recommend *Robert's Rules For Dummies* by C. Alan Jennings (Wiley).

Taking notes

Finally, as host or chair, you have to take notes. Taking notes isn't glamorous, but it's an important part of a successful meeting. Though other participants may take their own notes, those notes may not be comprehensive. As the meeting host, you want to make sure that everyone who attended the meeting ends up with the same record of what happened. If you're lucky enough to have an assistant at your disposal, you can ask that person to take the notes and then simply approve them. If not, taking notes is your job.

If you use a laptop computer to take notes, be certain that the noise you make typing does not distract the other participants in the meeting. You can do this by asking the chair and other participants at the beginning of the meeting whether using your laptop is distracting.

Unless your organization has a specific format for meeting notes, you can include this information:

✔ Time and date of the meeting

✔ List of participants

✔ Agenda and notes of the discussion about each agenda item

✔ Any motions made and the resulting decisions

When you're participating in the meeting

Some people arrive late at meetings, come in loudly, and start asking questions about topics that have already been covered. Don't ever be that person. If you arrive late, keep quiet, and ask a sympathetic soul to catch you up later — not while someone else is talking.

There's no question that we live in a hectic and quick-paced world. Punctuality is critical, however, not only for your career, but for your personal relationships as well. Time is our most precious commodity, and wasting other people's time by making them wait for you is extremely rude. Be on time for any meeting you're participating in. Period! If you can't help being late, call ahead, apologize, and let the other participants know when you'll arrive. Afterward, send an e-mail apology to the chair of the meeting.

As a meeting participant, follow the procedures that the chair or host adopts. If your host is running an informal meeting, your points of order are unnecessarily rigid. If your host is running a formal meeting, learn enough about Robert's Rules of Order to be able to participate effectively. (I discuss these rules earlier in this chapter.)

You should never interrupt other speakers, of course. Also avoid the temptation to sigh loudly, roll your eyes, or otherwise express your contempt when someone else is speaking. If you have a colleague who incessantly interrupts others, please refer to Chapter 16.

You're obliged to stay for the entire meeting unless you have another appointment or commitment. If so, at the beginning of the meeting, let your chair know when you'll have to leave, and leave quietly at that time. If you're unlucky enough to be a participant in a meeting whose chair has not set an adjournment time, and the meeting is dragging on and on, pass a note to the chair explaining your other commitment, stand up, excuse yourself quickly, and leave without making a show of it.

If you like taking notes, by all means do so. If you're not fond of note-taking, and someone else appears to be, don't take notes. You'll know after a couple of meetings how accurate other people's notes are. If you're concerned that the decisions made during the meeting diverge from the decisions reported in the notes and subsequent memoranda, offer to take notes for the meeting. You'll be doing your chair a favor.

Always think before you speak and weigh your words carefully. Whether you're running the meeting or are a participant, always stick to the agenda. Do your best to avoid harsh words, and don't repeat yourself, blather on for too long, or be offensive to anyone present.

One of the biggest mistakes in business today is acting rushed. This is particularly evident in a meeting when people begin looking at their watches or cell phones for the time, clearly showing they are distracted, which means they are not listening.

Chapter 11

Engaging in Business Meals and Parties

*W*hy combine food and business? At first, the answer may seem simple: time. Although it's true that you often don't have enough hours in the day to complete business unless you schedule some meetings during meal-time, sharing a meal is also a time-honored way of cultivating trust.

In a business meal, the devil and the deal are in the details. In this chapter, I show you clever ways to stay organized, save time, and build relationships. I also provide suggestions for entertaining at home without anxiety.

The more formal the meal, the more emphasis on the social aspects of your relationship. Informal meetings are for discussing business details, but formal dinners are for building personal rapport. In Chapter 12, I introduce you to the nitty-gritty of polite dining.

Organizing a Business Meal at a Restaurant

The most typical business meals are breakfast and lunch. Dinner usually is reserved for special occasions or out-of-town guests. Breakfast meetings are good if your time is limited and your agenda is short, but keep in mind that not everyone is an early bird. Lunch is the default business meal. Its neutrality implies neither the informality of a breakfast meeting nor the formality of a dinner meeting.

Assume that you've decided to take someone out for lunch. The following sections list the steps to follow.

Step 1: Schedule the lunch

Choosing the restaurant is your business, though you can make a couple suggestions for your guest and let him select one. If possible, select restaurants that you have been to, or choose a couple of restaurants that you think will appeal to your guest. See whether reservations are available on the day you want to take your client to lunch. Ask for two times: noon and 1 p.m. Also, the restaurant location should be convenient to your guest, not to you.

The actual invitation (extended during a phone conversation) can be phrased like this:

> *Chris, I'd like you to be my guest at lunch next week. Would Wednesday or Thursday work for you? Noon or one o'clock? Would you prefer Indian Garden or Chez Chez?*

After you've worked out the details, repeat them at the end of the conversation:

> *Great talking with you, Chris. I look forward to seeing you at Chez Chez at noon on Wednesday.*

Immediately call the restaurant to confirm your reservation and cancel any other reservations.

Step 2: Confirm

A day before the meeting, check with your guest and confirm the date, time, and location with either an e-mail or phone call, and confirm the reservation with the restaurant.

Step 3: Pay before you eat

Arrive early at the restaurant, and ask the maitre d' to take your credit card and run it through for preapproval right away. Sign the receipt; add a gratuity of 18 to 20 percent; and if you want, request that the receipt be mailed to you in a stamped, self-addressed envelope that you provide. You also can establish a house account at the restaurant. Either way, the bill never appears at the table, so there's no confusion about who pays.

Step 4: Be nonchalant

Arrive at the restaurant about ten minutes ahead of your guest. When the maitre d' or hostess asks you, "Would you like to wait in the bar, in the lobby, or at your table?" you choose the table. This way you can set the seating arrangements and make sure you aren't seated near the kitchen door or in some other inappropriate location. If the table is not ready and it's necessary to wait, at least check the table location and wait in the lobby. Greet your guest warmly by name and with a handshake.

Step 5: Take the worst seat

If you've not been seated at the table before your guest arrives and you've met him in the lobby, motion for your guest to follow the maitre d' to the table. Allow him to have the best seat. Guests should never sit looking at a mirror or toward the kitchen door.

Once seated, pay attention to your posture and body language. Always sit up straight at the table with your feet flat on the floor or cross them at the ankles, and leave your shoes on!

Step 6: Order carefully

Keep these guidelines in mind while you and your guest order:

- ✔ **Take a couple of minutes to get situated.** While you're perusing the menu, you can give your guest clues about the limits of your hospitality. You might say, "Hmm, I think I'll have a cocktail today" or "I think I'll have iced tea."

  You can help your guest by suggesting items from each course on the menu. You might say, "The shrimp dumplings here are good, and they're famous for their green-chile corn chowder." If you are on a tight company budget or company expense account, these suggestions can be in the price range that is allowable. If money is not a problem, then don't be stingy! Recommend one of the more expensive entrees. As the host you can encourage guests to order extra courses: "John, do have an appetizer, soup, or salad before your main course."

- ✔ **Always order the same number of courses your guest does.** If your guest orders an appetizer, for example, you should too. This action prevents the awkward situation that arises when one of you is eating and the other is not.

  If your guest is a light eater, so are you. You won't starve.

✔ **Once your food has arrived, be sure to use impeccable table manners.** See Chapter 12 for complete details.

Ordering at a business lunch has relaxed some in recent years. As encouraged by the host, everyone may order as many or as few courses as they want. However, it is a delicate balance. When in a group of three or more, it is best to make every effort not to appear too hungry.

As a guest, never order extra courses, until encouraged by the host. If the host says nothing, stick to ordering only a main course.

Step 7: Know when to start talking business

Unless the need to transact business is urgent and you and your guest have agreed to get right down to business, don't discuss business matters until the end of the meal. Yes, not until the end of the meal! Granted, in certain fast-paced businesses, this rule is broken so frequently that it's no longer a rule. Nevertheless, plenty of people still feel that business and dining don't mix. You should be able to get a feel for whether your guest wants to jump into business talk right away or would like to be social first.

Here are some more tips:

✔ During business meals, you often see memos and papers on the table. But resist the temptation to use cell phones or laptops at the table; the restaurant isn't your office. If you have to use all sorts of electronic devices to conduct the meeting, have the meal catered in a conference room or a private room in the restaurant.

✔ Don't forget that other people in the restaurant are dining. They don't want your business interfering with their meal. Try to find a table located at the edge or in the back of the dining area.

✔ Keep your voice low and pleasant.

✔ Don't load up the table with your sunglasses, keys, and electronic gadgets. Put these things in a briefcase or handbag, and put them under the table or on an empty chair.

✔ Turn off all beeping electronic gadgets, or turn on the vibrating option.

Planning the Perfect Social Event for Business

The time will come for you to welcome your business colleagues, bosses, or clients into your home. You'll want to make the experience as pleasant and as memorable as possible.

Whether your event is as simple as a weekend picnic for your colleagues and their families or as complicated as a formal dinner for the president of Venezuela and 50 corporate titans, your test as a gracious host is how you plan the event and whether you can deal with unexpected disasters.

Your budget determines the kind of event you can host. If you have enough money, you don't need to worry about budgeting time and energy, because you can hire people to do everything for you. If you're considering having a large, catered affair, read the suggestions about special events in Chapter 13. If your goals are more modest, you can provide a gracious ambience and good company all by yourself by following a few simple guidelines.

Staying organized throughout the planning process

Before pulling together your guest list, consider the reasons for having the party. Do you want to celebrate a promotion, bid farewell to a colleague, or have fun with some brews? Know your reasons, know your budget, and plan.

After you've determined the occasion and style, make a schedule to keep yourself organized. At least 45 days before the party, you will

- Determine the guest list (see the next section for details).
- Plan the menu; prepare your grocery and beverage list.
- Select decorations and supplies.
- Arrange for a tent, tables, chairs, and other equipment, if necessary.
- Select linens.

At least a month to no later than two weeks before the party, you will

- Mail the invitations.

At least two weeks ahead you should

- ✔ Check your dishes and glasses for chips and cracks, and replace them as necessary.

One week before the event, you will

- ✔ Select platters and serving dishes, matching each menu item to a container and utensils. If you will be replacing buffet items, select the second set of serving pieces, too.
- ✔ Choose appropriate music, and confirm that your extension cords are long enough to reach the cabana.
- ✔ Order flowers, if appropriate.

One or two days before the event, you will

- ✔ Wash dishes, glasses, and flatware.
- ✔ Call any guests who have not responded.
- ✔ Buy groceries and beverages.
- ✔ Polish the silver, if necessary.
- ✔ Clean the house and yard.
- ✔ Prepare any food items that can be made in advance, and refrigerate them.
- ✔ Coordinate last-minute arrangements with the caterer.
- ✔ Put extra hangers in the entryway closet, or provide a coat rack.
- ✔ Put away valuable and/or breakable items.
- ✔ Order ice, if necessary.

 Consider how much time you're going to have on the day of the party, and arrange to have things delivered. Also, have enough help. Consider "hiring" your own teenager or her friends to help you serve and clean up.

Assembling the right crowd

Sometimes, choosing the guest list is easy because the whole company should be invited to the party; it gets tricky when some people will be invited but not others. Try to make clear categories. You might invite the sales force and their spouses or guests, for example, or the company's clients, or the people on your floor. The point here is to have a ready, justifiable explanation for including some people and excluding others.

In the following sections, I explain how to assemble a great guest list and how to issue invitations that contain all the pertinent information.

Including all the necessary information in an invitation

An invitation is the first news of your intention to host an event. The way you word your invitations begins to set the tone for the affair. Invitations to casual events can be creative and unusual, but those to formal affairs should follow protocol. If the party has a theme, include it in the invitation.

Invitation basics include *who, what, where, why, when,* and *how:*

- ✔ *Who* is doing the inviting and *who* is being invited
- ✔ *What* you are inviting the person to do
- ✔ *Where* the party is being held
- ✔ *Why* the party is being held
- ✔ *When* the party will start and *when* it will end
- ✔ *How* to let your host know whether you will attend

If you plan an informal gathering of business associates, you can issue your invitations orally, either in person or by telephone, but make sure that you're clear about the date and time of the affair. Say something like "We'd love to have you join us for an informal brunch with a few others from work at our house a week from Sunday. We plan to get together at 11, have brunch on the deck, and play a little croquet in the yard for an hour or so."

If you are composing a written invitation, make sure that it has all the relevant information listed earlier in this section. See Chapter 8 for details on writing invitations and addressing envelopes.

Considering significant others and children

Many business parties are just for groups of employees, but occasionally more informal parties allow for significant others and children. Always mention exactly whom you're inviting when you issue invitations:

- ✔ For a married couple, mention both names.
- ✔ For a single adult whom you expect to bring a date, you do one of two things, depending on whether the invitation is oral or written:
  - • If you're issuing a phone invitation, say something like this: "Hi, Steve. This is Juanita. I was calling to let you know I'm having a party next Saturday at the beach house — a luau! Please bring a guest, if you'd like. The festivities will start around 5:00. Please let me know by Wednesday if you'll be able to make it. My office number is XXX-XXXX, or you can reach me at home at YYY-YYYY. Hope to see you."

- If you're issuing a written invitation or e-vite, first call the person you're inviting. Say that you're planning to send him an invitation, and ask whether he'd like to bring a guest. If so, ask him whether he'd be kind enough to tell you that person's name. Then send a written invitation or e-mail directly to the guest.

✔ For couples who live together, both names go on a separate line of the envelope. Roommates' names are also listed on separate lines.

✔ Generally, children aren't invited to formal parties, but sometimes they turn up anyway. If you want them to attend, your invitation can simply state that children are welcome.

Determining guest attire

A written invitation should include a freestanding line that specifies how you expect your guests to dress (see Chapter 4 for more about proper dress):

✔ If you want to see the gentlemen in tuxedos, the proper phrase is *Black Tie.*

✔ For suits and ties and cocktail dresses, people often use the phrase *Black Tie optional,* or *Semiformal,* although *Formal* is technically correct.

✔ For a reception after work at which you expect everyone to wear suits, use the phrase *Business Dress.*

✔ For slacks, sport coats, skirts, or pants, use *Business Casual.*

✔ For volleyball, use the phrase *Casual.*

If you're not sure what to wear to an informal or casual party, call your host and ask! Say something like this: "Hi, Sid. I'm looking forward to seeing you on Sunday, but I'm not quite sure what to wear. Any hints?" If you're the host, as people respond to the invitation, say, "I'm so glad you can make it. It really will be casual — shorts and T-shirts." Let people know how happy you are that they can come, and let them know what they can wear.

Providing directions and parking

Don't make your guests search and fumble through an unfamiliar suburb or area of town. Enclose a separate sheet of paper with accurate directions. If necessary, make copies of a local road map, and point out landmarks and distances.

One of your responsibilities as the host of a large affair is to provide parking. You can hire someone from a valet-parking service to park cars. Alert your neighbors to the event, and let them know that your guests probably will be parking on the street. If the parking situation is difficult, and your street or home cannot handle a large number of cars, consider limiting your guest list or hiring a shuttle for your guests.

If the event takes place at an establishment that offers valet parking, arrange beforehand to handle the fees and gratuities for your guests. The invitation should state that valet parking will be provided.

Dealing with RSVPs

If you're having a casual party, you can request phone or e-mail responses to your invitations. Include your own phone number and e-mail address.

If you're hosting an informal or formal party, send written invitations and request an RSVP. For all but the most formal occasions, you can include a separate response card — a note-size card that allows the recipient to respond quickly.

The most formal invitations require that you respond in writing on fine stationery, echoing the wording of the invitation.

If you haven't received an RSVP back from a guest within a week of the event, it's perfectly acceptable to call and ask whether he is attending. A guest should respond to an invitation as soon as possible — certainly, within a week of receiving it.

Finalizing preparations on the day of the event

On the day of the event, take care of last-minute details. Mentally walk through the event. Review the names of guests, spouses, and significant others; company affiliations; and interesting tidbits from the week's newspapers. Allow plenty of time to set up and dress. Try to give yourself half an hour to relax before the party begins. If you have a nonsmoking household, now's the time to make arrangements for smokers by reserving a place for them outside.

Above all else, maintain your sense of humor in the face of adversity. The most important things are your attitude, friendliness, and genuine pleasure in your guests' presence.

Greeting your guests

As your first guests arrive, greet them at the door. Use their names; shake hands; look them in the eye; and say, "I'm so glad you could join us." As the party progresses, you may have an associate or your spouse greet people by saying, "Hello. I'm Joe Cook — Lynne's husband. Lynne is on the balcony." Make sure that you're close by and that the person who's welcoming your guests knows where you are.

Introduce newcomers all around the room until the number of guests gets too large. When that happens, introduce newcomers only to the people who are closest at hand. Keep an eye out for shy guests who plaster themselves to the walls. Engage them in conversation, and introduce them to someone you hope can draw them out.

Offer your guests a drink, or show them to the bar. Always have both alcoholic and nonalcoholic beverages, including water, available during cocktail hour. Keep cocktail napkins close at hand, or offer them with the drink. Serve cocktails for no more than an hour, and provide appetizers and snacks while serving alcoholic beverages.

Serve the most senior guests first.

Running the meal

How you organize the meal depends on the number of guests and the atmosphere that you want to create. Your main options are a buffet meal and a sit-down dinner.

The buffet meal

A buffet works for 10 guests or 100. It is a great way to build camaraderie and allow people to mingle. A buffet can be a bit formal or casual, depending on the seating arrangements and style of food.

With a buffet, you can serve guests without having to traipse back and forth to the kitchen. Arrange everything on a side table, stack up the plates and silverware, and let your guests help themselves. Buffets can work beautifully if you avoid a few hazards that can turn a party into a nightmare. Be sure to

---

Handling the uninvited guest with grace

As a host, you face one of life's bigger challenges when an uninvited guest arrives at your carefully planned party. A guest may arrive with someone you didn't invite. Perhaps a relative from out of town showed up unexpectedly, and it seemed rude for your guest to leave him at home alone. Perhaps your cubicle-mate shows up with his brand-new girlfriend.

As a host, your job is to ignore your guest's breech of etiquette and to welcome any uninvited guest warmly, as though you were hoping for just such a visit. Say how wonderful it is that he can join you all. Begin making introductions immediately. Rearrange the seating to shoehorn the extra guest. SMILE! In the most absolute last resort, with much regret, a host may decline the additional guest if there are real circumstances that exist.

- ✔ Set up the bar away from the hors d'oeuvres and the buffet table to prevent congestion.

- ✔ Provide a drop-off table for cocktail glasses before the buffet.

- ✔ Think about traffic flow. Make sure people have enough room to get to and away from the buffet table. Consider setting up the buffet table so that people can serve themselves from both sides.

- ✔ Set up glasses and dinner beverages on the dining tables so that your guests don't have to juggle food plates and drinks.

- ✔ Organize menu items in standard menu order — main courses first and desserts last. (I describe the courses of a meal in Chapter 12.)

- ✔ Be sure to have backup serving dishes of each menu item so that they can be replaced easily. Guests shouldn't have to scrape the bottom of a serving dish.

Without exception, provide adequate seating for everyone invited. Rent enough tables and chairs, or arrange your own furniture to accommodate small groups. For very casual occasions, the floor and some cushions or the lawn and a few bales of hay are perfectly fine.

The dinner party

A dinner party is a small affair, usually with no more than 12 guests. Its business function is to provide a gracious climate in which to build relationships. The conversation at a dinner party should be general, social, and witty. The food at a dinner party should be prepared and served in courses — at least three and no more than five.

This type of party is an opportunity to use your wedding silver, your fine china, and your crystal. If you don't have enough matching plates and silverware, mix and match, or have a party-rental company or your caterer provide extra pieces.

If you can't even remember what the inside of a grocery store looks like, let alone attempt to provide a gourmet meal for 12 titans of industry, reserve a private room at a good restaurant or hotel. Or hire a caterer.

Certain rules govern where guests sit during a formal meal. The host sits at the end of the table. If a couple is hosting, the man sits at one end and the woman sits at the other. The male guest of honor sits to the hostess's right. The next most important man sits on the hostess's left. The female guest of honor sits to the host's right and the second most important woman sits to the host's left.

In many formal situations, guests are seated at round tables, which put everyone on an equal basis. Whatever the shape of the table, couples should be separated and men and women seated alternately.

As the host, you are the leader. When the time comes, move toward the dining room; your guests will follow. After you have properly directed everyone to their seats, you will take your seat as a sign that others should do the same. As soon as all the guests are seated, place your napkin in your lap, which is the signal that the meal has begun.

As soon as the wine is poured, offer a short opening toast. You might say something like "Here's to the great pleasure of dining with friends." If a special occasion has prompted the dinner, suit your toast to the event: "To a wonderful new vice president."

When it comes to serving food and drinks, if you remember only these three things, you'll do fine:

- Water glasses should be filled before your guests sit down at the table.
- Guests are served from the left, and dishes are removed from the right, unless the arrangement of the tables and chairs does not allow this system.
- Make sure that all the utensils for each course are on the table before the food arrives.

For further information about table manners, see Chapter 12.

When you rise from the table after dessert, so will everyone else. Make sure that the slowest guest has finished eating before you stand. When you lead the way from the dining table to the living room or other conversation location, your guests will follow. Try to engage every guest in at least a short personal conversation after the meal.

Ending the party

One of the toughest challenges for a gracious host is the delicate process of getting your guests to go home. Moving your guests homeward is really a two-sided issue, because they are expected to exhibit their own good manners by knowing when it's time to leave. The party should be over an hour after dessert is finished.

If your guests are lingering too long, you don't need to rely on hints or subtlety. Stand up, say "This has been such a lovely evening," and begin thanking your guests for coming.

As people begin to leave, station yourself at the door; accept their compliments; thank them for coming; and wish them a good evening. Don't apologize for the roast being overdone or for running out of tonic. Just say how pleased you were to have them at your party.

Drinks, Anyone? Understanding Cocktail Parties

Eating food while you're standing up and holding a drink can be a real nightmare. What are you supposed to do with those little toothpicks? Put them in that ficus-tree pot over there? And how are you supposed to shake someone's hand when you're holding a plate and a glass of wine?

Cocktail parties and receptions are among the favorite events for businesses to host because they last for a short period of time, and cocktails and hors d'oeuvres require a little less planning, less time, and less energy. And sometimes, if planned well, they're easier on your budget than hosting a sit-down formal dinner. Normally, cocktail parties and receptions have a larger guest list, which gives the host an opportunity to meet or get to know more people.

There are three kinds of cocktail parties, each of which has its own function and structure, as well as its own wardrobe expectations:

- **A true cocktail party** is usually about two hours long, starting sometime after 5 p.m. and ending sometime before 7:00 or 7:30 p.m. Dinner is not served at a cocktail party, but hors d'oeuvres are. A full bar is standard at a cocktail party, with nonalcoholic drinks available for those who don't imbibe. This type of cocktail party is the most flexible of the three types and can be casual to formal. Be sure to specify dress in the invitation. The primary function of the party is to provide a forum for mingling and meeting people.

- **A cocktail buffet** typically is held between 6 and 9 p.m. during the business week. A buffet dinner is served (hence, the name). Tables, chairs, and silverware are provided. Often, the food is varied, copious, and served from different locations. The function of a cocktail buffet varies from mingling to announcing a new product to thanking long-standing clients. The event usually requires business dress. Again, be sure to specify proper dress in the invitation.

- **A cocktail reception** traditionally is held for two hours before another evening engagement — say, from 5:30 to 7:30 p.m. before an 8 p.m. theater curtain, or it can be held after an evening event, usually for only an hour and a half. Champagne is usually served. Early cocktail receptions serve hors d'oeuvres; and the occasional late cocktail reception after a play or the theater often features egg dishes, such as omelets, fruits, and desserts. Cocktail receptions are the most formal of the three types of cocktail parties, usually reserved for making significant announcements, honoring someone, or celebrating an important event. Dressy or formal wear is in order. Again, be sure to specify proper dress in the invitation.

When you attend a cocktail party without seating, you will be challenged to hold on to your food and drink at the same time. Here's what to do:

1. **Hold your drink in your left hand so that your handshaking hand cannot be mistaken for a freshly caught mackerel.**

2. **If you are holding both drink and food and someone approaches you, put the food on a nearby table and offer your right hand (unless shaking hands would be awkward for the other person).**

   With a little practice, many people can master the art of holding a small plate and a wineglass in their left hand. If you are unable to perform this astounding feat, try to stay near tables or other surfaces.

3. **If you cannot comfortably shake hands, smile and nod or shrug in greeting; the other person will understand.**

   If you are the person making the greeting, it is rude to stand there with your hand out while the other person is looking around for a place to set his food and drink down.

Attending a Banquet

A banquet is a large luncheon or dinner typically hosted by a company or other organization; awards sometimes are presented at banquets. At the event itself, your job as host is to ensure that all your guests are satisfied. You will be milling, mingling, and massaging the situation most of the evening. You probably won't eat much. Don't fret. Your job is to talk to everyone, guarantee that people get what they want, and provide the necessary social skills to make the event a success for both yourself and your company. You can help yourself to food and drink, but only to the extent that doing so doesn't compromise your ability to be an effective host. (If low blood sugar is a problem for you, eat a substantial snack before the event.)

If you're the guest at a banquet, the guidelines that apply to any business function apply here as well. Don't overeat or overdrink; be polite to those whom you meet; and never forget that as pleasant as the surroundings may be, this event is a business function at which business conversation is going to happen, so be prepared to talk business at least some of the time. (See Chapter 5 for general information on meeting and greeting at business events; Chapter 13 has details on acting appropriately at special events.)

One other piece of advice: Leave before or at the stated ending time for the event. The polite guest knows when to leave.

In the following sections, I explain the responsibilities of a host and a master of ceremonies, and I give a few tips for giving a toast at a banquet.

Acting as host and master of ceremonies

The *host* is the person who represents the organization having the banquet — often, the president, CEO, or chairman of the board. The *master of ceremonies* announces and introduces speakers, those who offer toasts, and other entertainment. Sometimes, the host is also the master of ceremonies. When different people perform the different functions, remember to direct your logistical questions about the event to the host's office and any questions about entertainment to the master of ceremonies.

As a host for an event, make the appropriate contact people available to your speaker and guests.

Dinner speakers are common at large banquets and are often members of the company itself. Sometimes, they are celebrities or experts in other walks of life. The purpose of dinner speakers varies from providing reports on technical matters to offering comedy for the evening's entertainment.

Many professional speakers travel with an aide-de-camp or an entourage. Figure out who is in charge, and talk to that person. Some speakers like to make the decisions themselves; others prefer to delegate these matters to their handlers. Know your speaker's preferences.

If you're the host for a dinner speaker, your primary responsibility is to ensure that the speaker is at the right place at the right time and has everything he needs. This means making sure that the master of ceremonies knows how to introduce the speaker, that the speaker is aware of all the details of the scheduled appearance, and that any technology the speaker will use (such as a projector, laptop, and microphone) has been tested and is ready to go.

Remember to do the following as well:

- ✔ Ask whether the speaker would like instructions on using any of the technology.
- ✔ Ask the speaker whether he requires anything else.
- ✔ Introduce the speaker to important audience members during cocktails.
- ✔ Supply the speaker with water for the speech and be sure that their meal is served ahead of other guests, just following the guest of honor.

As master of ceremonies, you introduce the speaker. Introductions need not be long — good introductions usually are two minutes or less — but they should be prepared. Recognize that your impromptu witticisms may desert you as you face a thousand people in a brilliantly lit banquet room. Write something down ahead of time in a size large enough to read.

Making and receiving a toast

Toasts can be made with wine or any other beverage. Traditionally, you do not toast to yourself, although some people now think that it's okay to raise your glass in response. In either case, you do not drink if you're the one being toasted.

Toasting was once a man's job, and only the men drank the toast while the women nodded and smiled. Now it is perfectly appropriate for anyone to make a toast and for anyone to respond to the toast, regardless of gender.

Are there any rules left? A few:

- ✔ The host can and should propose the first toast (a welcome toast) to begin the dining.

- ✔ If the event has a guest of honor, the host proposes a toast to that person.

- ✔ If the guest of honor is a dignitary, a very important person, or a distinguished elder, it is a sign of respect for everyone to rise to perform the toast.

The guest of honor, regardless of gender, responds to the toast by thanking and toasting the host, and thanking everyone for their attendance. In fact, guest of honor or not, if you're toasted, you should always respond with a toast.

At large events where you want to command the attention of a room or of more than one table, rising for the toast is traditional. For smaller events, rising isn't necessary; simply ask for everyone's attention. When you have the floor, be respectful; take a minute or less to make the toast; and be seated again.

Clinking your crystal with a fork to get attention is gauche and potentially dangerous.

Chapter 12

Mastering Dining Etiquette

*W*ell done — you've been invited to the company's annual awards ceremony at the ritziest room in town. But instead of thrills, you've got chills. They didn't teach you how to go to one of these affairs in business school. When you ask your parents how to go to one of these things, they just laugh, recalling that in the commune, *formal* meant wearing shoes. No help there!

You need a quick course in dining etiquette. Not just in basic eating, either — you've got to know what to do with that place setting from *Titanic*. You don't know a Chardonnay from a Beaujolais, let alone how to locate your bread plate. Relax! Meals are supposed to be fun and entertaining — even business meals. They often aren't, of course, but by the end of this chapter, at least you'll know how to handle yourself with grace at any business meal. *Bon appetit!*

Starting Any Meal on the Right Foot

Whether you're having lunch with well-known business associates or sitting down to a formal dinner with complete strangers — who just happen to be your company's most important clients — knowing dining etiquette will help put you and others at ease. Good manners are like the handrails on a rope bridge. You may not be dashing across the chasm like Indiana Jones, but if you hang on tightly, you won't fall off!

Attending to preliminaries

As I note in Chapter 11, if you're the host, arrive early to make arrangements for paying the bill. Make sure that the table or room is what you had arranged, and decide on the seating plan. The guest or most important person sits in the best chair (normally, the one with the best view and location). The maitre d' can help you identify that seat. Everyone should be able to see everyone else and converse easily. Have large flower arrangements or other obstacles removed from the table by the waiter or maitre d' if you think that they will be distracting. Return to the bar or waiting area to greet your guests.

Do not order a drink before your guests arrive. Even if you have arrived 20 minutes earlier to make sure everything is in good order, it should appear to your guests that you, too, have just arrived. Don't start off by making your guests uncomfortable, thinking that they are late or have kept you waiting.

Some restaurants will not seat you until your entire group has arrived. In this case, for business lunches, you will wait in the lobby, not the bar. For dinner events, it is appropriate to wait in the bar and perhaps have one round of drinks before being seated for dinner.

As each guest arrives, get off to a good start by making formal introductions (see Chapter 5 for guidance). Unless doing so is unwieldy, everyone should stand for an introduction and exchange handshakes (if the parties are being introduced for the first time).

In the international business arena, business cards are never exchanged at the onset of a business lunch or dinner. The reason for the meal is supposed to be social and only at the end are business cards more appropriately exchanged.

Mentioning the purpose of the gathering is appropriate. Try something like this: "I know we're all thinking about the roll-out schedule, which we will get to. But first, I'd like to invite you all to just relax. We'll save that discussion for the end of the meal."

Coming to the table

After introductions, cocktails, and pre-dining chitchat are complete, you just sit down at the table, right? Wrong. At business meals, the host or lead businessperson should seat clients first and her business associates second. In formal business occasions, the seating is predetermined by place cards. In diplomatic situations, ladies are seated, but men do not sit until the host or guest of honor is seated.

Never switch place cards at a business function. You may be more comfortable, but considerable thought involving business strategy probably has gone into the seating plan. Moving the cards around might be a ticket to Palukaville.

Before sitting down, make sure that you know everyone at the table. If you don't, make last-minute introductions. Unlike in social situations, it is not necessary for men to seat women at a business meal. Regardless of your gender, however, if you are to the left of an elderly woman or man, or someone who requires assistance, you may always draw the chair for that person and assist as needed.

Behaving after you're seated

After you're seated, wait for your host to take up her napkin and place it on her lap. Then place your own napkin in your lap. Unlike in a social situation, in which guests wait for the hostess to touch her napkin, in a business situation, hierarchy replaces gender.

Opening a large napkin fully isn't necessary, and you should avoid flourishing it like a bullfighter's cape. The purpose of your napkin is to dab the corners of your mouth — not to wipe off lipstick or blow your nose. If you leave the table during the meal, place your napkin on your chair. When you've finished your entire meal and are leaving the table for the last time, place your napkin to the left of your place setting.

Posture at the table should be straight but not stiff. Lean slightly forward from the back of the chair, but never slouch. Sit on three quarters of the chair, with your feet flat on the floor. As you eat, bring the food to your mouth; do not bend forward to meet it halfway.

Sit up at the table throughout the meal, and remember not to support yourself with your forearms or elbows. Your elbows are never to be on the table when people are eating. This posture is permissible only when you are attending a casual social meal with friends and no food is on the table. In addition, never encircle your plate with one arm while eating. You may rest your wrists on the edge of the table, but lightly. Even though doing so may be tempting, don't rest your head in your hands between courses.

Don't fidget! That means don't plink on the table with your cutlery or play with the tablecloth, your napkin, cocktail stirrers, appetizer picks, your hair, your fingernails, or anything else that's close to hand.

As soon as you're seated, informal conversation is in order. Avoid discussing your personal life, sex, politics, or religion, and avoid telling jokes. You want cordial conversation, not controversy. See Chapter 6 for pointers on making polite conversation.

A drink or two before dinner as an icebreaker is perfectly acceptable and, for some, a way of life. If you intend to conduct business, however, protect your mental clarity. Remember, loose lips sink ships.

There's nothing wrong with ordering mineral water or iced tea, regardless of the choices others make. When you are the host, the best practice is to follow the lead of your guest. You can offer a cocktail, but if your guest doesn't order one, abstain as well. If you're a nondrinking host, suggest to your guests that they have cocktails, and offer to order wine during the meal.

It takes time for a productive discussion to develop. One purpose of chitchat during the meal is to warm up. This is the time to build rapport. If you've had a lively conversation during the meal, everyone will be primed to talk about the business plan over coffee. On the average, allow about two hours for a business meal. Be prepared to spend as much time as necessary at the meal. Don't book an appointment too close to the time when you think the meal should end, because you don't want to be rushed or appear to your guests to be preoccupied.

Beginning the meal

When should you start to eat? Almost every meal has a host (the person who invited you to the meal or the person in whose home you are dining). It's your turn to eat when — and only when — your host begins to eat. If it's a formal meal, unless you are choking, avoid having even a sip of water until your host does.

If you're attending an informal business lunch, it is acceptable for a guest to take a sip of water before the host does, but never at a formal dinner party.

If you're at a banquet or other group situation, wait until all those around you have been served the first course, and begin to eat together. If the first course is brought to the table in groups of two or three plates, and not everyone has food yet, wait until everyone has food. Sometimes, the host will encourage you to eat by saying, "Go ahead. Please don't wait." In this case, begin eating. Or, if you want, you can still wait for everyone to have the course before you begin, chatting with the other guests in the meantime.

The host may offer a toast before the meal. The toast should be simple and short. Something like "Here's to dining with esteemed colleagues" is fine.

A Primer on Basic and Formal Table Settings

The first step in intelligent utensil use is learning where the basic utensils and dishes go on a dining table and how to use them. Then you'll be ready for advanced utensil information — those additional utensils and china you may encounter in formal dining. At every meal, you have a plate, a napkin, several utensils — usually consisting of a knife, fork, and soup spoon — and at least one glass. Sometimes, you have a bread-and-butter plate. When you add a salad fork, you've filled out the simple place setting that most Americans recognize. Sometimes, a salad plate rests on the table rather than being delivered with the salad, and the dessert utensils, dessert plate, and coffee or teacups and their spoons may appear after the meal. See Figure 12-1 for an illustration of a basic table setting.

The basic setting is an abbreviated version of a full or formal place setting, which can have any number of other utensils, plates, and glasses.

Figure 12-1: An American basic table setting.

The most important rules to learn in dining, whether casual or formal, are

- Drinks right, bread plate left. (Another version is liquids to the right, solids to the left.)

- Fork is a four-letter word, as is the word "left." Knife is a five-letter word, as is the word "right."

- Start by using the utensils placed farthest from the plate and work inward with each course. By examining the formal place setting in Figure 12-2, you get a good idea of what each course will be.

Plates

The *place plate,* or main dinner plate, is in the center in front of each chair setting. In formal dining, you usually find a *charger* (underplate) as well. The bread plate is always to the left, slightly above the forks, with a small knife across the top. That knife is the butter spreader. If soup is served as a first course, the soup bowl will be on a service plate. A salad, if served as a first course, may be placed on the service plate, and the salad plate will then be removed. The charger or underplate is removed from the table before the dessert is served.

Toward the end of the meal, you may find a small plate with a doily and a small bowl above your dinner plate. These items are the dessert plate and finger bowl, respectively. A small fork and spoon — your dessert spoon and fork — will be resting on the edge of the dessert plate.

Utensils

Forks are to the left of the plate, and knives and spoons go to the right (with the exception of the tiny cocktail fork, which is placed on the soup spoon or to the right of the soup spoon). The dessert fork and spoon are above the dinner plate.

If a salad is the first course (as is often the case in the United States but rarely the case in other countries), the salad fork, which is smaller than the dinner fork, will be farthest to the left. If fish is being served as the first course, a fish fork comes first. Next is your dinner fork for the entree. Salad sometimes is served as the third or fourth course, in which case your salad fork is closest to the plate. The butter spreader is on the bread plate on the left above the forks.

To the right of the plate, starting from the outermost utensil, are a cocktail fork, a soup spoon, a fish knife, a dinner knife, and (nearest the plate) a salad knife. The sharp edge of the knife is always turned toward the plate.

Figure 12-2:
An American formal table setting.

A dessert fork is placed horizontally above the place plate, tines right; a dessert spoon is placed horizontally above the place plate, bowl left. All these additional knives, forks, and spoons have specific functions — and to add to the confusion, a few look slightly different in Europe than they do in the United States.

If you're unsure which utensil to use or do not know how to eat a certain food, it is best to delay by having a sip of your beverage and watching what the others are doing.

Glassware

In a formal setting, you usually have lots of glasses at the table. These glasses are to the right of your plate. Each glass is slightly different in shape and size. Their purposes are fairly easy to master; your waiter will fill the glasses with the correct beverages in the right order. As long as you are not drinking from an empty glass, you will be fine.

The glass farthest to the right may be a sherry if one is served to accompany the soup course. This glass will be the first one you use. When each course is finished, allow the waiter to remove the glass, as well as the plate, for that course. Next is the white-wine glass, which is used during the fish course or appetizer. Behind the white-wine glass is the red-wine glass. This glass is larger, with a fuller bowl that allows the red wine to breathe. The largest glass is the water goblet, which sits closest to the center of the dining table, often, just above the dinner knife. Finally, behind and to the right of the water goblet is the champagne glass, if champagne will accompany dessert. You may also find a champagne glass in the first position, perhaps served with oysters as an appetizer.

Salt and pepper

Most table settings include salt and pepper shakers or grinders. At formal meals, you'll see individual salt and pepper dishes with tiny spoons.

In some situations, where there is no salt or pepper on the table, do not ask for any salt; this is considered an insult to the chef. It is fine to ask for pepper, however, because it is considered a condiment and salt is considered a flavor enhancer.

Thoughtfully taste your food before you add any seasoning. The chef has tried to achieve perfect seasoning, and when you reach for the salt and pepper immediately, you indicate that perfection was not quite achieved. Always pass the salt and pepper as a pair so that they can stay together throughout the meal.

The Meal: Managing Basic to Formal Dining

Knowing proper dining etiquette and using table manners simply gives you more confidence in embracing new dining experiences, especially important in business situations. Dining graciously, whether it's a job interview over a meal, dining at the White House, or dinner at your boss's home — not only makes you more comfortable, but it also makes a positive lasting impression.

If the food or the wine is especially good, mention it to your host, but keep complaints to yourself.

Ordering food

As I note in Chapter 11, you may suggest items from the menu for the guests, but when the time comes to order, follow the lead of your guests. Order an item similar to theirs and in the same price range. If they order appetizers, you should order one too, so that your guests don't have to eat alone. At a formal dinner, a menu card will be presented to you, with each course to be served printed on the card. The date, location, and purpose of the dinner appear at the top. This card is the main (or only) keepsake for guests.

Avoid selecting the most expensive item on the menu. If a client or your employer will be paying for the meal, it's best to order from the mid-price offerings. If you dine in restaurants that specialize in international cuisine, and you don't speak the language, take the time to learn four or five food items ahead of time. It's also acceptable to request assistance from the waiter.

During a business meal, your mind is on business, even if the preliminary chitchat is about Tiger Woods. Don't overburden yourself by ordering foods that challenge your table manners and your wardrobe. As you survey the menu, be alert to the following hazardous foods:

- Deeply colored sauce or gravy
- Spaghetti
- Food that requires on-the-plate management, such as whole lobster, crab, and spare ribs
- Finger foods such as hamburgers or French fries
- Unfamiliar foods that may challenge your digestion or allergies

If you have special dietary needs, and you know in advance where you will be dining, call ahead and discuss your needs with the restaurant personnel.

Serving food

In banquets or banquet-style serving, platters of food are served from the left. A serving spoon and a serving fork usually are on the serving platter, spoon with bowl up and fork with tines down. Take the fork in your left hand, tines remaining down, and use it to steady the food. Using the spoon in your right hand, lift the food, and steady it with the fork while bringing it to your plate.

Serve the food in individual portions, as it is presented on the platter. Don't take more than one portion. If the food is presented as a whole — mashed, grouped, or in gels — take a portion with the spoon, using the spoon sideways to cut if necessary. Return the spoon and fork to the serving plate as they came to you: spoon bowl up on the right, fork tines down on the left.

Distinguishing between American and Continental dining styles

There are two methods of handling and using the silverware at a meal: the American style and the European or Continental style. Either version is fine in the United States.

In both the European and the American style, you cut your food as follows:

1. **Hold the knife in your right hand.**

2. **Place your index finger on the handle and a little of the blade, if necessary.**

3. **Hold the fork with your left hand, prongs facing down (with the curve pushing up), as shown in Figure 12-3.**

4. **Eat your food one or two bites at a time.**

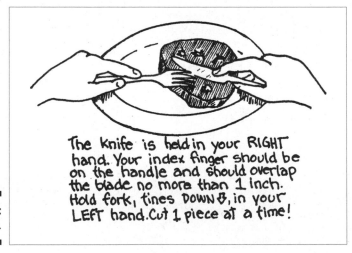

The knife is held in your RIGHT hand. Your index finger should be on the handle and should overlap the blade no more than 1 inch. Hold fork, tines DOWN ⊕, in your LEFT hand. Cut 1 piece at a time!

Figure 12-3: Cutting food.

At no time should you hold your utensils in any fashion other than those suggested in the following sections. Whether you're left-handed or right-handed doesn't matter. Never saw your food; simply request a steak or meat knife. Never cut all your meat into bites at the same time. Don't place your utensils on the edge of the plate by their tips, letting them hang onto the table; after you pick up your utensils, they should never touch the table again. And don't wave your utensils around while you're talking; you're not conducting an orchestra!

The American style

In the American, or zigzag, style, after you finish cutting, you lay the knife on the plate near the top of the plate, cutting edge facing in, and switch the fork to your right hand after cutting your food. Holding the fork with your thumb over the end and your index finger underneath, and the prongs up, you pick up the food, either with the prongs, as shown in Figure 12-4, or by slipping the food onto the prongs.

Hold your fork like a pencil. Steady it between your middle and index fingers. (Turn your thumb up, not down, like you would a pencil.)

After you cut the meat, lay your knife on your plate. The cutting edge should always face the center of the plate. Switch the fork to your RIGHT hand before you raise it to your mouth.

Figure 12-4:
Eating American style.

When you finish a course, you place your knife and fork side by side, knife on top, in the 4 o'clock position on the plate, the blade of the knife facing in (see Figure 12-5). This way, your server knows that you have finished this course and she can remove those dishes and utensils.

Figure 12-5:
Cutlery
placement
when you
finish a
course
(American
style).

If you want to rest between courses, you use the same position, but space the utensils farther apart and slightly higher on your plate, as shown in Figure 12-6.

Figure 12-6:
The rest
position
when eating
American
style.

The European or Continental style

In the European or Continental style, you simply use the fork to prong the bite and bring it to your mouth with your left hand. Raise the fork to your mouth with the tines down but turning your forearm toward your mouth. The knife stays in your right hand, ready to be used again, as shown in Figure 12-7. If you put something on the tines of your fork, use a gentle nudge from your knife. You may also rest your wrist on the edge of the table while you hold your cutlery.

Figure 12-7:
The
Continental
style of
eating.

To rest your cutlery in the European or Continental style of eating, you cross the fork (tines down) across the knife, cutting edge in, in the 4 o'clock position, as shown in Figure 12-8. Place your utensils in either of these positions if you must leave the table, take a drink, or use your napkin. The finished position is the same as in American style, but with the fork tines down.

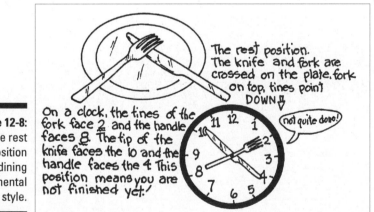

Figure 12-8:
The rest
position
when dining
Continental
style.

Taking bites of food with grace

Conversation will continue during the meal, so be prepared to participate. Don't get caught chewing a large hunk of pork chop when the company president asks you how your children are doing in school. Remember the sage advice of President George Washington: "Put not another bit into your mouth till the former be swallowed. Let not your morsels be too big for the jowls."

Eating French fries in France

American table manners allow for considerable latitude in the use of fingers while dining informally. European etiquette, however, is much more formal, even during a casual meal. Americans will eat French fries with their fingers, for example. But in France, *pommes frîtes* are eaten with a knife and fork. When you dine overseas or with an international group, be especially watchful for the behavior of your foreign companions. When in doubt, use a knife and fork.

Take small bites, always remember to chew with your mouth closed, and don't talk while you have food in your mouth. Though it's acceptable in some cultures, in the West it's never acceptable to pick your teeth while you're at the table. Excuse yourself and go to the restroom if you have food stuck in your teeth.

Following etiquette for basic courses

The following sections cover the basic courses diners encounter most often.

After finishing a course, don't push your plate or bowl away. The way your cutlery is placed informs the wait staff that you've finished. If you've placed your cutlery properly in the 4 o'clock position, the staff also can pick up your plate easily. Never "help" the wait staff by handing them plates or holding glasses for them to fill unless you're asked to do so.

A sorbet or intermezzo may be served between courses to cleanse the palate. You need to have only a small taste; finishing the entire dish isn't necessary. If you're planning a personal menu card for your guests, you don't have to include the intermezzo in the menu. If you think that some of your guests may be confounded by the course, however, list it. Think of your guests' comfort.

Bread

As a guest, if a bread basket or bread plate is sitting in front of you, you may generally begin by taking one slice or roll, as directed by the host, then passing it. If the table is round, offer the bread to the person on your right. As the host, you will not take bread first, you will wait to take bread until the bread comes back around at the end.

When bread is served half sliced in a basket with a napkin, take a portion of the napkin with your left hand and hold a section of the bread, without touching the bread, while you tear off one piece with your right hand. The napkin is in the basket to cover or protect the remaining bread.

Place butter from the serving dish on your bread-and-butter plate, not directly on the bread. Never use the knife with the butter dish to butter your bread. If no knife is with the butter dish, you may use your own butter spreader or dinner knife.

Break off a piece of bread only when you're ready to eat it. Do not butter the entire slice or roll at the same time. Break off one piece, hold it over the plate to butter it, and eat it. If you're eating a crunchy hard roll, keep it as close to your bread plate as possible; it's not the end of the world if a few crumbs get on the table. The wait staff will take care of them later in the meal.

Whether at an informal or formal meal, dipping, dunking, or wiping sauces with your fingers holding bread is not polite. Instead, you are allowed to place a small piece of bread into your soup or on your plate, but use your soup spoon or fork to move the bread around and then carry it to your mouth to eat, except in the most informal gatherings or with certain dishes that are designed to do just that — such as fondues, certain au jus dishes, and olive oil. If you are dipping your bread into a communal plate of olive oil, never, ever double dip! Take smaller bites.

Soup

Soup is served in a variety of bowls and cups, hot or cold. Clear soup is served with a small round soup spoon; cream soup and soup with ingredients such as chicken or vegetables will have a medium, more oval soup spoon.

Occasionally, you may be served consommé, served in a small bowl with handles on each side, without a spoon. Pick up the delicate bowl by the handles, and sip.

All other soups should be handled this way: Hold your spoon the way you would hold a pencil, between your index and middle fingers, with your thumb up. Spoon the soup away from you toward the center or top of the bowl, and then sip the soup from the side — not the point — of the spoon. You may rest the spoon in the soup bowl (not cup) while you pause. When you have finished, place the spoon on the saucer or plate beneath the cup or bowl. Don't leave the spoon in the bowl or cup.

Blowing on your soup to cool it is not polite. You may gently stir it or spoon the soup from the edge of the bowl first, or hold your spoon with the soup in your hand for an extra moment or two. Never add ice from your water glass!

A small glass of sherry is often served, or aperitif may be served with your soup. It is polite to sip the sherry slowly. It's not necessary to finish the entire glass.

Entree

Your main course normally is beef, chicken, duck, or lamb, and you eat these foods with a knife and fork. Finger foods, such as fried chicken or barbecued ribs, are not served at formal occasions.

If you happen to be served a very large steak, in the American style of eating, you may cut it into two or three sections, but not into many small pieces at the same time. In the Continental style, you will cut one bite at a time.

Salad

Salad may be served before or after the main course; the placement of the salad fork will tip you off. A basic American table setting (which I describe earlier in this chapter) usually has only one knife. For this reason, some Americans seem to think that the knife is for the main course and that they cannot use it for the salad.

A fine restaurant or considerate host always serves the lettuce in bite-size pieces. If you're served large pieces, however, cut one bite at a time by using the knife provided. Using your knife to cut lettuce is perfectly fine; just request a clean knife when the main course arrives.

If salad is the main course, such as at a luncheon, use the entree fork. If the salad is served before or after the main course, use the smaller salad fork. When a salad is served during a formal meal, you always have a salad knife. Notice that this knife usually is smaller than the dinner knife.

Here's a trick to eating cherry tomatoes on a salad without making them fly off the plate: With your fork, pierce the top where the stem was located.

Finger bowl

First place the dessert fork and spoon on the table beside you, to make ready for the dessert service. Then it will be up to you whether you want to use the finger bowl at this time or after dessert. If after dessert, you will dip just your fingertips in the water and dry them on your napkin. Remove the doily and bowl and place it to the upper-left side of your place setting. After dessert, you will then bring the finger bowl back to the center to gently dip the fingertips of one hand and then the other to wash, drying each hand with your napkin. You will not dip both hands at once as though you are washing your hands from a basin. The server will then remove it following the dessert.

Dessert

When the main-course plate is removed, you may have a spoon and a fork left above it. It is your responsibility to move the fork down to your left and the spoon down to your right. If you do not have silverware above your plate, it will be brought to you before dessert. If you're served ice cream, use just your spoon; if you're served cake with a sauce, use both the spoon and the fork. In a Continental-style setting, you hold your spoon in your right hand and the fork in your left hand, tines down.

Fresh fruit and cheese sometimes are served either as dessert or before dessert. You eat these foods with a knife and fork.

Excusing yourself from the meal

If you must leave the table for any reason, rise from your seat, put your napkin on your chair, and say a simple "Excuse me" as you depart. When you return, resume your seat without comment.

Don't announce a visit to the "john" or the powder room, or the need to make an important phone call.

If an occasion arises in which you must quit the meal permanently before it is over, make a brief apology, indicate when you will next talk with important guests or clients, and then leave with as little interruption as possible. Anyone else leaving the meal temporarily should return and gracefully and discreetly re-enter the meal and conversation.

Silence your gadgets! If an emergency arises, briefly explain the situation to the others before excusing yourself: "I regret the interruption, but my wife has been involved in a traffic accident. I'll be in contact as soon as I take care of the emergency."

Scoring High Marks for Wine Savvy

Wine enhances food. Like music, wine can be as much a pleasure for the blissfully ignorant as for the expert. The only danger with wine is knowing that your knowledge is so limited that you won't order the right one. Relax! Nearly everyone is curious about wines, and most people are delighted to try new kinds. You can read more about choosing the right wine for your meal in Mary Ewing-Mulligan and Ed McCarthy's *Wine For Dummies,* 4th Edition (Wiley).

Selecting a wine to complement your meal

Think of wine as the final seasoning of the dish. Normally, you order red wines with red meats and other robust dishes, and white wines with fish and other delicate entrees. Delicate foods usually are better with delicate wines. But some of these rules are changing. Wine experts sometimes simply drink what they like. What if you order oven-roasted sea bass served with a veal-reduction sauce? If a dish has a wine base, such as a Pinot Noir, a buttery Chardonnay is an excellent choice. Or try to choose an appropriate Pinot Noir to match the sauce; you will find it a sure hit. If you're not certain, ask the waiter to make a suggestion.

Taste, learn, and drink what you enjoy. Personal preference should be the deciding factor.

Basic wines

Wine and food go together. The key to choosing a wine is finding one that won't overpower the food or be overpowered by it. In general, the following are examples of wines that complement certain foods:

- Light meat dishes (such as pork), poultry, or full-flavored fish (such as salmon) go well with a red wine such as a light-bodied Pinot Noir or Burgundy.

- Lighter fish and shellfish dishes are fine with a light-bodied white wine, such as Chenin Blanc, Sancerre, Pinot Grigio, or German Riesling.

- Lobster or richer fish dishes are complemented by a full-bodied Chardonnay, Semillion, or Viognier.

- Chicken and pasta can take either red or white wine, depending on the sauce. A heavy meat sauce will be better complemented by a medium-bodied red wine, such as a Merlot or Cabernet Franc.

- Stews, roasts, game, duck, and other full-flavored dishes go best with full-bodied red wines, such as Cabernet Sauvignon, Petite Sirah, or Zinfandel.

Sparkling wines

Champagne is for celebrating and normally is served before a meal or with dessert. But champagne is the ultimate "power beverage" and also can complement appetizers and first courses. Just opening a bottle of champagne injects zest and signals the importance of the meal and your guests.

Champagne is distinguished by its degree of dryness. Brut is very dry, extra dry is slightly sweet, sec is medium-sweet, and demi-sec is sweet. Dry champagne and rose wines are served chilled. Champagne is bottled in various sizes of bottles, all but one of which have Biblical names: magnum, jeroboam, rehoboam, and methuselah. You are unlikely to need more than a magnum, which holds about 1.5 liters.

Everyone loves hearing the pop when a bottle of champagne is opened, but you need to open the bottle with a minimum of fanfare to protect your guests from a flying cork. Holding the bottle at a 45-degree angle from your body, making sure not to point it toward anyone, follow these steps:

1. **With your thumb over the cork, remove the foil and wire hood from around the cork.**

2. **Cover the top of the bottle loosely with a clean cotton napkin.**

3. **With one hand about two thirds of the way down the bottle and the other over the cork outside the napkin, twist the bottle (not the cork) while pushing down on the cork.**

4. **As the cork emerges, continue putting pressure on the cork so that it makes only a quiet hiss as it's released from the bottle.**

Dessert wines

Dessert wines often go unnoticed or neglected. These rich-flavored sweet wines go well with desserts of cheese, nuts, and fruit. They're best served at cellar temperature — with the exception of champagne, which is served chilled. Particularly outstanding are sweet Chateau Y'quem, Marsala, Angelica, Tokay, Malaga, Cream Sherry, Port, and Madeira.

Holding the glass: Stem or bowl?

Wine is served in clear glasses to show off its colors. The type of wine served determines which glass to use.

✔ Rhine and white-wine glasses have long, slender stems so that you can hold the stem and avoid warming the wine with the heat from your hand. The bowl of the glass is smaller than that of a red-wine glass, with a more fragile look to complement the wine's delicate flavor and clear color.

✔ A red-wine glass has a shorter stem with a bulbous bowl. The bowl is large to allow the wine to breathe. Hold the glass close to the bowl.

✔ Sherry and port glasses are small and open, because these wines are more potent in aroma, flavor, and alcoholic content.

✔ Champagne glasses are tall and narrow, and are designed to emphasize the effervescence and flavor of sparkling wines.

Many restaurants preset the tables with at least two wine goblets: a long-stemmed glass for white wines and a tulip-shape glass for ordinary red wines. When you order wine, the server leaves the appropriate goblet on the table and removes the other.

Mastering the ritual of ordering wine

You and your guest have been seated, and you've been presented a wine list. Uh-oh! All those French words! All those grape varieties! All those fancy descriptions! Now what?

Deciding who selects the wine

In traditional business settings, the official host or hostess navigates the wine list and orders the wine. If you know that one of the guests is a wine connoisseur, it is considered gracious or flattering to ask the guest to select the wine; however, I don't recommend this if you are on a limited company expense account. If you are the host and are not especially knowledgeable about wine, you can ask for suggestions from the wine steward or sommelier. What happens if your important client makes a comment that one of her favorite wines is on the list? Say no? Of course not! By all means select her favorite; if it's beyond your company budget, you can explain it to your boss later or you can contribute the difference.

If you conduct business regularly at a favorite restaurant, consider calling ahead and having the restaurant staff plan a menu and select the wine, or arrive early to discuss the menu, wine choices, and prices.

Wine adds flair to a meal and communicates to your guests that they are valued and important associates. The effort you put into wine selection not only helps you entertain successfully, but also helps you appear confident and in charge. Do your homework!

Determining how much to spend

If you are a beginning wine drinker, you may want to enlist the help of your waiter in making a selection. Fine restaurants will have a wine steward, or sommelier, on hand to assist you.

Have a price range in mind before you order. A sensible guideline is to spend about as much on a bottle of wine as you spend on one complete dinner. Fine wines can vary in price from a few dollars to hundreds of dollars, so make sure that you know what you're doing if you select an expensive wine.

Most restaurants price their wines by doubling the retail price and adding $10. The most expensive wine on the wine list isn't always the most impressive. When looking for value, don't follow the trends; select lesser-known varieties or local wines, which normally are priced lower.

A good rule of thumb is to order the second least expensive wine on the wine list because many times this is the owner's pick or the wine buyer's pick. Upscale restaurant wine buyers normally are careful not to allow the consumer or customer to be ripped off, so the wine price is in line with quality. But, remember, the price isn't always a good indicator of the value.

One bottle of wine contains approximately four glasses. Make sure to request an adequate number of bottles for the number of guests. If more than four guests are present, order a second bottle.

Asking what your guests want

Ask whether your guests have any preferences. It's fine to offer or make suggestions on an apéritif, champagne, or white wine to be served with the first course.

Also ask your guests about their meal choices. If everyone decides to have a rich red-meat entree, a red wine would be appropriate. If guests are having lighter chicken or seafood dishes, suggest a lighter-bodied white wine. Occasionally, you may have a guest who does not drink red wine. If the majority of your guests prefer red wine, suggest individual glasses of white wine, or order one bottle of white and one bottle of red for the table.

Red wines normally are served at room temperature, though not the normal 67°F standard but rather cellar temperature, around 55°F to 60°F. White wines are served chilled so that their flavor and aroma are at their peak. If the restaurant is hot, a slightly chilled light red wine may be more desirable than a heavy Cabernet.

Handling the presentation

The server will present the wine to you, as the host or hostess. Now is the time to examine the label, making certain that it is the correct wine and vintage. If the wine is acceptable, the next step is for the server to remove the seal, take out the cork, and place it on the table. Visually examine the cork. You don't have to sniff or smell it to tell whether the cork is in good condition. Unless the cork bears a different name from the label or is dry and crumbly, you have nothing to worry about.

In recent years, more wines are using plastic or no corks. Screw tops are increasingly popular with many wineries throughout the world and are no reflection on the quality or level of the wine.

A crumbly cork is a sign that air may have leaked into the wine and spoiled it. The bottle should be replaced with another.

Tasting the wine

The person who orders the wine normally is the taster, although the host may ask one of the guests to taste instead, if she knows the guest is knowledgeable and interested in wine. A small amount of wine will be poured into your glass. Color tells you a lot about the age of the wine, so look carefully before you taste. Red wines lose their color when aged. The younger the wine, the brighter the color; the older the wine, the deeper the color and the more concentrated the flavors. White wines become deeper yellow or gold with age.

Gently swirl the wine by holding the stem firmly and rotating the bowl. This motion is a small one, not at all akin to preparing to lasso a steer. Swirling wine provides it oxygen, which assists in releasing its aroma or nose. Now sniff. Most of what you need to know about wine, you can determine by its perfume. If you like, take a small sip. Although you don't have to swish the wine through your mouth, you may want to hold the wine in your mouth for a moment before swallowing.

Tasting allows you to discover the overall impression of the wine. If the wine has been spoiled — or, as it is commonly known, *corked* — you will know that upon tasting. It will taste terrible, not just strange. If the wine tastes off to you, don't hesitate to say so. The waiter or sommelier may also taste it to confirm. He will then bring another bottle of the same wine. If that vintage is not available, the waiter or sommelier will suggest or bring a similar wine. Establishments do not ask guests to pay for spoiled wine. Fine restaurants always replace truly spoiled wine without hesitation.

Returning a bottle of wine only because you dislike it is gauche.

Coping with Difficult-to-Eat Foods and Unusual Utensils

Some foods are tough to eat without looking too much like an animal gnawing away at bones or tubers. In the following sections, I offer some advice on how to eat these difficult foods while maintaining your dignity.

A couple of general tips to begin with: In an informal setting, when you're eating fowl of any kind, separate the bird at its major joints. With small animals such as frogs and game hens, pick up the tiny legs and wings by a protruding bone, and eat the meat as finger food. When you finish, place all bones to one side of your dinner plate.

Specific foods

The following sections discuss the biggest troublemakers for those of us who are unsure about dining etiquette.

Japanese soups and noodles

Soups are often served after the appetizer as the first course. The soup should not be so hot that you have to imbibe quite a bit of air with your sips to avoid being scalded.

Noodles are often served so hot that they can't be eaten in puckered silence. Open your mouth wide to accommodate the slippery pasta, and suck in with a fair amount of gusto! For a Westerner, picking up the knack of noodle eating depends on how quickly you can abandon the American taboo against noisy eating.

Pitted foods

Olives are finger foods. Large stuffed olives are best eaten in two bites. You may pick up olives and other foods that have pits with your fingers when they are on your plate. Discreetly remove pits with your forefinger and thumb.

Shellfish and mollusks

Follow these guidelines for eating shellfish and mollusks:

- **Lobster and crab:** Whole lobster and crab are almost always served in informal situations. The host provides bibs. Everyone accepts that a lot of finger work is forthcoming. When in doubt about the correct method, ask your host for guidance. If you're unfamiliar with the procedure for tackling a whole lobster, and you find yourself confronted by one, the other guests are likely to have plenty of good advice. Don't be shy about asking for suggestions.

- **Mussels:** Steamed mussels may be eaten with a fork and spoon or a cocktail fork. Spear the mussel, dip it into the sauce provided, and eat it whole. Place the empty shells in the shell bowl.

- **Oysters:** Oysters are attached to the bottom shell by a slender membrane. To free the meat from the shell, slip your oyster fork underneath the meat, and wiggle it back and forth a time or two. If you want, you may dip it into the sauce on your plate. Eat the oyster in one bite — usually, more of a swallow. You may pick up the shell with your fingers and drain the juice directly into your mouth. Try not to slurp.

- **Shrimp:** If shrimp is served ready to eat in a cocktail appetizer, pierce the shrimp on a little cocktail fork, and bite off a succession of manageable pieces. If the shrimp are large, place them on the plate and cut them with the provided fork before dipping them into the sauce. Steamed shrimp served in their shells, however, are definitely finger foods. Before you tackle a serving of shrimp in their shells, make sure that you have a large fabric napkin on hand. Ask for a bib if you fear for the safety of your shirt or blouse. Usually, a large bowl is provided for the empty shells; otherwise, pile them neatly on your plate.

- **Snails (escargot):** If the escargot is served in the shell, tongs to hold the shell will be provided. Use the escargot tong to secure the snail, pick up one escargot shell at a time, and remove the snail from the shell with your cocktail fork. Dip the snail into the butter sauce provided. Many restaurants serve escargot already removed from the shell and placed in special dishes with sauce or melted butter.

Spaghetti

It may look difficult, but eating spaghetti is easy: Spaghetti is normally twirled on the edge of your plate with your fork and secured with your knife before bringing the bite to your mouth to eat. However, a fork and a place spoon may also be used (though you rarely see this method in most of Italy. It is primarily used in Southern Italy, as in Sicily). The place spoon serves as a base of operation. Place a forkful of spaghetti strands — not too many — in the bowl of the place spoon. Then twirl the fork around until the strands are firmly wrapped around the fork in a bite-size portion.

Using chopsticks

In many Asian countries, chopsticks are used instead of the Western knife, fork, and spoon. Chopsticks come in a wide variety of finishes, from plain wood to ornately decorated lacquer.

Using chopsticks involves a certain technique. Hold them between your index finger and thumb, with the lower stick resting in the web of your hand and the top stick being held like a pencil (see Figure 12-9). The top stick does most of the moving. Use your two middle fingers to maneuver it. Holding chopsticks too tightly restricts mobility; holding them too close to the tip makes you lose leverage.

Figure 12-9:
Holding
and using
chopsticks.

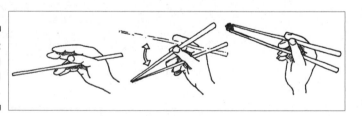

If your food is too big for a single bite, you may use your chopsticks to cut it or you may hold the food with your chopsticks while you take a couple of bites. Between bites, either place your chopsticks on the rest provided or lay them diagonally across the lower dish or plate.

Here is a brief list of chopstick don'ts:

- ✔ Never point, gesture, or talk with chopsticks.

- ✔ Do not leave chopsticks pointed upright in your rice or soup bowl.

- ✔ Do not pick through the common food plate to find your favorite piece; select it visually and then help yourself.

- ✔ Never take food from another person's chopsticks.

And remember — if you're not ready to tackle chopsticks, it is perfectly fine to request a fork and knife if you are in the United States. When traveling to Asian countries, it's good to take time to learn to use chopsticks (properly) ahead of time. In most traditional restaurants, they won't have forks, though many of the newer restaurants and hotels in large cities will provide a fork if requested.

Managing Dining Mishaps

Eating in any social setting may result in mishaps. The following tips may help you steer yourself out of common mishaps that can occur:

- ✔ **You drop a utensil on the floor.** Never lean over and pick up the utensil. Beckon a waiter, and politely ask for a new one.

- ✔ **You're served a piece of food that is not cooked properly.** Do you send it back or live with it? Depending on the time allocated and the type of meal you are attending, business lunch or dinner, it may be best to say nothing and just eat it. If you choose to send it back, be aware of the delays you may cause to the overall meal. Let the server know by discreetly explaining the situation, and remember to keep your voice low. Trust the server to reappear with a different plate of food for you.

- ✔ **You find a foreign object in your food.** Again, find a waiter, and tell her about the problem in a very discreet manner. Rest assured that your meal will be replaced quickly.

- ✔ **You dislike the food that is being served, or you are allergic to it.** The polite thing to do is try a little of everything, but if you are allergic to a food, just smile and say, "No, thank you." It's not necessary to say anything critical.

- ✔ **You have a piece of bone, gristle, or some other unwanted food item in your mouth.** Discreetly place the item on the tines of your fork and lay it on your plate, hiding it under something if possible.

- ✔ **You notice that your dining partner has spinach in her teeth or a crumb in his beard.** Catch your dining partner's attention, and discreetly motion to that part of your face where the offending morsel is lodged on his or her face.

If you have a mishap, always be discreet and apologetic — use a little light humor to keep the mood upbeat.

Chapter 13

Attending Conferences, Trade Shows, and Special Events

....

In This Chapter

▶ Remembering that you represent your company

▶ Mingling at social events

▶ Being social after hours

▶ Planning or attending a special event

....

Most people end up attending work-related special events at least once in a while. Depending on your perspective, these events are enlightening and energizing, or they're a big fat bore. Regardless of how you feel about these events, certain guidelines exist for how to act when you're at one of them.

In this chapter, I show you how to be a good company representative, how to mingle at conferences and conventions, and how to avoid embarrassing yourself after hours. I also explain how to plan and participate in a special event for your company.

Being a Stellar Representative of Your Company

It may not be fair, but it's true: When you're at a conference or a trade show, your actions are not completely your own. If you are an employee of Big Fish Corp., the people you meet will see you as a Big Fish representative, even if you see yourself as a guppy. Make sure you conduct yourself in a way that's fair to the people who sign your paycheck.

Perhaps your most important responsibility is to avoid making negative comments about your company. You don't have to lie, but you shouldn't slander your employer either. Even if you hate your job or think that the company is mismanaged, it's not your place to say so in this environment. Politely change the subject. If someone says something like "I had a friend who worked for XYZ Co., and he says the CEO spent all the company's money on exotic sharks for his personal pool," you could respond, "Hmm. I haven't heard that. Did you say you work for Mega Technology? I've heard lots of interesting things about your new product. Is it really going to revolutionize the frozen-burrito industry?"

Come up with a few stock answers for questions about your company — explanations of what the company does (if this question is common), positive comments about the new CEO, or information about new products.

Obviously, you should never reveal any kind of confidential information about your company. If you're not sure whether something is a secret, assume that it is. What you're saying may not seem to be especially important, and the person you're talking to may seem to be inconsequential, but you can never be sure. You should discuss interesting and exciting news that's public information, however. Making comments about how much you like working for your company or making other positive comments is always appropriate.

Your behavior at mealtimes, during meetings, and after hours also reflects on your company. To be a good representative, follow the other rules you find throughout this book.

Schmoozing and Networking

Industry events such as conferences and trade shows are great places to make contacts in your field and to find out more about what's going on at other companies. In fact, your company may be paying your way to the event in part so that you will learn more about your industry. If you're naturally confident and outgoing, the social aspects of work probably aren't that difficult for you. But if you're a little shy (or a lot), the idea of navigating a room full of new faces may be terrifying. Instead of hiding in your room watching HBO, take a deep breath, and try these strategies.

First of all, slap on a name tag. These events almost always provide them, and they make you more approachable. The name tag should go on your right shoulder, the idea being that when you shake hands, the other person's eyes will be drawn up your arm to your name tag. If the tags are the self-adhesive kind, and you're concerned about damaging a silk blouse, ask whether any clip-on holders are available. Better yet, try to remember this problem when you're packing, and bring something a little sturdier.

Next, you should establish some goals for yourself. If you're in sales, your goal might be to gather as many business cards and sales leads as possible. If this conference is your first, your goal might be simply to practice introducing yourself. If you don't have a specific need to meet people, your goal might be to have a good time and sample the shrimp toast.

If introducing yourself to a stranger is daunting, keep in mind that saying hello and telling someone your name are not major commitments. For some people, speaking to a stranger is as scary as asking for a first date. It shouldn't be. All the people in the room have at least something in common with you: They don't know many people either, they're a little nervous, and they're not sure what to say. They will be very grateful if you break the ice by starting the conversation. All you have to do is extend your hand and say "Hello, I'm Johan Otto." This introduction will prompt the other person to respond with his name. Then you can say "What did you think of today's speaker?" or "What company do you work for?" or even "How's the artichoke dip?" What you say doesn't have to be something profoundly interesting; it just has to be something. The other person responds, and then you're off.

Unless you're attending a convention of Nobel laureates, no one is expecting you to be outrageously witty or wise — just friendly.

If someone approaches you and starts the conversation, good for you! Smile and be pleasant. Share some information about yourself and ask questions in return. If you have a business card, hand it out. You're doing great!

Now it's time to remember your goal. If you're trying to meet the maximum number of people, stay on task. Although you want to be polite, you don't want to spend too much time with any one person. After you've chatted with someone for a few minutes and learned a little bit about her, it's all right for you to move on. You can say something as simple as "Mary, it's been nice getting to know you," hand her your business card, and ask whether she has a card. If it makes you feel more comfortable, you can make up some small excuse, such as "I really wanted to make sure I met this afternoon's speaker, and I see him over there." Making excuses really isn't necessary, though; you don't need to apologize for wanting to meet a variety of people at the event.

If you're not concerned about making lots of contacts, you can be a bit more relaxed. An interesting conversation could last all night, or you can end a boring one and move on.

Whatever you do, avoid the temptation to look around the room while you're talking to someone. This can be difficult at a busy party, because so much movement is going on — like sitting at a sports bar and trying not to watch the hockey game. You have to discipline yourself, though. Seeing your eyes darting around the room is very disconcerting for the other person.

If you have a friend or a colleague at the event, you may want to buddy up, provided that you don't talk only to each other. When you're introducing yourself to someone, introduce your friend at the same time. What you shouldn't do is stand together in the corner like cellmates looking out at the world. You're there to meet new people and expand your boundaries.

Flip to Chapter 5 for more details about the art of meeting and greeting. Chapter 6 has the goods on making polite conversation.

Socializing after Hours

Whether you're at an industry conference or at a meeting that's only for your company's employees, work lasts for only so long. In many cases, you're on your own in the evenings. You may want to use this opportunity to get to know the people you work with — or want to work with — a little better.

Deciding whether to socialize

Before you get down to serious socializing, you should decide whether you want to attend any social event at all. How should you decide?

- ✔ If your boss or another influential person asks you out to dinner, don't say no, even if you have a stack of work and a big headache. Although such opportunities are not strictly part of the work day, they're an important part of your career. Even if the invitation is from a peer, you usually should accept. If you routinely turn down opportunities to socialize with your colleagues, you risk getting a reputation for being aloof or not a team player.

- ✔ On the other hand, if you're craving an evening alone, you may not make a very good dinner companion. Particularly on long trips when you're working long days, you may be tired, cranky, and overwhelmed with work. On those occasions, it's all right to tell colleagues, "I'm really not up to dinner this evening; I'm planning to get some work done and turn in early." Politely stick to your guns if they try to change your mind. You have every right to use your evening the way you want to.

A busy executive for a telecommunications company travels frequently, and he almost always has dinner with colleagues. He's learned to recognize his own limits, however, and sometimes lets others know that he's going to slam and click: shut his hotel-room door, click the lock shut, and open it for no one but room service! As long as you don't use it too often, the slam and click can be a great strategy for renewing your energy.

Sticking to a few simple rules

So you've decided to go out with some colleagues after work. Great! When dining with colleagues, you should follow the standard rules for business dining outlined in Chapter 11. Here are a few additional guidelines for socializing after hours:

✔ When you're with people from work, the conversation often drifts toward office gossip. Watch your step, keep your own comments to a minimum, and resist the temptation to say anything vicious or untrue. Although you may be forced to respond to a question like "Is it true that you heard Sam getting chewed out because he messed up on the IPO?", avoid wallowing in your own contempt for Sam and his incompetence. Just say something like this: "I heard that he and Sue had a big talk about the offering, but other than that, I don't really know what happened." Your colleagues may be disappointed if they can't get some good gossip, but that's their problem, not yours.

✔ If you're with your boss or some other senior person, you should follow that person's lead in ordering. If he orders an appetizer and an additional side dish, you should too. Keep courses balanced so that everyone is eating at the same time.

✔ Although you can always drink less than the senior person, you should not drink more. Two or three glasses of wine during a business dinner are plenty for almost everyone. (It isn't even necessary for you to drink to make your clients comfortable, as long as your behavior in no way suggests disapproval of their drinking.)

Be careful! Getting drunk in front of your colleagues will make you look pathetic and out of control, not fun and sophisticated. Know your limit, and stay well under it. If you're having drinks at cocktail hour or later in the evening, drink slowly, and have at least one glass of water for each alcoholic drink. When you're drinking wine or beer with dinner, savor it slowly. If you feel even close to woozy, stop drinking, and keep eating.

✔ In addition to keeping your conversation under control, staying sober can keep you from doing things you will regret back at the office. Even if you haven't had a thing to drink, however, being out of town can make you feel that a liaison with that attractive coworker isn't so far out of reach. Resist, resist, resist! You shouldn't do anything out of town that you wouldn't do back at home. Why?

• If your colleague isn't interested in your advances, you may find yourself facing a sexual-harassment claim or, at the very least, an awkward situation.

• Keep in mind that you have to work with this person for the foreseeable future.

• Stories about your after-hours activities may — and probably will — find their way back to the office gossip, and possibly to your boss or members of your family. Even if you think you're being very discreet, you may well be the subject of next week's nudges and smirks.

Questionable behavior with consenting adults from other companies may be slightly less risky, but not much less.

Planning and Participating in Special Events

Myriad reasons exist for having special events in the business world — boosting employee morale, celebrating company successes, recognizing employees, entertaining and impressing clients, launching new products, and many more. When you're on the planning end of these events, you play a key role in their success. Even as a participant, you are an important part of the proceedings. The following sections give you some guidelines for each role.

When you're the planner

Planning special events is such a huge task that some people make a career of it. A few simple tips, however, go a long way toward helping you plan a successful event.

Begin planning as far in advance as possible

Start as far in advance as you can. In many cases, you don't have much control of the schedule — many an executive has said something like "I'd like to take our top ten clients ice fishing in Alaska two weeks from Saturday; get on that, won't you?" — but you should control it as much as you can. If you know that an event is coming up and that you will be in charge of organizing it, get as much information as possible right away. What's the purpose of the event? Approximately how many people will be there — 50 or 5,000? Will it be casual or formal? Where will it take place? Is a budget allocated? Take a cue from the experts: Planning for some huge events, such as the Olympics, begins years in advance.

If someone is reluctant to discuss the event with you because he doesn't have all the facts yet, explain to him that you will get started with whatever facts are available now. The earlier you begin planning, the greater chance of success you have.

Get organized with detailed to-do lists

Be as organized as possible. You can't put together a successful event by keeping everything in your head and on those tiny sticky notes. Professional event planners are known for their extensive, detailed to-do lists and ubiquitous clipboards. Many professionals start a project by putting together a huge list of every single thing they can think of that will need to be done. From that list, they develop the following:

> ✔ **A timeline, working backward from the event:** The timeline includes a list of tasks from booking the location (months in advance) to sending out invitations (weeks in advance) to having fresh flowers delivered (the

morning of the event). The timeline must include reminders to get the necessary approvals — everything from your fireworks permit from the city to your boss's okay on the menu.

✔ **A list of assignments:** With any luck, you'll be able to find someone to pick up the keynote speaker from the airport while you're busy cutting 10,000 egg-salad sandwiches into the shape of the company logo.

✔ **A list of the vendors needed:** Even if you don't know right away who these vendors will be, such as caterers, limousine services, travel agents, sound-system experts, florists, belly dancers, and balloon-animal technicians, you should make sure that you have all the categories in mind.

✔ **A list of contingencies:** What if extra attendees show up? What if the speaker is late? What if it rains?

Share your big list of things to do with at least one other person, who will act as your backup if needed. And have a list of contact people at the various service-providing organizations, including notes about what's been arranged with each of them. As the event gets closer, you may want to review this list with your backup, or at least send it to him, on a weekly or even daily basis. Most events require lots of last-minute preparation and on-site management. If you wake up with a debilitating rash on the day of the event, your backup will appreciate having this list.

Think through every aspect of the event

Walk through the entire event in your mind, and if possible, walk through it physically. How long does it take you to walk slowly from the conference room to the gazebo? Take that figure and multiply it by four; that's how long herding your guests will take.

A new employee at a large company thought he had planned for everything — prompt airport pickups, vegetarian meals for those who didn't want Iowa beef, fresh flowers on every table, and welcome letters in each room. What he didn't plan for was a huge speaker's event in the room next door. For his next event, he added "Check on other events in hotel" to his big list.

You dramatically increase your chances of pulling off a successful event if you take into account that people will act the way they want to, not the way you want them to. Most people cannot sit still for three hours without a break, for example. If you plan a meeting without sufficient break time, you can be assured that it will be interrupted by a steady stream of participants leaving to smoke, powder their noses, and make phone calls. Many others will not eat certain foods — especially red meat — so you should always offer at least one vegetarian choice. Most people also refuse to wear bathing suits, sing, or do the limbo in front of coworkers.

When you're an attendee

When you're a guest in someone else's home, you're probably gracious and polite by instinct. Your instincts at a special event should be no different. Even in a hotel ballroom or in the middle of a wheat field, you're someone's guest, and your behavior is important.

✔ **Be on time.** If the event starts at a certain time, you don't want to be the one walking in late and disrupting the speaker. Be sure to allow time for getting a name tag and finding a seat, as well as for regular concerns like traffic and parking.

✔ **Do what's asked of you.** If a chair is marked "reserved," don't sit in it. If someone asks you to move into the dining room, don't keep standing right where you are. Even if you're used to being in charge, take this opportunity to see how the other half lives.

✔ **Stay seated, pay attention, and remain quiet.** If the event involves a meeting or a sit-down program, sit down, and do your best to pay attention. Turn off your pager and cell phone, just as you would during a business meeting or meal, and refrain from jumping up to make calls. You should also avoid talking during the presentation. Talking is distracting to the speaker and to those around you. (These rules go for outdoor concerts, too.)

✔ **Be polite to the staff.** If you have a problem that can be fixed, mention it politely to your server. A knife, if you didn't get one, and refills of coffee should be easy. Some food-related requests, however, just don't make sense at a banquet. Your server probably won't be able to correct an overcooked steak while taking care of 79 other guests in a fixed period. Accept that fact, and give thanks that you don't have to eat in a hotel ballroom every night of the week. Likewise, ask the buffet attendant whether more shrimp will be coming out, but don't complain to him; he can't do a thing about it.

✔ **If you're at an outdoor event, don't leave your manners inside.** Paper plates and napkins belong in the trash can, not on the ground. Your mouth should be firmly closed while chewing, even if you're eating corn on the cob and fried chicken with your fingers. Casual dress doesn't mean frayed, see-through, or tight clothing — at least, not at a business function. When you're back in the office next week, you don't want your colleagues contemplating the image of you in a Metallica T-shirt with the arms cut off.

Unless you've been given very special treatment of some kind, thank-you notes usually are not required for business special events. A nice note to the host and/or event planner, however, will be treasured for a long time and is preferable to an e-mail. See Chapter 8 for details on thank-you notes and other types of business correspondence.

When you're part of the action

If you're an important part of the special event — a speaker, entertainer, or guest of honor — congratulations! You've obviously earned the respect and admiration of your hosts. By following a few simple rules, you can be sure that they will still respect and admire you after you leave:

- **Try not to be extraordinarily high-maintenance.** Asking your hosts to pick you up at the airport — which they probably will offer to do anyway — is well within bounds. Asking them to pick you up, drop you off for an afternoon of skydiving 40 miles in the opposite direction, and then pick you up again later is out of bounds. If you want to combine the event with other personal business or pleasure activities, offer to arrange your own transportation. If your hosts are in a position to assist you, they will offer to do so.

- **When traveling long distances for an engagement, plan extra time for travel delays.** If allowing extra time leaves you with an extra half-day of down time, ask your hosts to help you out with finding temporary office space, setting up a videoconference room, or getting whatever you may need. They would much rather do that than have you arrive after the event because of a weather delay.

- **Don't commit to an engagement unless you're sure you can make it, and don't cancel unless circumstances make it absolutely unavoidable.** A parent's sudden hospitalization is a reason to cancel; a golf game with an old buddy at a really great course is not. Canceling plans because you got a better offer is never polite, but it's especially impolite when hundreds of people have arranged their schedules to hear you speak.

- **If you have a problem with your accommodations, speak up, but know when to quit.** It's one thing to call the front desk of your hotel and complain about the temperature, cleanliness, or smokiness of your room. It's another thing to rant at your host about the inferior quality of the hotel he chose. At that point, it may be too late for him to do anything about it, and he'll only feel guilty (or annoyed). After the event is over, and his stress level has receded, you could follow up with a polite note to let him know that a different hotel might be a better choice for the next speaker.

- **Don't be the boring presenter everyone talks about for years to come.** If you've agreed to be the keynote speaker, you've agreed to do your very best work onstage. This rule may seem to be elementary, but it's important: Prepare for your presentation! If you're the main event, your audience expects an interesting, articulate, and enlightening presentation. Unless you are extremely good on your feet — and most people aren't — don't plan to get on stage and wing it. Outline your presentation, and practice it as many times as necessary to make it shine. In addition, having an outline may make it possible for a colleague to make your presentation in case of an emergency.

When attending a trade show or convention, be sure to bring along three times the number of business cards than you normally would take. You can always take home what you do not use; it's better to have too many than too few. You don't want to miss out on winning that special prize or not having a business card for that VIP.

Chapter 14

Taking Part in a Variety of Social Off-Site Activities

In This Chapter

▶ Hosting business outings

▶ Going over special etiquette for a variety of sports

▶ Covering your bases at sporting and cultural events

*W*ith the new flexibility in the workday, business isn't restricted to the office or the restaurant anymore. The contemporary world has as many venues for business as it does activities that colleagues and associates can share. Whether you and your best client are avid ice climbers or fanatical golfers, at some point in your career you're likely to find yourself in a situation in which you never thought you'd be doing business.

In this chapter, you get advice on some of the most common out-of-the-office venues for business. Your list might include paragliding or heli-skiing in Bugaboo State Park. But take heart: At least for now, trips to Mount Everest are not de rigueur.

Hosting Group Outings

Just as the workday is more flexible than it used to be, so are the places where you can conduct business. You may work for an engineering firm that encourages employees to take after-lunch group bike rides to the city overlook. Your boss may like to take small groups to her house so that you can discuss strategy in the privacy of her backyard. You may visit a high-tech firm in Portland and be invited on a walking tour of Horsetail Falls in the Gorge. Come prepared with the appropriate clothing if at all possible.

If you're the host of an off-site outing, take care to think things through ahead of time. Schedule off-site outings at least two weeks in advance and notify the guests of the plans. In the invitation, clearly state the equipment needed (if any), as well as the purpose and length of the outing. Unless you provide ample warning, respect people's right to decline if the outing radically deviates from the time and place of the regular workday. That way, an employee won't be stranded on a granite face 10 minutes before she needs to pick her daughter up at day care.

Also take the time to learn about any other personal or practical impediments to the off-site outing. Perhaps your guest is asthmatic, and the trip you'd hoped to take to the sea lions' caves would only make her miserable. Perhaps reservations have to be made months in advance for that ferry ride across Puget Sound; if you show up without reservations, you'll embarrass both yourself and your guest. Whatever the event is, think things through, and always consider the weather.

If you are hosting a guest from out of town and want to take him to see some of the local sights and landmarks, discreetly inquire as to his willingness to undertake such an excursion. Say something like this: "Mr. Ferrari, I would like to offer you the opportunity to see our wonderful art museum and the local arboretum tomorrow. Would that be of interest to you, or is there something else you would prefer?" If Ferrari has some restrictions that would prevent him from enjoying walking, this phrasing of the question allows him to back away gracefully. It prevents embarrassment to you as well, because the way you've phrased the question doesn't put your guest in the position of having to admit that he'd rather not join you for reasons he'd rather not reveal.

Avoid planning strenuous outings unless your guest is a health nut. There's no point in jeopardizing a business relationship by possibly humiliating your guest.

Displaying Good Manners, No Matter the Sport

Civility is fundamental and essential to survival, because it preserves our basic human values. Lately, this ideal has been challenged in sports, with the debasement of the traditional values of good sportsmanship. Almost every week, you see TV and newspaper reports about both players and spectators yelling, using vulgar language, and engaging in physical altercations.

Yes, losing is disappointing, and most people don't like it. But we can all find ways to control our behavior in reaction to a loss. Players and spectators alike should practice these basic guidelines:

- Even if you lose, don't make excuses or walk away angry; be a good sport, smile, and hold your head high. No one likes a whiner or complainer.

- Treat your opponent(s) respectfully, and always try to avoid arguments.

Combining cruises and business meetings

An increasingly popular place for off-site meetings is — believe it or not — the cruise ship. More than just conventions and trade shows happen on board; day cruises from major and minor ports and river cities for business meetings are at an all-time high.

The reasons for the newfound popularity of business cruises aren't hard to find. Unlike hotels and convention centers, cruise ships provide few distractions. Also, managers find that business meetings held on board are focused and efficient, and everyone has a good time to boot (at least, as long as the weather is good).

- ✔ Accept judgment calls from the officials, and follow their directions.
- ✔ Abide by the rules of the game. Play fair.
- ✔ Offer encouragement to teammates; never criticize them if they make a mistake.
- ✔ Play your best without showing off.
- ✔ Win without bragging or gloating.
- ✔ Never throw anything in anger. In addition to being rude and childish, this behavior could be dangerous.

In the following sections, I discuss the etiquette of a variety of sports that you may engage in during your career.

Admitting that you don't play a sport you've been invited to play is perfectly all right. Rank beginners and fakes aren't appreciated. It's better to decline than to embarrass yourself in a sport you don't know how to play at least passably well.

Golfing

Golf and business are like hot dogs and baseball: They naturally go together. The relaxed pace, bucolic surroundings, and handsome appointments of the clubhouse provide an elegant way to get to know other people and to strike deals.

Golf works well as an icebreaker and deal-maker only some of the time, of course. The game is immensely frustrating on occasion, so it's a remarkably accurate test of a person's stress-management abilities. If your partner doesn't lose her cool after a quadruple bogey on the par-3 fifteenth hole, chances are good that she'll be cool under other kinds of fire.

As old as the game is, golf is loaded with expected behavior and attire. Except on public courses, you rarely see jeans on a golf course, for example. About as casual as things get is business casual.

When you're golfing, keep in mind two codes of conduct: the etiquette of golfing and the etiquette of combining golf and business.

General golf etiquette

When you golf, you should know that:

- ✔ Women wear knee-length skirts or long shorts or pants, shirts with collars and sleeves, and golf shoes with soft spikes.

- ✔ Men wear slacks or long shorts, shirts with collars and sleeves, and golf shoes with soft spikes.

- ✔ Colors never found in nature or in the office are acceptable on the golf course. Some clubs favor more muted, conservative attire, however. If you're in doubt, call the club and ask.

- ✔ Don't talk when someone else is playing a stroke.

- ✔ Be ready to play when it's your turn.

- ✔ The player with the lowest score on the preceding hole is first to tee off on the next hole.

- ✔ Everyone in your group should be behind you when you hit.

- ✔ Let faster groups play through.

- ✔ If alcohol is allowed on the course, go easy! Drinking too much while playing golf with clients is as dangerous as it is at any other company function.

- ✔ Take your practice swings before you get to the tee.

- ✔ Repair divots and pitch marks, and rake away your footprints in sand traps.

- ✔ Avoid offering bets, but accept them if they're offered by your client or boss. Win graciously, and pay promptly if you lose.

- ✔ Don't cheat on your scorecard.

- ✔ In general, the host tips, but if you have a personal caddie, you may tip your caddie even as a guest.

- ✔ Keep your off-color jokes to yourself, as you would at the office. (See Chapter 2 for more about general office etiquette.)

- ✔ Don't stand with your group on the green after you've all holed out. "Holed out" means that everyone has finished their putt. Move off the green so the next group can continue to play. You don't want the players behind you waiting around unnecessarily.

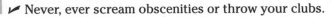

✔ If the golf cart is suppose to hold two people, put no more than two people in the cart and drive it slowly, keeping it on the cart path and off the green unless you have special needs and have made special arrangements.

✔ Never, ever scream obscenities or throw your clubs.

Business golf etiquette

Putting golf and business together is supposed to be fun and productive at the same time. You can achieve both goals more effectively if you remember that the golf outing is first and foremost a business event and that your boss and clients have to look good if you're going to get what you want. Keep these tips in mind:

✔ Don't outplay the boss or client, even if he's a 15 handicap and you're a 4.

✔ Avoid talking business until the group members are settled into the game and are comfortable with one another.

✔ Avoid talking business if a companion is facing a difficult shot.

Playing tennis, racquetball, and squash

Racquet sports are popular in large cities because they happen inside and don't require a lot of space. A dress code usually is involved. Make sure that you know ahead of time what the dress code is for the club you are going to attend.

White is always appropriate at a racquet club, so you will be dressed correctly if you wear a white knit shirt with a collar and sleeves tucked into white shorts. Women may also wear tennis dresses. Tennis shoes are the appropriate footwear. Some clubs' dress codes are less restrictive than others. When in doubt, check with the club.

If you're hosting a client at your club, be sure to arrive early so that your guest will not face quizzical looks from the staff. Escort your guest to the locker room, supply her with towels and a locker, and allow her some privacy for changing.

When you're the guest, you should arrive with the right gear and the appropriate attire. Bring your own racquet, balls, and protective eyewear, and check ahead about the club's dress code.

John McEnroe notwithstanding, racquet sports are known for genteel play. And with the exception of professional or refereed competition matches, racquet sports rely entirely on the honesty of the players to enforce the rules. This feature requires you to observe the following codes of conduct:

- Show up on time.
- Call out-of-bounds shots on your side of the net.
- Don't return serves that are out.
- Say nothing if your opponent makes a lousy call.
- Announce the score after every point when you're serving.
- Return stray balls from other courts when you have a break in your game.
- Stay in your court, and don't interrupt other players while they're playing; wait for a break in their game.
- Never, ever scream obscenities or throw your racquet.

Although playing someone at your own skill level is fun, you will not always have this luxury. If you are playing with someone at a different level, try to make the game enjoyable for your guest. If you're a beginner and your guest is an accomplished player, let him know your status, and ask for advice. On the other hand, if you're an experienced player and your guest is not, don't destroy her in the game. Be encouraging. Remember, the point is to have fun.

Sailing and motorboating

Sailing and motorboating can be opportunities for the boss or client to show off his latest toys. They can also be enormous fun, so long as you know what you're doing on the boat:

- Never call a yacht a yacht! All boats, from the smallest motorboat to the largest yacht, are simply *boats* to their captains.
- Becoming proficient at sailing takes years of practice, and if you are a novice, no amount of confident bluster will cover for your ignorance of the difference between a line and a halyard. Faking it simply isn't in your strategic interest; admit your landlubber status, and ask for directions. Most captains will be more than willing to tell you what to do.
- If the captain asks you to stay put and stop helping, stop helping. Uninformed "helping" on a sailboat can result in an unintended swim.
- If you're the host of a day at sea, advise your guests ahead of time about what they should wear and whether they're likely to get wet. Let them know whether they will be sailing, motoring leisurely, or attempting to break the sound barrier.
- Don't invite more people than your boat can accommodate.

✔ If you're a guest, remember that the boat is your captain's. The captain is boss at all times on the boat, which is not a democracy. Follow directions.

If your work will involve frequent sailing or boating expeditions and you grew up in Nebraska or some other landlocked area, familiarize yourself with the terms by browsing through an introductory handbook on sailing or boating (such as *Sailing For Dummies,* 2nd Edition, written by J. J. Isler and Peter Isler, and published by Wiley).

Here are some other guidelines to know:

✔ Wear clothes that will protect you from the elements and can get wet. Layer! If the weather is reasonably warm, wear a bathing suit, shorts, T-shirt or polo shirt, a hat, and sunglasses. Bring a windbreaker and a sweater or sweatshirt if you will be out in the evening or out on the ocean. You may take most of your clothes off, but having the right kind of clothes on hand can help if the weather goes bad or you're out after dark.

✔ Wear deck shoes or simple tennis shoes. Sandals, hiking shoes, or leather-soled shoes are inappropriate and sometimes dangerous.

✔ Never smoke below deck; ask if you may smoke above deck.

✔ Bring only gifts that can be shared while you're on board. If you're not sure about the galley facilities, ask.

✔ If you fear that you'll be seasick, take medication along. If you are very prone to motion sickness, it's better to decline the invitation.

Skiing and snowboarding

The rules of skiing and snowboarding are, like many other etiquette guidelines, based on safety — yours and that of others. Begin by acknowledging that skiing happens in winter and requires warm clothing. You have to be outfitted properly to enjoy skiing. Necessary clothing items include thermal underclothes, pile shirts and sweaters, wool/nylon-blend socks, moisture-wicking pants, breathable waterproof parkas and ski pants, gloves or mittens, and a hat. Sunglasses or goggles (or both) and sunscreen are also necessary.

Skiing and boarding may look easy, but they aren't. (Ask any orthopedic surgeon!) If you've never been on skis or a snowboard, counting on your natural athletic ability to get you down the slope isn't smart. Do the sensible thing, and take a lesson or two. With parabolic skis now being the norm for recreational skiers, learning to ski is easier than ever before. The same goes for boarding.

If you're a skier or a boarder, you already know the etiquette rules. If you're a beginner, memorize the following:

- ✔ Don't crash the lift line. Stay in order. Offer to ride with singles, or offer to share a ride with a single.

- ✔ If you've never been on a lift, tell the operator at the bottom of the lift, who will slow it and show you how to get on.

- ✔ If you've never gotten off a lift, motion to the operator at the top to slow it so you can get off. Then move away from the off ramp immediately.

- ✔ Ski and board under control at all times. Skiing and snowboarding can be lethal sports.

- ✔ Don't go on runs you're not prepared to go all the way down under your own power.

- ✔ The skier or boarder below you has the right of way at all times. If you want to pass, yell "Left!" or "Right!" before you do so.

- ✔ If you get in over your head on a slope, side-slip down the edge of the slope to safer ground.

As a skiing host, be aware of your guests' abilities. Don't cajole them onto a double black diamond run to impress them with your skill. Always be prepared to ski well below your level to ensure the comfort and safety of all your guests. Again, remember the point is to have fun. You're not at the Winter Olympics.

Hosting social sporting events for business can be beneficial for your career and company. If done properly, these occasions can make a positive and lasting impression. With good planning and a bit of practice, you will shine as a gracious company representative — all while actually having fun! Remember, the goal is to build client and customer relationships, trust, and a rapport. To accomplish this, it isn't always necessary to discuss business.

Participating in extreme sports

The etiquette of extreme sports is more than that of most other sports, due to safety concerns. After all, a significant risk of injury or death is attached to extreme sports. Your strict adherence to the sport's etiquette may well save your life and almost assuredly will save you from injury. Your knowledge of specific safety concerns will help you enjoy the sport more and make it an effective social activity for business.

Each extreme sport has its own set of etiquette guidelines. I won't cover them here. But I can say that the key business-etiquette issue is, again, to take care not to outdo your guest or boss. If you and your guests are both kayakers, but your guest is capable of handling only Grade IV water and you can manage Grade VI, either don't take her on a river with Grade VI water, or confirm that the Grade V and VI rapids can be portaged. Your guest may be humiliated if she tries to run water she can't run, and she may even get seriously injured.

It is always advisable for the host to introduce the etiquette of a particular sport to his guests. And if you're uncertain as a guest, don't hesitate to ask. (If you doubt this advice, read *Into Thin Air,* by Jon Krakauer. Need I say more?)

Attending Sporting and Cultural Events

Corporate boxes at football and baseball stadiums and at basketball arenas are more popular now than ever. These facilities are impressive places to entertain clients, and companies in major cities spend lavishly to impress clients with their firms' prestige.

In the same vein, cultural events such as plays and concerts have become popular activities for business entertainment. In the following sections, I provide guidelines on behaving appropriately at such events.

Be on time

When you're attending a play, concert, or other indoor event, it's never appropriate to arrive late — or leave early. Doing so is unfair to the artist or performers, not to mention very disruptive to other members of the audience. Many theaters now require latecomers to remain in the hallway or the lobby until the end of the first act. Yes, sometimes being late is unavoidable, so always confirm the start time of the event or performance, and plan accordingly.

Know who pays for what

As host, you invite clients, employees, or friends to your box or club expecting them not to pay. Your invitation carries with it the presumption that you will pay for the time your guests spend there and for their food and drink, if any. This extends to tips.

The presumption that the host pays does not extend to buying equipment for your guest, however. If you invite a client to a game of tennis at your club, you pay for his time on the court and for his refreshments and rental equipment, but your guest is expected to arrive ready to play.

Dress the part

Wearing cutoffs, jeans, a T-shirt, or a halter top to a private box for a sporting event or to play sports at a private club is inappropriate. If you're participating in sports, make sure that you have the right wardrobe and equipment for the sport you will be playing. If you're unsure, call ahead to ask about proper attire. If you are attending an event as a spectator, don't wear clothes that make *you* the spectacle. Dressing appropriately and wearing proper clothing, clean and neatly pressed garments, and well-matched accessories is a sign that you're professional and in tune with whatever is going on. The key when attending sporting or cultural events is to ask about proper attire. You should never be uncomfortable or present an image that isn't you or that may be a negative image for your company.

If you stick to the rules or category of *business casual* or slightly less than business casual, you will make a positive impression. (For more tips on various styles of dress, see Chapter 4.) Overdressing or under-dressing will send a strong message either way.

Respect other people's space

Share space with others courteously. Always be aware of your surroundings, and adapt your actions when necessary. For example:

- ✔ If someone in front of you is moving too slowly, walk around on the outside, saying, "Excuse me, please." But don't push through the middle of people walking together. Pushing and shoving at a public event are unacceptable.

- ✔ Don't hog the seats. When you're in a stadium with unassigned seats, make sure that you're not taking up more space than you need. Move down, and allow others to sit down or let them pass you easily.

- ✔ Sit up straight in your seat, too. Do not lean too far forward in your chair so you crowd or are in the space of the person in front of you.

- ✔ If you're wearing a hat while seated, be certain it isn't obstructing the view of the people behind you.

- ✔ Keep your elbows, knees, and feet within your designated space.

These rules also apply when you're entering or exiting moving walkways, escalators, elevators, and open stairways.

Monitor your noise level

Audiences enjoy events in a variety of ways, such as by eating, talking, cheering, clapping, and whistling. Depending on the event, you need to strike a certain balance between behaving graciously and being an overly enthusiastic fan, drinking too much and acting obnoxious. Be aware of and sensitive to those around you. Try not to distract others by talking when you should be watching, or cheering too loudly. Monitor noise levels, especially if you are with a large group of your colleagues.

If you attend an indoor event, try not to distract those around you by rustling the program or eating food loudly. Leave alarmed watches or any dangling jewelry at home. The same goes for cellular phones; turn them off, or turn on the vibrate feature.

Watch what you say

Refrain from using any form of obscene, foul, or disrespectful language when you're out in public, especially where other people are within earshot. Children or others nearby (including your coworkers) may find your words offensive.

Dispose of trash properly

It is obvious that we all know the consequences of leaving litter behind when we're outdoors. Not only is it an eyesore for others, it pollutes our environment and can be a danger to wildlife. The same thought should apply when you're attending an indoor event. Not only is leaving litter around an eyesore, it can create a danger, and it shows you're inconsiderate of those who have to clean up after you. Yes, they may be paid maintenance personnel, yet it's courteous to think of others by making their jobs easier (this goes for servers in restaurants). Show that you are aware of your surroundings and you care about others by throwing your trash in the proper recycle bin or receptacle, not on the ground. Extremely courteous folks will also pick up after others.

Chapter 15

Marking Life's Major Events and Passages

*W*hen the heat is on and everyone is working full force, a break to celebrate a colleague's new baby can seem superfluous, but it may be just what everyone needs. Some people tend to dismiss office celebrations or to look at them as contrived affairs that no one really enjoys. But recognizing major events in the lives of your colleagues helps establish camaraderie and cooperative working relations; it also lets you acknowledge your colleagues as individual human beings.

People often feel uncomfortable at such gatherings, not because they don't like their colleagues, but because they're not sure what to talk about. In this chapter, you come to see that the social gatherings that occur in professional life can be handled with grace.

Making the Most of Company Parties

General office parties are useful for building morale and celebrating accomplishments. They can also be held for special occasions, such as a colleague's 50th birthday.

Office parties should be given for a reason and should be reasonably short. Once or twice a year is plenty for the entire company to celebrate together with a big bash.

When you're planning an office party, the first thing to do is verify with your boss that the time and day you want to have the party are open. Failing to do this can throw the shadow of your boss's displeasure over the party, and you wouldn't want that.

If your division or department is going to host an office party, send invitations in the form of memos or e-mails if the party will be held in the office; send formal invitations if the party is to be held outside the office. (See Chapter 8 for details on invitations.) The invitation should include the reason for the party, where it's to be held, and its start time and duration.

Delegate the details of the party as you require, but guarantee a successful party by putting one person in charge. If donations will be involved, designate one person to collect the money, and specify whether the money will be used for a gift, refreshments, or both. Don't ask for too much money; if you can't get by with less than $5 or $10 from each person, look for some other way to supplement the party kitty.

In the following sections, I provide specific guidelines on hosting an office party and on attending an office party as a guest.

Hosting a restaurant gathering

As the host of a restaurant gathering, you're responsible for the invitations and the reservations. Select a restaurant where you've dined previously so that you know what to expect. If the restaurant is new, try it out beforehand to familiarize yourself with the menu and service.

When you arrive at the restaurant, make arrangements to pay the bill privately, so that no one else has the opportunity to dispute your generosity. If everyone is pitching in for the meal, the bill can come to the table. But remember to clarify this matter before the meal.

For larger groups, the host can arrange ahead of time for a set menu with two or more menu choices in each category ordered, at an all-inclusive set price that everyone brings on the day of the event. This way, no one is caught off guard by not having enough money on hand, and no one is upset at having to fund those individuals who ordered one of everything off the menu. The key is informing everyone of all the details before the event (such as whether wine and cocktails are included or will have to be paid for separately) so there are no surprises.

As host, you must dress in appropriate business attire. Being a little overdressed is better than being underdressed. If the restaurant is on the formal side, you need to include this information in the invitation so that guests don't show up in jeans and T-shirts.

As host, you're also responsible for making sure that no one gets out of hand and that even the wallflowers have as good a time as they can. Do your best to greet all your guests at the entrance (if possible) with a welcoming smile and to thank them for coming. Try to introduce guests to one another as they arrive and give a little information about each person to keep conversations going. Also do your best to spend a few minutes with as many of the guests as you can and keep an eye on the seating and the flow of the group — this task can be essential for ensuring that all guests feel included. For more on entertaining, check out Chapter 11.

Make sure, too, that no one drinks too much punch. Remember, "Loose lips sink ships." If you're a nondrinker, don't give in to social pressure to drink, and don't expect a nondrinking guest to indulge. Being drunk on company time is a very bad idea, and as host, you can try to prevent it. In some situations, the host can be held legally responsible if something happens to an intoxicated guest.

Being a well-behaved guest

When you're a guest, your normal guest responsibilities are in order at the office party. Behaving in a professional and considerate manner is important. Being rude or thoughtless is never in style and can do serious damage to your career. Whenever you're a guest at an office party, you should treat the host and other guests as you would want to be treated.

Here are tips that will leave a positive impression and surely will please your host:

- ✔ **Respond to invitations promptly.** A timely response is vital because the host plans the menu and cost of the meal around the number of people attending. I recommend responding within a day or two of receiving an invitation; however, a response within three to four days is acceptable.

- ✔ **Dress appropriately.** Dressing appropriately shows respect. A well-mannered host will let you know what the attire is for the event. However, if you're unsure of the attire, contact the host and ask.

- ✔ **Don't be late.** Being fashionably late is unfashionably rude. Being prompt is a guest's most important responsibility. The host carefully chose a time for the event to begin, and you must respect that choice by showing up at that time. When an invitation specifies a time, you're supposed to arrive at that time.

    You shouldn't arrive later than 15 minutes after the scheduled start of an event. If the event is a dinner party and you're running late, phone ahead to request that the host start without you. Arriving too early is as unacceptable as arriving too late.

✔ **Don't bring an uninvited guest with you.** If an unexpected houseguest happens to show up on the day of the scheduled event, you can call the host and ask whether it's possible for you to bring a friend. Present the question in a manner that doesn't put the host on the spot.

✔ **Be pleasant and cheerful.** Introduce yourself to other guests if you don't know them (a possibility if significant others have been invited to an office party). If everyone knows one another, mingling is still important (and polite). Don't spend the evening speaking to the same people you hang out with at work. Take advantage of the opportunity to network, and get to know the other employees.

✔ **Watch your conversation.** Conversations should include interests that most people share. Confidential company information is off-limits; so are tasteless jokes and any subjects that may be politically incorrect and could cause others to become uncomfortable (such as office gossip).

✔ **Stay sober, and avoid illegal drugs.** Consume alcoholic beverages in moderation in all business and social situations. Nothing spoils a good party faster than forcing a host to deal with an inebriated guest who creates a scene.

✔ **Mind your behavior.** Even if everyone is feeling giddy, avoid baring your soul to your favorite shipper, displaying a little too much affection for your romantic partner (or that attractive new accountant you wish were your romantic partner), or making aggressive sexual advances to any of your colleagues.

✔ **Don't complain or make negative comments about the room or the meal.** If something was wrong with the food, speak to the server or your boss quietly and discreetly.

✔ **Know when it's time to leave.** If the majority of the guests have already left, thank the host and head for the door. Try not to engage the host in a long goodbye that keeps him from the other guests.

✔ **Follow up with a thank-you note, e-mail, card, or letter of appreciation.** You're expected to send a thank-you note within a few days (the sooner, the better!).

Employee Birthdays, Weddings, Babies, and Deaths

Although many people keep their work lives separate from their private lives, everyone has a birthday; many people get married and/or have babies; and many people will lose someone dear to them while you know them at work. What are the best ways to mark these milestones with colleagues, clients, and bosses?

Birthdays

There is no general requirement to mark every coworker's birthday. From a company perspective, celebrating the anniversary date of someone's employment is more appropriate; the celebration of someone's birthday should be left as a personal celebration among coworkers.

Also keep in mind that some people prefer not to have others know their exact age. Unless you know that people have personally spoken about their birthdays and revealed their ages publicly, birthdays shouldn't involve anything relating to age. If a person has acknowledged his birthday, a card signed by everyone in the office and perhaps a group lunch or a gift are in order.

Birthday gifts from a boss to an employee are always acceptable, but a birthday gift from a subordinate to a boss at the office needs to be handled with utmost care. Others may perceive the gift as sycophantic behavior. So if you're giving the boss a gift, be discreet and do it privately. A group card or group gift for a special birthday is better.

Weddings

Colleagues, clients, and bosses get married, and you won't be invited to all the weddings. Unfair? Maybe. But not everyone shares everything with coworkers: Plenty of people draw a sharp, bold line between work and home. Rather than being hurt, acknowledge that some people are just plain different from you. If you're invited, send a gift by all means. But even if you're not invited, organizing an office gift for your fellow worker is a nice gesture.

Try to be gracious to coworkers even if you're hurt because you're not invited to their weddings. Often, a wedding budget is tight, or the couple have their own reasons for limiting the guest list. Assume that the omission wasn't personal.

If you're invited to a colleague's or client's wedding, remember that being asked to attend is an honor. Act accordingly. Respond to the invitation promptly (and with the same formality as the invitation itself), and send a gift either to the bride's parents or to the bride herself before or shortly after the wedding. Don't take gifts to the wedding. If the invitation is to you alone, go alone; don't bring an uninvited guest. And be on your best behavior at the wedding.

A gift of money in the form of a check is always proper for weddings. On the other hand, asking for money as a wedding gift is always wrong.

Babies

Anticipating the birth of a baby can bring out the very best in people; unfortunately, it can bring out the weirdest in people too. Occasionally, office showers are painful experiences for all involved. The reason is simple: Having a baby is necessarily an intimate affair, and you may not be on intimate terms with all your coworkers. Yet there you are, discussing things with your colleagues that even some of your closest friends don't know.

Avoid making the following mistakes:

- Touching a pregnant woman's stomach.
- Asking a new parent detailed questions. Demanding a play-by-play description of the delivery or subjecting others to every detail of your own experience is not appropriate.

Unless you and others in your office are good friends with the person having the baby, group gifts are preferable to office baby showers. Most parents-to-be have gift registries at local department stores and/or online, so check them ahead of time.

Funerals

At some point in your career, someone you work with will lose someone dear. The death of a loved one is a wrenching, debilitating event for the survivors as they confront not only their loss, but also their conflicted feelings toward the person who died.

It isn't at all unusual for survivors to go through a prolonged period of mourning after the death, during which sociability and probably even performance will lag. As a coworker or superior, you can help the grieving person by offering to help, either in a condolence card or in person.

As soon as you hear about the loss, draft a letter of condolence in black ink on a plain white fold-over card or a plain monarch sheet. (See Chapter 8 if you need to brush up on your business stationery needs.) In this letter, your compassion for the survivor should be apparent, as should your own lack of ego. You should focus on the loss of the loved one and offer to do what you can to help the survivor through the period of mourning. Be prepared never to get any such request, however; most people mourn alone.

Don't get caught making these mistakes:

> ✔ Talking about your own loss of a loved one in a letter of condolence is uncaring and mean.
>
> ✔ Offering ribald memories of the dead person is inappropriate.

As a manager or boss, watch the griever carefully. Offer to help with the griever's job if necessary, and if it's clear that she cannot work, offer time off. It will be welcome.

At funerals or memorial services, your dress should reflect the somber nature of the occasion. Wear a dark gray, black, or navy blue suit with a white shirt and dark tie if you're a man, or a dark dress or suit with subdued jewelry if you're a woman. Check with the funeral home or church about the appropriateness of flowers. Often, the obituary explicitly states that flowers aren't preferred. Please take that advice seriously. If a memorial is suggested, send your donation to the given address. You don't need to mention that you have done so. The organization receiving the gift will send an acknowledgment card to the bereaved.

At all times, your comportment should be quiet and dignified. If there is a receiving line, shake hands with everyone in it. If you're unknown to the family, identify yourself. If you don't know the family, say something simple and genuine, such as "I am so sorry for your loss."

Widows and widowers often forget to eat in the weeks following their loss. Taking food to them is a kindness. You don't need to stay long when delivering it; you can even call ahead and leave it on the porch.

It's important to be sensitive to any specific cultural customs, observances, and rituals that grieving members may have during their period of mourning. Find out what will take place and what may be expected of you during the ceremony ahead of time, so you'll be knowledgeable and act appropriately.

Pondering Whether to Give or Not to Give

Giving and receiving gifts cause considerable concern in business, for obvious reasons. Gifts can be used appropriately to thank clients for business, to reward someone for a job well done, to celebrate a promotion, or to commemorate a long-term relationship. But gift-giving can also veer into undue influence and bribery.

Two kinds of gift-giving occur in business. The first kind — between colleagues and/or supervisors — is easier to justify and is less fraught with danger than the second kind — gift-giving between companies.

Gifts at work

Gift-giving between coworkers, especially during the holiday season, is a common practice at many companies. If you work for such a company, you'll be considered churlish if you don't participate. This situation is one of those coerced acts of generosity that you really can't ignore or belittle, so bite the bullet and join in.

Avoid making holiday gifts explicitly religious.

Gifts for coworkers don't have to be lavish and ought not to be too personal. Something a colleague can use in the office, such as a coffee mug or a picture frame, is just fine.

Group gifts for weddings, babies, and retirements are the norm. Here again, don't presume to know your recipient so well that you get him something personal. Focus on the utilitarian and the practical, not the exciting or the alluring.

Gifts for bosses are a different matter altogether. There is cause for concern with giving a gift to a boss. You may look like you're trying to curry favor with her or, worse, bribe her. Besides, if you spend too much, your boss — who, after all, knows what you make — may decide that you're a toadying fool. Follow these simple guidelines:

- ✔ Extravagant gift-giving is both bad strategy and poor taste. Others may not share your love of lavish gifts, and they may resent you for going overboard.
- ✔ Send group gifts rather than individual gifts to bosses.
- ✔ Sending a card or flowers to your boss if he has been ill or in the hospital is all right. However, flowers aren't always allowed. Check with the hospital first.

Gifts between companies

Gift-giving between companies or between employees of different companies is a thorny issue — so thorny, in fact, that most organizations have explicit rules governing the practice. The following sections discuss two kinds of corporate gift-giving: gifts that you or your company presents to others, and gifts that you or your company receives from others.

Giving gifts

Companies commonly give gifts to clients and customers during the holiday season. So long as the gift isn't ostentatious, this practice doesn't seem to be an attempt to curry favor, and so long as the gift is reasonably well made, it doesn't seem like an attempt to dump promotional items.

Be careful with humorous gifts. If you aren't sure that the recipient will be pleasantly amused, don't send it.

Receiving gifts

You really have only one thing to consider: Know your company's policy about receiving gifts! Some companies don't allow employees to receive any gifts worth more than, say, $25; others require all gifts worth more than a specified amount to be disclosed to supervisors or other managers.

Problems arise when you receive a gift that violates company policy. If you receive season tickets for the Green Bay Packers, for example, and your company forbids acceptance of any gifts worth more than $100, you're painfully obliged to decline the gift. Ouch! If you're in this predicament, you probably will have to write a letter declining the gift.

Compose the letter in which you decline a gift carefully, focusing on your company's policy on receiving gifts, rather than on your personal feelings. The company's policy prevents you from accepting the gift, not your own displeasure. Say so.

Finding Appropriate Gifts for Every Occasion

After you figure out when giving and receiving a gift are appropriate, you may still be mystified by the prospect of choosing a gift. Luckily, you have only a few choices to make.

Make these distinctions between personal and business gifts:

✔ If you know a client or colleague well, socializing outside a business context on a regular basis, you may want to give a personal gift for a birthday, promotion, or holiday. Send or deliver such a gift to the person's home.

✔ If you want to give a business gift, first familiarize yourself with your firm's gift policy, if any. Professional gifts can be quite varied, from food or wine to small conveniences (such as a business-card holder or a new pen) to office items (such as a picture frame or a computer accessory). If you know your client well enough to have visited her office many times, you may have had the opportunity to divine a welcome addition.

Just as a distinction exists between personal and professional gifts, a distinction exists between perishable and lasting gifts:

✔ Perishable gifts are, as the name implies, gifts that have a short life, such as food, flowers, and wine. Perishable gifts are fine for most professional gift-giving between companies and between people who don't know each other well.

Flowers can be great gifts, but if you send long-stemmed roses to an administrative assistant as a thank-you for her outstanding accomplishment in getting everyone organized, you send the wrong message. Roses traditionally have romantic overtones, which isn't a professional message. Tulips, a tasteful mixed bouquet, or a flowering plant would be a better choice.

✔ Lasting gifts are intended to last longer — perhaps even a lifetime. Lasting gifts are better reserved for especially significant events and for events you want the other company or person to remember for a long time.

Whether a gift is temporary or permanent, personal or professional, take care to present it competently wrapped and with a card. Otherwise, your intentions will be sabotaged by your shoddy presentation. If you can't wrap a box, get someone else to do it, such as the customer-service counter at the store where you purchase the gift.

It is better to give than to receive. In giving, you extend your everyday kindness to an act whose only goal is kindness.

Part IV
Overcoming Work-Related Challenges

The 5th Wave   By Rich Tennant

"You're not going to go into one of your nit-picking, hotheaded, blowgun-hating rants, are you?"

In this part . . .

I present tips and strategies to help you maintain your integrity and keep your sanity in the workplace. I also cover office conflicts and ways to find a smooth resolution, as well as ways to deal with difficult personalities.

This part also discusses some ethical dilemmas that occur at work and gives you advice to illustrate the right and wrong ways to handle them. I close with a discussion of office romance and sexual harassment, and ways to approach these issues and draw the line between the two.

Chapter 16

Coming to Terms with Difficult People

*Y*ou know who the difficult people are: the manager who can't control his temper, the assistant who spreads malicious rumors about others, the shipping clerk with the social skills of a mollusk, the colleague who stabs you behind your back, the leering network-technology specialist. They're in every business and at every level, and they can make your life miserable.

Some people are difficult because of their personalities; others are difficult because of their positions in the company. In this chapter, you discover some helpful techniques for coping with both types of people. By the end, you still won't be a qualified therapist, but you'll know enough to help yourself and others through a wide range of challenging situations.

Getting a Grip on Work Dynamics

Most businesses have a defined hierarchy; even businesses that don't appear to have much of one normally do. With a hierarchy comes competition for the top spots, and with competition come rivalries and the need to cope with them. Some companies reward intraoffice competition; others work to defuse it through team-building and training on how to have fun at work.

Teams

Many companies organize teams of people to work together to defuse competition among employees. Although this strategy may help the company in some ways, productive individual initiative is always valued. Everyone knows this, so everyone tries to find a way to both be a good team player and stand out from the group.

Some people get recognized by engaging in outrageous stunts and by practicing crude self-promotion. Sometimes these tactics work, but for the most part, they don't. The trick is to get yourself recognized while not losing your status as a team player. That trick takes good manners.

Good manners are important for your rise to the top. You'll get noticed simply by respecting other team members and by being gracious. Your fair-mindedness and graciousness, all by themselves, set you apart from most of your colleagues. They show others — managers in particular — that when you're a member of a team, you aren't a credit hog and thief (a personality type I describe later in this chapter). You share credit where credit is due.

Rivals

Most people aren't interested in your interests or in hindering your progress. But some people have the same goals that you have. If you're at roughly the same level of the hierarchy, these folks are, in some sense, your rivals. Your respect for others and good manners are among your best allies in handling them. You can even use manners to defeat the bad apples who play dirty.

Some rivals play rough. They blast away at you in meetings; they go behind your back to superiors; they spread rumors about you. Rough players scope you out to see whether you're willing to play their game. If you're not well-versed in their techniques, you'll lose, for they rely on their knowledge of you and their ability to bait you into doing something you'll regret.

You don't want to play this game for three very good reasons:

- Rivals who play rough probably have been doing it since childhood. They're good at it.

- Good managers recognize rough players for what they are and don't tolerate them long.

- The most effective countermeasure against rough rivals is demonstrating that even though you recognize them for what they are, you won't be ruffled and can't be bothered to lower yourself to their level.

Your best bet is to expose the rough players for the bitter so-and-sos they are by killing them with good manners. When they arrive at the office before you do, compliment them on their initiative. When they criticize you in a meeting, thank them for their views, and politely point out the existence of other pertinent facts that, had they only known them, may have changed their minds. When they maneuver to oust you from the A team, counter with your credentials and your track record of teamwork.

Luckily, most rivals aren't that rough. Almost everyone is interested in getting promoted, but most people rely on their good work and their good reputations to get a promotion. Again, good manners are an integral part of your good reputation, so use them to your advantage.

If — just out of obtuseness — someone picks on your work and your input in meetings, stand up to her politely and firmly. The workplace is governed by professional civility; you're under no obligation to be the butt of someone else's meanness. If you have to, go to the offender's superior, and ask that the offender be notified that you've had enough. If the carping is persistent, keep a written record of the offenses, and submit your concerns to a superior. If the superior is the one who's picking on you, go to *her* superior.

Understanding Problem Personalities

A few people will take your best behavior as a weakness to be exploited. Show them otherwise. No better gauge of your strength of character exists than your unfailing politeness. The person who treats others with respect is a walking refutation of social cheaters. The hothead, the rumormonger, the credit hog and thief, the braggart, the bully, the manipulator, the malcontent, and the Machiavelli are the ones who show that they're weak. By acting the way they do, they betray their own belief that they can succeed (if they succeed at all) only by abandoning control.

I know what you're saying: "That all sounds fine, but you have no idea how the jerks I have to put up with treat me. Having good manners sounds fine in theory, but when the chips are down, I'm gonna have to fight back, aren't I?"

True enough, you need to know how to handle colleagues and superiors who are problems. But you can defeat these problematic people in lots of ways other than fighting back on their terms.

The hothead

Hotheads have a hard time controlling their tempers. Most hotheads are embarrassed by their bad tempers and, after flailing away for five minutes, apologize profusely.

The way to deal with a hothead is to let him blow his stack . . . privately, if at all possible. Suggest that he vent in his office. This suggestion won't go down well with the hothead, because he probably requires an audience. If you're well suited to it — that is, if you have a hide as thick as an elephant's — offer to listen to him. If not, tell him that you're sorry, but you prefer that he not let off steam in your presence. This tactic won't always work, but at least you'll have expressed your disapproval, and if it happens again, you can politely leave the room.

The rumormonger

Gossip is unavoidable and, for the most part, benign; it's just people's way of showing that they're interested in other people. You do yourself no favors by standing proudly aloof from all the tidbits that fly around an office. On the other hand, you don't want to be labeled a gossip. So although you can be receptive to gossip, it's not in your best interest to spread negative or potentially damaging information about other people. Instead, focus on positive gossip.

The rumormonger is a different story. She lives on gossip, using it to skewer others and to advance her own career. She's trouble for you because you may become the subject of some juicy bit of her gossip.

When a rumormonger's attention turns to some salacious tidbit regarding you, you have only one strategy: Confront her. You're under no obligation to confront her if the gossip is about someone else, although you may want to come to the defense of a friend or a colleague. But if the story is about you or yours, confront the rumormonger politely and publicly — politely because you don't want to embarrass her, and publicly because you want to ensure that others hear her recant. Malicious gossips rely on staying in the shadows to flourish. Confronting them publicly forces them out of the shadows. Most will wilt on the spot.

The credit hog and thief

The credit hog tries to take all the credit when some is due to others. The credit thief takes any credit he can find, even when it belongs to someone else. Dealing with either requires the same skill: Ensure that you get the credit you deserve. This is easier said than done sometimes, but you can do it. A private chat, in which you point out that other people helped on the project and deserve credit, sometimes works. If it doesn't, offer to write the update memos so that the credit hog doesn't have the opportunity to monopolize reporting on the project. If that tactic doesn't work either, talk to a superior. Point out the problem, and ask what to do.

The braggart

The person who brags or name-drops can be incredibly annoying. When you look closer at this personality type, you normally see an insecure person who exhibits a lack of self-esteem and self-confidence by trying to impress others with their accomplishments, their travel, or the people they know. Bragging also can be a form of intimidation. Sometimes, braggarts are just trying to be friendly, but unfortunately, they just don't know that their excessive bragging is unacceptable and many times makes them look foolish.

You may want to avoid the braggart, but the best approach is to respond with short comments, such as "Oh really?" or "That's interesting." Then change the subject or ask a question unrelated to the braggart's comments. Try your best not to encourage her to continue bragging if you're not really interested. Eventually, she may get the hint if you aren't showing that you're impressed.

The bully

The bully tries to threaten you into doing things you'd rather not do and aren't required to do. The only way to deal with a bully is to stand up to him on the first occasion and continue standing up to him. The problem usually is that you're so astonished by what he's doing that you can't think of a snappy comeback.

Luckily, you need no more of a snappy comeback than your good manners. Always be ready with a calm and polite retort that offers some compromise between what the bully wants and what you're willing to do. When your supervisor tells you on Friday to get those reports ready by the end of the weekend, or you're toast — and you know that the reports don't need to be ready until the following Friday — reply that sadly, you have firm plans for the weekend. But couple that politely phrased refusal with the offer to take the reports with you and to do whatever is necessary to have the reports ready by, say, Wednesday.

If you're unlucky enough to work for an unrepentant bully, look for another job. Things will never get better.

The manipulator

The manipulator tells half-truths. She lies; she reveals only what she thinks is in her interest to reveal; she routinely conceals information from you. She's a royal pain-in-the-you-know-what. The manipulator focuses on others' weaknesses and tries to take advantage of those weaknesses to make herself look better.

Manipulators are masters at their craft, and you're not going to outdo them. Have your ducks in order so that when a manipulator starts her little game, you can counter with the facts. Be prepared to say no or do whatever it takes to avoid being used.

Some manipulators sugarcoat their machinations with offers of generosity. You'll soon find out that a tit-for-tat expectation is always attached to these offers. Learn quickly, and be safe: Refuse the offers!

Here are some more ideas for dealing with a manipulator:

- ✔ If the manipulator tries to get you to do something that you think is against policy, put her off long enough to check on the policy yourself.
- ✔ If the manipulator tries to slide something unwanted past your team, challenge her in public to defend her suggestion.
- ✔ If the manipulator succeeds in getting you to do something that you know is a mistake or is against your interests, put the facts in writing, and submit them to the proper manager.

The malcontent

The malcontent is the kind of person who, when you say "Good morning," accuses you of being friendly because you secretly hate him. His responses are so far from the norm that you can't anticipate them — and don't even think of protecting yourself from them.

Malcontents are impossible. Fortunately, most malcontents aren't threats and don't require you to do anything other than continue to be your usual friendly and polite self. They can stew in their unhappiness, if they want.

If a malcontent slides into manipulation or bullying to feed his perverse happiness in resentment, action probably is required. But the best defense against manipulation and bullying is blithe disregard of the attempts to goad you into doing something you'll regret. Let the malcontent try to irritate you. Mom was right: Just ignore him!

The Machiavelli

The Machiavelli is your worst enemy, because she wants power and nothing but power. Worse, she's smart, calculating, and tenacious. She'll adopt whatever pose she needs to so she can get more power.

My advice: Stay far, far away. Most Machiavellis self-destruct, and those who don't are poison to you. The truth is that most Machiavellis are pretenders.

They're crude, and sooner or later, they'll make a fatal miscalculation. When they do, you can watch them free-fall out of the company without going along for the ride.

Machiavellis who are successful rise only to a certain level, beyond which their naked lust for power is harmful to the company. There, they fester, becoming malcontents. And you already know how to deal with malcontents!

You can't always stay away from Machiavellis, of course. Some people work for power junkies, and others have no choice but to work with one. These environments are among the most difficult you can work in. If the Machiavelli is your boss, know ahead of time that power, for her, is something that only one person can have, and that person is her. She has no extra power to share with you. If you find this kind of working relationship intolerable, my advice is that you look for another job.

Taking a Deep Breath and Relaxing after an Irritating Run-In

No, you really didn't deserve that dressing-down from your boss. And you certainly didn't deserve being called an "incompetent moron" or any of the other names he saw fit to utter. But he's your boss, and except for these tirades, he's a pretty good one. Besides, the problem probably is just the stress he's been experiencing.

Petty annoyances are inevitable consequences of being with other people in confined spaces. You encounter hundreds of irritants in a workday — the person who smacks her lips eating breakfast at her desk; the person who's a drummer for Nine Inch Nails during all your phone calls; the person who puts his dirty running shoes up on your desk when he talks to you; the boss who yells too much; the colleague whose cologne permeates your cubicle like smoke; and all the problem personalities I write about earlier in this chapter.

What are you supposed to do? The first thing to do is count to ten and relax. Other people will irritate you; you just have to be ready for irritations. If you're constantly surprised by the strange things people say, eat, or smell like, your first change should be of your expectations. People are different — often, irritatingly so. Deal with it! Remember the morning affirmation of Marcus Aurelius, an emperor of Rome: "Today, I will be surrounded by people who irritate me. I will not demonstrate my irritation."

The next thing to do is figure out the most helpful strategies for cooling your temper when the temperature starts to climb. I talk about this matter in more detail in Chapter 17, but here, I present some simple suggestions for those first few minutes when you're worried that you're going to explode.

When someone does something that really bugs you:

- ✔ Look away and count to ten. Repeat as necessary until you calm down!
- ✔ Excuse yourself from the situation to get a drink of water.
- ✔ Imagine that you're doing your favorite activity in your favorite place.
- ✔ Remind yourself that in a certain number of hours, you'll be on your way home.
- ✔ Return to your desk or office, sit quietly for a few minutes, and plan your response.
- ✔ Kill 'em with kindness. In other words, rise above the situation, and always demonstrate calmness and patience.

If you're in a position in which you have to make an instant response to an incredibly annoying comment, swallow hard and be polite, but remember to stick up for yourself and your ideas.

It's never necessary to respond to rudeness with rudeness. Always take the higher ground. You'll not only feel better about yourself, but it also makes a positive impression on the job. There are lots of ways to defeat these problematic people other than fighting back on their terms.

Helpful hints for dealing with an invasive question

Some people just don't know any better than to ask questions you have no interest in answering or to engage you in conversation on topics you would rather not discuss. Sometimes, these people are just trying to be friendly. Unfortunately, they don't know that their excessive inquisitiveness is unacceptably invasive.

Suppose that your colleague Raul asks you about the story he saw in the paper about your dad's recent arrest for gardening in the nude. You're embarrassed by the question (and by your father!). You'd hoped that the matter would never come up. What do you do?

a) Say that it's a long family tradition to garden in the nude, and wink.

b) Give Raul a withering glare.

c) Apologize, but reply firmly that you won't answer the question.

d) Ask Raul why he's asking ("So why do you ask?").

Not surprisingly, any of these responses is fine. Each has its advantages, and each has its disadvantages. But generally, the best approach to responding to impertinent questions is politely asking the questioner why he's asking. Also, smile — which usually embarrasses the other person enough to withdraw the question.

Chapter 17

Managing Office Conflict

In This Chapter

▶ Seeing why conflict can be good

▶ Resolving conflicts with your peers or boss

▶ Handling conflict when you're a manager or a spectator

For many people, conflict — at work or at home — is difficult. You probably know people who would rather move than confront a neighbor about his barking dog or the annual Summer Picnic and Bagpiping Competition. But believe it or not, some conflict is actually helpful. In this chapter, you find out why. The chapter also introduces some effective conflict-management tools. You and your colleagues can get along better by knowing these tools. More important, you and your boss can get along better, too!

Realizing That Conflict Can Be Good (It's True!)

Though having a conflict takes guts, it can be useful — even energizing. At work, conflict can help bring up issues that need attention, such as processes that don't make sense anymore but are "the way it's always been done." Conflict can also give birth to excellent ideas. If everyone agrees with the first idea the boss tosses out, that idea may be the only one that ever comes up, even though it may not be very good. When the team debates an issue, however, many more thoughts and opinions emerge, often producing a superior result.

Pick your battles. Debate can be productive, but after a decision is made, you need to get in line. Don't undermine the team by saying things like "Well, it wasn't my idea, but I guess we're going to go with that stupid ad campaign anyway."

R-E-S-P-E-C-T. Aretha demands it, and your colleagues deserve it too. In fact, perhaps the single most important key to effective conflict is respecting others' opinions and their right to speak up. If someone works in the same place you do, chances are that she's done something right to get there. Even if you disagree with a colleague's opinion, you can still respect her intelligence and integrity. If you're sure that she's a moron, keep that conclusion to yourself — even when you chat with your office buddies.

Showing respect for other people's opinions is more than just biting your tongue on witty putdowns. It also includes controlling

- **Facial expressions:** Even when your mouth is closed, rolling your eyes and smirking show a lack of respect.

- **Body language:** Refrain from shaking your head or looking around the room as though you can't wait for the other person to finish.

- **Other actions:** You're not fooling anyone when you kick other colleagues under the table and give them significant looks.

When the conflict involves people and their behavior, however, it usually becomes significantly more challenging, and it's often a serious drain on energy and resources. These types of conflicts can be destructive rather than productive because, in many cases, people with personality conflicts simply don't have much respect for each other, which can make for a difficult situation.

Managing Conflict with Your Peers

You've been working for months to get promoted, and you've finally made it to that corner cubicle near the snack room, the restroom, and the parking lot. Life is good for the first few days as you work on the great new strategy you'll present at Friday's meeting.

You make your presentation, and you feel great. Then a voice pipes up from the back of the room: "We tried that last year, and it didn't work." Maybe the speaker is the person who was passed over for the promotion you got. Maybe he's the person who takes a pessimistic view of everything. Maybe she's the woman you stood up on prom night in high school and who's returned 15 years later to haunt you. Whoever it is, that person has scratched and dented your shiny new idea.

You can manage office conflict ineffectively in lots of ways. Locking your door and blasting your radio is one way; taking aim with coffee is another. Try a more productive solution. Thinking some evil thoughts is okay at this point, as long as they stay inside your head and don't appear on your face or fly out of your mouth. It's also okay to go home and complain to your long-suffering spouse, friends, or dog. Pretty soon, however, you're going to have to discuss the issue with your detractor in a mature and professional manner.

Vent if you must, but not at work

Complaining about this person to someone else may help — if you can find someone who's willing to listen. But avoid venting to other people at the office or to other people who know the person. Even if you trust the person you're venting to, your comments may eventually get back to their target, causing an even bigger problem.

Many companies today now have mentoring programs in which each employee is assigned to a designated mentor. This person is perhaps the best person to whom you vent your issues and who can help you in the best way.

The privacy of your car is a great place to vent your frustrations, as long as you don't vent them on other drivers by driving aggressively. Use your commute time to say all those things you would never say at the office. After you get them out, you'll probably feel better. Just ignore the people in the next car who are pointing and gaping; you're emotionally healthy.

Put yourself in the other person's shoes

Try to understand where the other person is coming from. Are you new to the department, newly promoted, much younger or older, or much more beautiful than your peers? Consider the fact that some people may be intimidated by you, and be professional and respectful until they get to know you better.

Has the other person in this conflict been in his job for a long time? If so, a certain weariness may have set in after years of the daily grind. You can't fix that problem. You can be willing to listen and compromise, however, without letting him affect your own attitude.

You can discover a lot by paying attention to how your boss or coworkers react to you. Take notice if you've had the same response from more than one person. Perhaps you need to extend yourself beyond your comfort zone and make an effort to be open to others' advice or recommendations.

Practice active listening

Most of us spend plenty of time talking but not much time hearing what other people have to say, especially during an emotional conflict that may push a few buttons. Here's how to become an active listener:

- **Set the stage by setting your phone to "do not disturb," turning away from the computer or other distractions, and facing the person you're talking to.** If people have a habit of barging into your office, close the door or find a conference room or a quiet corner of the cafeteria to have important discussions.

- **Sit in a neutral position.** Sitting on opposite sides of a conference table puts you on equal footing; sitting behind your desk while the other person sits in front of your desk gives you more perceived power. That perception is just what you *don't* want the other person to have in this situation, because it immediately puts her on the defensive.

- **Clear your mind of your own point of view.** Your goal is to listen and understand your partner's point of view without considering how it stacks up against yours. During discussions, people often miss someone else's point because they're busy thinking about what they want to say next. If you're concerned about being able to respond to everything later, take notes. (If you take notes, you may want to explain that you're doing it so you can really concentrate and remember. Otherwise, your partner may think that he's undergoing a psychological profile.)

- **Encourage the other person to keep talking by nodding or asking her to continue, but don't interrupt.** Wait until the other person has said everything she wants to say. At that point, you should understand her point of view, even if you still don't agree with it. That's your basis for negotiation and compromise.

Ask clarifying questions

So you tried some strategy before, and it didn't work. Ask your partner to explain more about how or why it didn't work. Were the circumstances the same? Was the project funded and supported by upper management last time? Was the plan given enough time to work? You should be open to accepting that your plan really won't work and that you need to start over. On the other hand, you may be able to identify problems that could be fixed this time around.

Be willing to compromise your ideas, but not your ethics

Somehow, *compromise* has turned into a bad word in our culture. Although you may not want to compromise your ethics, most work situations don't require you to do so, and you can almost always find some areas where you're willing to give up an idea to gain something else. Another term for this concept is *consensus-building*.

One thing you should never compromise, however, is your ethics. If a peer suggests that you cheat a supplier, for example, let him know that you're not comfortable doing it. If he insists, you may need to involve your manager. If the manager also insists, it's time to use your company's open-door policy to go over your manager's head. It also may be time to find a new job.

Always try to manage peer conflict by yourself first. Involve your manager only if absolutely necessary. Handling the situation yourself is good experience for your next move up the organizational ladder.

Restrict your comments to behavior, not personality

Never say something like "You're a loudmouthed jerk, and I can't understand how someone like you ever got into management." Instead, say something like this: "When you interrupt me during meetings, I feel like I can never finish what I have to say. I think that's one of the reasons we can't seem to get past this conflict." The next time the person interrupts you, call her on it. Some people — especially those from families of ten children, who are accustomed to fighting for every shred of attention — aren't even aware that they're cutting other people off.

Watch your language

If you're in the habit of swearing at work, stop. Even if you do it only when you're angry, many people will be so shocked by your inventive variations on the *F* word that they'll be unable to concentrate on what you're trying to say. Swearing does not make you appear to be more intelligent.

Look at the big picture

Perspective is important. Yes, work is a big part of your life, but it's not your whole life. Keep in mind that this challenging person is only one person and that in today's job-switching environment, you probably won't be working with him forever.

Resolving a Conflict with Your Boss

Need to resolve a conflict with your boss? Again, the answer comes down to respect — on your part, on your boss's part, or both. She may see you as a threat, a loudmouth, unintelligent, or just plain obnoxious. You may view her as incompetent, unfeeling, or a young whippersnapper with nothing to teach you. But she has a direct effect on your future, even if you think of her as Machiavelli on acid.

What should you do? Look for her good points; she does have at least one, and probably more. Try to understand her point of view and the pressure she's under as a manager. Concentrate on her behavior and her treatment of you, not on her annoying laugh or unsettling physical attributes. Most of all, remember that she's the boss — a fact that's not likely to change.

If you feel that you're being treated unfairly, address the problem with her directly and politely. As a manager, she should be open to constructive criticism. If she refuses to acknowledge your concerns, weigh your options:

- ✔ You could put up with your current situation.

- ✔ You could look for another job.

- ✔ You could talk to human resources for advice — and if that department has had numerous complaints about her in the past, one more complaint could be what is needed to take action.

- ✔ You could approach *her* boss, which may help significantly but which puts you at risk of alienating her.

Unfortunately, no single answer is right. Use your best judgment.

To maintain work stability and job security, avoid annoying your boss. Make every effort to be part of a positive work environment. Keep the following tips in mind:

- ✔ Study your boss's behavioral profile. Try your best to anticipate his needs and wants. Is he a micromanager? Does he prefer written or verbal reports?

✔ If you have a problem to discuss with your boss, always take a positive approach, and try to have a solution to the problem.

✔ Do your best to understand your boss's priorities.

✔ Make sure that you're both on the same page by keeping the lines of communication open.

✔ If a conflict arises, as with your coworkers, always keep your cool.

Managing Conflict If You're the Boss

Managing people isn't always easy, especially when you have to handle disputes and conflict within the office. That chore is why you're getting the big bucks. Two reasons why you're a manager in the first place are that you get along well with others and that you've demonstrated your coolness under fire in the past. So get ready . . . the qualities that got you the promotion will now be put to the test on a regular basis in keeping those two brilliant hotheads you hired from ripping each other to pieces. And while you're keeping them from engaging in their favorite pastime, you have to protect yourself from becoming their next victim.

A manager at a large tech company was dealing with two employees, Sally and Phil, who were at each other's throats continually — arguing loudly in staff meetings, spreading vicious gossip, even threatening each other with bodily harm. He was tired of these disruptions, but so far, his reprimands hadn't worked. Finally, he blew up in a staff meeting, called both of the employees idiots, and suggested that they go back to the sandbox where they belonged. Phil immediately made a call to human resources, and the manager ended up with a reprimand.

What did this manager do wrong? He violated two of the cardinal rules of employee relations: Never ridicule an employee, and don't discipline an employee in front of other people. I provide additional tips for managing conflict between employees in the following sections.

Address small problems before they become big ones

As a good manager, be proactive and polite about small problems so that you don't have to be reactive and rude when they fester into big problems. If a new employee is listening to loud music at her desk, don't wait for another employee to complain. Instead, you could say something like this: "I'm not sure if you've had a chance to read the employee handbook yet, but we suggest that people listen to music with headphones." Chances are that she'll be happy to comply, and you'll have nipped a problem in the bud.

Try a one-on-one chat

If the problem seems to be primarily one employee, meet with him alone. Find out what the problem is without being accusatory. Instead of saying "Everyone here knows that you and Sally can't seem to get along, and it's damaging our productivity," say "It seems to me that there's something going on between you and Sally. Is that true?" If so, ask the employee to tell his side of the story. If he insists that there's no problem, talk to Sally.

Try sitting the employees down

After you've had a chat with both employees individually, try speaking to both of them together. Again, your approach should be exploratory, not accusatory. If they try to interrupt each other, say something like this: "Sally, I promise to listen to everything you have to say, but at the moment, Phil has the floor." Make sure that you've scheduled plenty of time to hear both employees out. If one or both of them want to meet with you alone, make time for that too. No, conflict resolution probably isn't how you want to spend your time — but that's management.

Don't play favorites

You may like Phil better because he has a better sense of humor or because he brings bagels every Friday. Put that preference aside, and focus only on the behavior in this particular conflict. If Phil is the one who's acting inappropriately, you need the maturity as a manager to let him know, even if doing so affects your friendship.

Appeal to the employees' sense of teamwork and fair play

Let both employees know that you have faith in their intelligence, ethics, and ability to work things out. Ask each of them to identify an area or two where they could compromise to make things work, and ask them to commit to changing that behavior.

Let the employees know you're serious

Be sure that the employees know that maintaining the status quo isn't acceptable. You'll be watching, and if they don't follow through on their mutual commitment to change their behavior, they'll be hearing from you.

Don't be afraid to ask for help

Your manager relies on you to handle what you can, but he's also there to help you when you need it. After the current crisis has cooled down — or before it happens — ask about management training that will help you deal with these situations. If your company doesn't have a formal training program, plenty of training outfits would love to help you. Check your local telephone directory or the Internet.

Employees in a professional environment very rarely resort to physical attacks, but they've been known to happen. Be ready to cut the discussion short and call human resources or security if matters get really out of hand. (If you suspect that a problem may arise, consider informing security in advance.) Whatever you do, don't participate in the violence yourself.

If in the end, the warriors just can't get along, you're going to have to make a painful decision to split them up, either by reassigning one or both of them or by firing one or both of them. A good manager knows that she has to bring the ax down when, despite her best efforts and the best efforts of the warriors, the situation just doesn't get better.

Staying Out of the Fray If You're a Spectator

Whether you're a manager or not, don't allow yourself to be sucked into conflicts that don't concern you. Many people who have good conflict-resolution skills themselves — and many who don't! — can't resist the temptation to "help" others with their problems. Don't do it! At least one of the parties probably will resent your intrusion, and other people will perceive you as a meddling busybody without enough work to do. People who try to solve other people's problems at work often find conflict oddly titillating and like to gossip. Even if you don't deserve that reputation, you may get it if you're not careful.

Maria, a computer programmer, had always prided herself on the good advice she gave her friends about their relationships at work. In fact, many of her friends came to her for advice. Maria knew that she would make a great manager, but so far, she hadn't had that opportunity. So when she saw two people at work who were continually angry at each other, she wanted to help. She talked with Venkat and Bill separately to find out their respective sides of the story; then she served as a go-between.

Unfortunately, her good intentions backfired. Both Bill and Venkat thought that she was taking the other person's side, and they both stopped talking to her. Her manager got wind of the situation and asked Maria to please concentrate on her own work. Maria was crushed, because she was only trying to help. That fall, however, she started back to school and is now a licensed corporate conflict manager. She has gained the authority and expertise to do what she loves: helping people work out their differences in the office.

If your peers come to you for advice at work, resist the temptation to get involved. You may be safe in suggesting strategies that have worked for you in the past ("When I had a problem with one of my colleagues last year, I just sat down and had an honest discussion with her, and it was really helpful. She just didn't realize that she was bothering me, and I learned some things I did that bothered her."). But never get involved in the current situation or make comments like "I've heard that Ronnie's a total nightmare to work with. I feel sorry for you." That sort of comment only polarizes the situation further. Don't take on other people's problems. Instead, give yourself a pat on the back for having learned how to resolve your own conflicts!

Chapter 18

Managing Ethical Dilemmas at Work

*N*o one is immune from ethical dilemmas at work. If the company you work for is well organized and has a clear set of policies, ethical dilemmas can be minimized, but they can no more be eliminated than can the pleasure you get from doing a good job. Ethical dilemmas are part of life, so they are part of your professional life as well.

No single chapter in any book can capture every nuance of the ethical issues that emerge in the workplace, but I offer some suggestions about some of the most common ethical issues arising at work. In this chapter, I introduce some of the ethical issues that come from your role as an employee.

Billing the Company for Expenses

Pretty obviously, when you work for a company, you're employed to work for that company. In return, you receive a salary and the opportunity to learn a great deal. While you're at work, you should spend your time doing what you are expected to do — not straightening out your private life or browsing the Internet for hours on end, looking for interesting facts about Tahiti.

Your company may ask you to travel. While you're traveling on business, you are expected to remain focused on your job. You may incur expenses while doing the company's work on your travels, of course, and you may ask the company to compensate you for those expenses.

If you're a manager, it's your responsibility to be educated about your company's expense-report policies. If your company doesn't allow gifts or alcohol charges as expenses, for example, inform your employees of that rule before they travel. If exceptions arise, employees need to know what those exceptions are. Suppose that one of your sales representatives stays at a friend's apartment when she travels to New York for a convention, saving the company $280 a night for five nights. Can she claim as an expense the $20 bottle of wine that she gave her hosts? How about the cost of the taxi rides between her friend's apartment and the convention site, the taxi ride back from the Broadway play to which she took a client, or the ticket for that play? Make the rules clear.

When you're doing the company's work and spending money as an employee, you may ask the company to reimburse you, and when you're not doing the company's work or not spending money as an employee, you may not ask to be reimbursed. Always confirm with your boss and CFO what will and won't be allowable expenses before the trip.

Keep these tips in mind:

- ✔ Clarify acceptable and unacceptable expenses before going on your trip.

- ✔ Most companies appreciate any reasonable ways to cut costs.

- ✔ Keep expense-report receipts safely together. Use a credit card rather than cash so you have an additional record on your credit card statement.

- ✔ When you fill out your expense report, attach all the receipts for money spent while you were on company time.

If you host a business dinner while traveling, you usually can include that in your expense report. If you work for a company that doesn't compensate for alcohol, not even wine at dinner, try to separate the alcohol portion of the bill from the meal portion. If you can't do that, compute the amount spent for the meal and the proportion of the tip that went to the waiter for the meal, and submit only that expense.

Don't pad your expense reports. If you rent a car for a business trip and add three days to the trip for a little sightseeing, you aren't entitled to charge the company for those three days. If you buy your daughter a gift at the airport gift shop, you aren't entitled to charge the company for it. Smart accountants have seen most of these tricks before, and you're unlikely to get away with them. But the heart of the matter is that padding your expense report is unfair to the company. Even if the company isn't always fair to you, you have no reason to be unfair in return.

Understanding Loyalty, Confidentiality, and Security

Typically, you work for someone else, who pays you a salary. That relationship establishes the expectation that you owe your professional loyalty to the company or person you work for. It almost certainly means that you'll learn things that, if disclosed, would damage others or the company. But what are you supposed to do when, in the name of loyalty, you're asked to do something wrong? And how far are you obliged to respect confidentiality?

Loyalty

Loyalty is a valued commodity in the business world. Many employers list it as the most important virtue that an employee can have. It's not surprising that loyalty is so valued; employees who look to promote the business's interests and defend it against competition are essential for a successful company.

When the company's values overlap with your own, being loyal to the company is easy. Trouble arises when either a colleague or a boss asks you to do something you know is wrong and invokes your loyalty in making the request. This kind of request or demand can come camouflaged in many ways and may never be explicit. But the implication is always clear: You're expected to do something that you know is wrong to demonstrate your loyalty to your colleague, your boss, or that amorphous entity, the company.

People in positions of authority shouldn't ask their subordinates to lie for them. If you're a manager, and you're doing something on company time that you shouldn't be doing, just tell your assistant that you're unavailable. Don't try to take advantage of someone else's loyalty to you or to the company.

Likewise, subordinates shouldn't agree to lie for their bosses. Loyalty is one thing; lying in the name of loyalty is something else entirely. If your boss asks you to lie for her, politely give her an opportunity to back away from the request. Tom could, for example, have asked: "You want me to tell the owner you're in Denver arranging financing when in fact you're in Pebble Beach?"

If your boss doesn't back down from the request that you lie, ask an even more pointed question, such as "You want me to lie?" If your boss doesn't get the hint that you're unwilling to comply by now, tell her politely that as much as you respect her and enjoy working with her, you won't lie for her.

Be prepared for the worst. Some bosses will take your refusal in stride; others won't. If your boss does, you've established a ground floor, and she'll respect you for it. If the boss is angered by your refusal, you can expect anything from a grunt of disapproval to a campaign of discrimination.

Confidentiality

As an employee, you know things that, were they to be disclosed, might hurt you, your colleagues, your bosses, or your company. Many companies have nondisclosure and confidentiality agreements written into employment contracts. Many others discuss confidentiality in their employee guidelines. Take confidentiality seriously!

Generally speaking, two kinds of confidential information exist: proprietary company information and information about people.

Company information

Every business has proprietary information — information about jobs, layoffs, and performance reviews; information about patents and contracts; information about sales and earnings; information about product developments. The list goes on and on. What should you do, as an employee, to avoid disclosing confidential business information?

If your boss is on the ball, she'll inform you about confidential information. She'll give you answers to the following questions:

- ✔ Which documents are confidential? Are there degrees of confidentiality? If so, what are they?

- ✔ Are you and your boss the only people who can look at these documents? If not, who else can look at them?

When you won't break the rules for your boss

When your boss goes after you because you won't do something wrong, the following tips may help:

- ✔ Keep a record of all incidents and your responses when your boss asks you to do something unethical.

- ✔ Keep your records at home. Don't keep them at work, where they could be stolen.

- ✔ Follow the instructions in the company's policies-and-procedures documents (if your company has them) for combating unethical behavior.

- ✔ Direct your concerns to the human resources department, if your company has one.

- ✔ Look for a new job.

✔ Do you have the authority to open packages marked "Personal" or "Confidential"? If not, does anyone other than the addressee have that authority?

✔ Should you clear with your boss all requests for confidential materials? If not, under what conditions can you exercise your own judgment? If so, what should you do if your boss is unavailable?

✔ Does anyone have permission to remove things from your boss's office? If so, who? If not, how should you handle such requests?

Having this kind of blunt discussion with your boss will show her that you care about confidentiality and are willing to work to protect it.

If you're privy to confidential proprietary information, you bear a duty not to disclose it. This duty requires, among other things, that you learn how to live with secrets. Learning to live with secrets in turn requires that you be alert to what you say in the company of others and that you be alert to others' attempts to get information from you. Don't take these duties lightly! Your job depends on doing them well.

These guidelines can help you:

✔ Know who's authorized to discuss confidential matters, and discuss confidential matters only with that person.

✔ Practice self-control by being the model of discretion in all situations.

✔ In public, speak softly so that others do not overhear you.

✔ When you're asked for confidential information, reply that because it's confidential, you can't divulge it. If the other person persists, politely point out that he's out of line. If that doesn't work, try a blank stare.

✔ Don't allow others to read your computer screen or peruse your desktop. Put confidential documents face down or in a locked drawer when you're not looking at them.

✔ Don't tell your spouse or life partner all the details, even if you're tempted to do so.

Personal information

The other kind of confidential information that you can gain is personal information of an embarrassing sort. Everyone knows that administrative assistants sometimes learn things they would really rather not know about their bosses, and that bosses sometimes ask employees to report things about colleagues that are really none of the boss's business.

These kinds of breaches are entirely avoidable, but only by those who are responsible for committing them. Whenever someone else — through what he says or what he does — discloses something that you would rather not know, you're placed in a coercive position, in which you either keep the secret or snitch. Both options are unpleasant.

To keep this kind of situation from happening to you, the first line of defense is to stop someone from saying something before she says more than you want to know. You can do this in two ways:

- ✔ Distinguish between friendly exchanges of benign information and malignant exchanges of harmful information.

- ✔ Ask whether, given your professional relationship, the other person really wants to give you the information. Most of the time, this tactic prevents the conversation from going somewhere both of you will regret. Having avoided the issue, make sure that it never comes up again.

Sometimes, of course, preventive measures don't work. A colleague may just blurt something out, or you stumble onto something you shouldn't see, or you find yourself overhearing something you shouldn't hear. In these kinds of cases, you're stuck. Through no fault of your own, you know something about someone that you shouldn't know. The best general advice is to act as though you never had that bit of knowledge in the first place. This method isn't always easy and won't always succeed, but at least you'll have tried to not act on something you shouldn't know.

Here's more advice that can help:

- ✔ Ask yourself, "Do I want what I'm about to do to be on videotape?" If the answer is no, don't do it.

- ✔ If someone discloses confidential information about clients or patients to you, your best recourse is to keep quiet. If the disclosure continues, you could consider approaching the other person's supervisor with the breach of confidentiality. Correcting the problem is the supervisor's responsibility, not yours.

Security

If you read the earlier sections about loyalty and confidentiality, you know most of what you need to do to ensure that confidential information isn't leaked. But I still have a few loose ends to tie up.

Stealing from your company — whether you're taking a product or some office supplies — is wrong.

Another serious issue is maintaining the security of hard copy and electronic documents. Luckily, you can take some straightforward steps:

- ✔ Don't leave confidential documents unattended on your desk. At a minimum, turn them face down when you leave. Better still, put them in a locked drawer.

- ✔ If you have confidential documents at a meeting, keep them under wraps until they're needed. Return them to your briefcase or portfolio as soon as they are no longer needed.

- ✔ When you're transporting confidential documents anywhere, put them in an envelope or folder. If you leave the office with them, put them in a locked briefcase.

- ✔ When you mail confidential documents, place them in an envelope marked "Confidential," and place that sealed envelope in another envelope also marked "Confidential." That way, no one can pretend that he didn't see the warning.

- ✔ Never throw confidential documents away. Shred them.

Your computer support team will no doubt develop security measures to protect sensitive electronic documents. Various encryption codes, password procedures, and clearance procedures may already be in place. Follow those procedures, and use the codes consistently.

You can also take or recommend additional measures if you think that electronic security is lax. Ask your manager for suggestions. Information security is, after all, her responsibility. Talk to the resident information technology officer about what he does to protect documents, and then recommend that everyone follow his example.

Here are some ways to protect confidentiality while using computers:

- ✔ Remove printouts from shared printers as soon as possible.

- ✔ Store document and program disks in a locked drawer.

- ✔ Turn your computer off at night.

- ✔ Don't share disks.

- ✔ Don't send confidential documents by e-mail unless you're certain that your system is secure.

Mixing Personal Business and Work

In many businesses, the workday is much less structured than it used to be. Flextime, personal days, home offices, and the conveniences of electronic devices have worked together to make the 9-to-5 workday a thing of the past in some companies. Even companies that have rigid structures offer much more flexibility than before.

Additional flexibility in the workday is a huge change and a real boon. But the flexible workday has introduced some new problems into the business environment and exacerbated some existing ones.

For employees, the line between work time and private time has blurred, and the desire and need to take care of personal business during the workday has become acute in some cases. If you have a lot of autonomy in structuring your day, and if you act in a professional manner, mixing private and professional activities isn't likely to cause problems. If you don't have much autonomy, or if you allow your personal business to interfere with your real business, you'll end up in a bad situation.

Doing personal business on company time

Many employers understand, and even encourage, employees to take enough time to do short personal errands during the day, so long as they complete their work. If you're the manager, you're responsible for making company policy clear. Some companies offer electronic concierge services that perform personal errands for their employees or arrange for dry cleaning to be picked up at the office or home. These services are a real boon to employees.

The difficulties introduced by children call for sympathetic managers and understanding colleagues. If your colleague leaves work early every Wednesday to take his son to violin practice, that doesn't mean he's getting a perk that you're not. He may have to compensate by working on the Saturday that you spend ballooning in New Mexico. This kind of rearranged workweek is a common feature of the contemporary economic landscape.

In the following sections, I explain how to handle a few personal tasks on company time.

Personal calls

Abusing phone privileges is a recurring employer complaint. Spending two minutes talking to your daughter about her pet mouse is fine; spending half an hour talking to your best friend about your latest round of golf while a deadline is looming isn't. Keep personal conversations short and to the point, especially if you're in a cubicle. Avoid having screaming arguments with your spouse.

E-mails

Your work e-mail account is for work-related e-mails. If you want to join chat rooms or dating services, do so from some other computer (such as the one you have at home). Also, refrain from sending racy or highly critical (or flaming) e-mails on your business computer. I cover this topic in more detail in Chapter 9.

Your e-mail is company property and may be monitored. If your boss finds questionable e-mail, she may have grounds to discipline or dismiss you.

Computer games

Some people are addicted to computer games. This includes some professional adults, and this fondness can impinge on work. Don't let yourself get bug-eyed and irritable when you realize that you've been playing for two hours and that the Webding report is due this afternoon. If you have to, remove the games from your work computer and put them where they belong — at home.

Web browsing

In the past ten years, employers have lost untold work hours to employees' Web browsing. No doubt, looking at the Himalayan Adventure Outfitters Web site will get you stoked for your next climb in Nepal, but this site probably can wait until you get to some other computer — such as the one at home. Also, save your browsing for just the right office coffee mug until you get home, because that task can take hours. (Believe me, I know!)

At work, your Web browsing should be confined to the personal time that you're given. Managers bear responsibility for letting employees know the expectations. If it's okay with you for an employee to watch a Sam Donaldson Webcast on his break, by all means say so. But also say that when break time is over, it's time to get back to work.

Finally, I have to say it again: Stay away from porn sites while you're at work. If you get caught looking at them, you'll be in big trouble, and chances are increasingly good that you will be caught. Employers everywhere are installing software that tracks the Web sites visited by employees. Is getting a cheap thrill really worth a dressing-down from your boss? Is it worth your job? Probably not.

Separating personal space and business space

One consequence of the additional flexibility in the workday is that the line between personal space and professional space is fuzzier now than it has ever been. There's no doubt about it — the new casualness has caused more than a few privacy problems.

Keeping your personal life personal

Taking care of too much personal business on company time is a bad idea. You also have to be careful about involving your business colleagues in your personal life.

No specific rule governs how much of your personal life to reveal to your colleagues and your employer. You can divulge it all if you're comfortable doing so. But remember that some people would rather not know about your latest Atlantic City escapade. Most people are better off not knowing how much you hate your ex-wife. Also, what you divulge today could come back to haunt you tomorrow.

Keep in mind that your lifestyle can become relevant to your employer if that lifestyle has a negative impact on your performance. If you publicize your long tradition of leaving work and getting drunk every Friday while you're still in uniform, you could be called into your boss's office to hear a lecture on the virtues of sobriety and the importance of being a good company representative at all times.

Some personal issues probably are best kept from colleagues and supervisors. Your family's health history, for example, is nobody's business at the office. If you are rash enough to tell someone that the men in your family have a history of prostate cancer, you shouldn't be surprised when the human resources person asks you about it one day while she's filling out an insurance questionnaire. And if you're vain enough to tell your supervisor that your uncle is Bill Gates, you shouldn't be shocked when he tells you that he has a great idea for Microsoft; he just needs your help setting up a quick interview with your uncle.

Keeping your professional life professional

Just as keeping some of your private life away from the office is wise, keeping some of your professional life away from your private life is also wise. Your romantic partner doesn't need to know everything about petty office politics to know that you're stressed in your job. And if you have business information that you can tell your friends or your romantic partner only by violating client confidentiality or company policy, you're obligated not to tell.

Not telling your closest friends or your romantic partner something can be very hard. Psychiatrists, physicians, and lawyers face this dilemma on a regular basis. A sympathetic friend or romantic partner will acknowledge the difficulties entailed by professional codes of conduct and won't pry. Pressing for personal information from someone who's bound to professional confidentiality may cause the end of the relationship.

Violating client confidentiality is grounds for dismissal in some professions and grounds for expulsion from some professional organizations.

Drawing the line between the personal and the professional

Not only are there things about you that your colleagues don't need to know, but there also are some things about you that no one at your workplace has any right to know. Your political views, for example, are irrelevant in the vast majority of business situations. So are your religious beliefs, your ethnic background, your family's lifestyle, your sexual orientation, and your hobbies. And although your moral values may be pertinent, try to keep the dogmatic elements out of your workday environment.

Here's some advice to keep in mind:

✔ No one at work is entitled to know everything about you. If someone asks you to reveal a private matter, just say, "I prefer to keep my private life private, thank you."

✔ If someone persists in asking impertinent questions despite your repeated refusal to answer them, report the matter to a supervisor.

✔ If your supervisor is the one who won't let up on the impertinent questions, report the matter to her supervisor.

Saying "No" and Maybe — Just Maybe — Keeping Your Job

Some ethical dilemmas come not from your taking advantage of your employer, but from your employer taking advantage of you. These problems are tough because you're no longer in control. If you routinely browse the Web while you're at work, you can change that situation. But if the owner of the company asks you to falsify employee records to avoid paying Social Security taxes, you're no longer in control. Not only is the request unethical, but also, it's combined with the implicit threat that if you won't do it, you won't have a job.

This situation is a classic professional dilemma. Millions of workers face variations on it every year. Your success or failure in dealing with situations like this depends more on your tact, diplomacy, and good manners than on anything else.

First, try to defuse the situation by giving the other person the option of retracting the request or demand. Try one of the following methods:

✔ Repeat the request. Say, "Let me make sure that I heard you correctly. You would like me to misreport our earnings this quarter. Is that correct?"

✔ Give the other person a blank stare.

✔ Say nothing.

✔ Say, "I'm not sure I heard that."

✔ Say, "I'm sorry. Let's look for another solution."

✔ Say, "Excuse me a minute. I'm going to go for a drink of water. When I get back, we can start over."

The aim of all these maneuvers is to get the person who's making the improper request to think twice and retract that request.

These techniques won't always work. You may face a choice: Go along with the unethical request and compromise yourself in the process, or refuse to go along with it and face the consequences.

It's almost always in your self-interest and in the interest of your company to refuse an unethical request from another employee.

If you stand by your refusal, no doubt you will face some criticism and some discrimination from the person who made the request or demand. He may brand you as being disloyal or not a team player. Let him do so. Others will notice when you're being persecuted for no apparent reason, and more often than not, they'll guess what happened.

You may lose your job. That outcome is unlikely, but it does happen. Most of the time, the only result will be that the other person tries to get someone else to go along. Maybe she'll find a co-conspirator; maybe she won't. But you won't be going along for the long tumble out of the company that she's likely to take when her shenanigans are discovered — as they probably will be.

You could face lots of other ethical dilemmas at work that aren't covered in this chapter. Some excellent resources are available for understanding the difficulties you face in your job. I recommend the following:

- *The Bully at Work,* by Gary Namie, PhD, and Ruth Namie, PhD (Sourcebooks)

- *Ethics at Work,* by Alice Darnell Lattal, PhD, and Ralph W. Clark, PhD (Performance Management Publications)

- *Honest Work: A Business Ethics Reader,* by Joanne B. Ciulla, Clancy Martin, and Robert C. Solomon (Oxford University Press, USA)

- *When Good People Make Tough Choices: Resolving the Dilemmas of Ethical Living,* by Rushworth M. Kidder (Harper Paperbacks)

Chapter 19

Handling Sexuality in the Workplace

- -

In This Chapter

▶ Recognizing sexual harassment

▶ Dealing with sexual harassment

▶ Dating a coworker

- -

Romantic attraction is a fact of life, so it's a fact of professional life. Sometimes, though, the attraction is one-way rather than mutual, or the romantic attention is forced instead of consensual. In the workplace, either situation can come coupled with unequal power, leading to sexual harassment. Although never condoned by company policy, sexual harassment occurs in the workplace with frightening regularity.

Most of the time, romantic attraction is mutual or at least consensual. But you may have plenty of reasons not to let others know about a romance, not the least of which is that you may not know whether it's going to work out. Unfortunately, no secret is more likely to be exposed and become the subject of gossip than a romance. Few office romances remain under wraps for long, and when they're exposed, trouble sometimes follows.

In this chapter, I cover what sexual harassment is, how to avoid it, and what to do if you encounter it. I also give you a few pointers for handling office flirtations and romances.

For more information about sexual harassment, visit www.eeoc.gov/facts/fs-sex.html.

Defining and Avoiding Sexual Harassment

Sexual harassment in the workplace is considered to be an expression of intimidation and perceived power by one person over another and can be a threat to a victim's job. The behavior creates an offensive and hostile environment, which interferes with the victim's work performance. Sexual harassment can be described as any unwelcome physical, visual, or verbal sexual advance; it also can be a request for sexual favors. The following sections cover what constitutes sexual harassment and how you can avoid it.

Defining sexual harassment

A difference exists between office flirting and romance on the one hand and sexual harassment on the other. Flirting is sometimes annoying, and romances are sometimes forbidden by company policy, but sexual harassment is always illegal.

Even today, after sexual-harassment laws have been on the books for more than 40 years, many people are uncertain and confused about what sexual harassment actually is. Many companies have mandatory sexual-harassment seminars for all employees. If you're not in such a company or haven't yet attended one of these seminars, here is a definition of sexual harassment derived from Title VII of the Civil Rights Act of 1964.

Sexual harassment occurs whenever:

- Someone promises you a job or a promotion in return for sexual favors.
- You are demoted or fired for refusing to comply with a request for sex.
- You are explicitly required to engage in certain sexual behavior to get or keep a job.
- Someone else's sexual behavior creates a hostile or abusive work environment that changes the conditions of your job.

There are three kinds of sexual harassment: quid pro quo, the creation of a hostile workplace, and explicit harassment. The following sections describe them in detail.

Quid-pro-quo harassment

The first kind of sexual harassment is by far the easiest to understand. It's *quid pro quo* (this for that), in which one person — usually, a man in a position of authority — asks another person — usually, a woman in a subordinate position — to provide sexual favors in return for a job or a promotion.

Although male-to-female harassment is the most common form of quid-pro-quo harassment, it's not the only kind. Gays, lesbians, and transgendered individuals increasingly face sexual harassment as well, and more men are facing sexual harassment from women as women climb to positions of power.

The U.S. Equal Employment Opportunity Commission's (EEOC's) Sexual Harassment Charges Web page (`www.eeoc.gov/stats/harass.html`) states that in fiscal year 2006, the agency received 12,025 charges of sexual harassment, 15.4 percent of which were filed by males. The EEOC resolved 11,936 sexual-harassment charges in 2006 and recovered $48.8 million in benefits for the plaintiffs and other aggrieved parties (not including monetary benefits obtained through litigation).

Quid-pro-quo harassment has a long history, having long been a favorite practice of people in positions of authority. But it's wrong, and you don't have to comply with it. Period. (I explain later in this chapter how to confront sexual harassment.)

The creation of a hostile work environment

The category of harassment that's most difficult to pin down is a hostile work environment. In recent legal cases, findings showed that unwanted touching or flirting, nude pictures of men or women, lewd gestures or comments, and certain comments about appearance or dress all rise to the level of creating a hostile work environment; therefore, they qualify as instances of sexual harassment.

A female employee of a municipal utility company told a dirty joke to a male coworker. The male coworker was not offended, but another employee passing them in the hallway overheard the joke and was offended. She claimed that the two people in question had a practice of exchanging dirty jokes within earshot of other employees. Despite her protests to them, she claimed that they continued the practice. Management sided with the offended employee and placed formal reprimands in both of the other employees' files. Subsequently, both were denied promotions.

The ribald camaraderie that used to exist among many men in male-dominated workplaces is a thing of the past. The old-boy practices of telling dirty jokes and pinching secretaries are, like racist comments, strictly out of place in today's workplace.

Explicitly stated sexual harassment

The third kind of sexual harassment rises above the other two forms in severity. A supervisor might hint that sexual favors will be rewarded with a promotion, for example. But if the quid pro quo is made explicit, the matter rises to the third level of harassment, and you need to turn it over to another supervisor or the human resources department immediately.

If you're a woman working in a mechanic's shop, and a fellow mechanic has a couple of pinups posted on the wall next to his workstation, that display probably rises only to the level of creating a hostile work environment. If you walk into work one day, however, and find the walls of your workstation liberally plastered with offensive pictures, the conditions of your job have changed materially. That situation qualifies as harassment rising to the actionable level.

Avoiding sexual harassment

Pretty clearly, you don't want to work in a hostile environment or in an office where the managers think that having their pick of the latest recruits is an executive perk. How, then, do you avoid harassment?

Supervisors and managers set the tone of the workplace, so the first responsibility is theirs. If your manager makes it clear that sexual harassment won't be tolerated, you're lucky. He may allow some frivolity, but he should state explicitly that predatory behavior won't be tolerated. If he doesn't, you may have no choice but to go over his head.

Other tips for avoiding harassment include the following:

- ✔ **Conduct yourself professionally at all times.** If you treat others courteously and professionally, and make no sly allusions to sexual matters, chances are good that you'll be treated the same way.

- ✔ **Take care with your appearance.** Women should avoid clothes, makeup, and accessories that send sexual messages, such as heavy mascara, plunging necklines, supershort skirts, and nosebleed high heels. Men should avoid tight pants and muscle shirts. (See Chapter 4 for guidelines on creating an appropriate work wardrobe.)

- ✔ **Remember that some people's personalities change when they travel.** During business trips, avoid meeting other people in hotel rooms, and leave bars and restaurants if your colleagues are clearly more interested in getting drunk than in relaxing after a hard day. (See Chapter 13 for details on behaving properly during special events.)

- ✔ **Keep your ears open to rumors about sexual harassers.** Rumors often are unreliable, but if you keep hearing the same thing about the same supervisor, you'd be wise to check out the rumor with the human resources department and — if it's verified — to stay away from private encounters with that supervisor.

- ✔ **Check to see that your company has developed a sexual-harassment policy.** If so, ask that the company provide information on what the policy covers and whether it's effective.

- ✔ **Don't discuss your sex life at work.** "Don't ask, don't tell" applies to everyone.

Confronting Sexual Harassment

Your attempts to avoid sexual harassment won't always work. If you're being harassed, you're entitled to protection. Unfortunately, taking that protection before you give the harasser an opportunity to change her behavior instantly brands you as a troublemaker. So the first thing to do if you're being harassed is to confront the harasser as politely as you can. Tell her that the behavior is unwanted and unappreciated, and that you want it to stop.

If the behavior is a simple misunderstanding, telling the harasser to stop ought to do the trick. But this technique won't work in plenty of cases. Suppose that you're in the boss's office, and no witnesses are around. Telling him that his advances are unwelcome may not deter him. In such a case, you have no alternative but to leave his office as soon as you can, with as much dignity as possible. As soon as you get back to your desk, write down the date of the harassment and what happened. Take it home. Keep it there. He may never harass you again, but if he does, you'll be keeping a record of it.

Here are some additional guidelines for confronting harassment:

- ✔ Keep — at home — records of all incidents of harassment. Don't keep them at work, where they could be stolen.

- ✔ If your company has policies-and-procedures documents, follow their instructions for combating harassment.

- ✔ Direct your concerns to the human resources department.

- ✔ Get counseling and support as soon as possible from someone you can trust. Sexual harassment has a huge impact on your emotional and physical well-being.

- ✔ Don't ignore harassment, hoping that it will go away. It won't.

If you feel unsafe, or if the harasser is threatening you or trying to discredit you and your job performance, filing formal charges may be your only option. In such a case, contact the EEOC (www.eeoc.gov) or the National Organization of Women (www.now.org). Both organizations can help you determine whether your case is strong enough to pursue and, if so, how you should pursue it.

If you love your job, love working for the company, and want to stay there, don't let yourself be intimidated by the prospects of filing a harassment charge. Sexual-harassment charges aren't to be undertaken frivolously or under false pretenses, of course, but don't avoid them out of fear if they're well founded.

In filing a harassment charge, you have to rely on your supervisor to set the tone. Your supervisor's responsibilities are twofold: ensuring that you're treated fairly and neutrally, and ensuring that the person you're charging is treated fairly and neutrally. Fulfilling this dual duty is one of the hardest things a supervisor has to do, but it's essential if the people involved are to avoid premature vilification. If your supervisor is the one doing the harassing, you really have no choice: You have to report her to her supervisor.

Having said all that, I must also say that levying charges against others can have a negative impact on you. You not only have the burden of proof in any legal proceedings, but you also must bear the burden of being thought a disloyal rabble-rouser by some of your coworkers.

- ✔ **The legal burden is hard to bear:** You must prove that you were treated worse than others, that the harassment was intentional, and that the only reason for the employment decision was your refusal to accept the quid pro quo. That's a lot to prove.

- ✔ **The social burden is worse:** Some of your colleagues will ostracize you. Bringing a sexual-harassment suit against a coworker or a superior also could result in your being fired on trumped-up charges.

As hard as it is to bring to light, sexual harassment cannot be tolerated. If you file a sexual-harassment charge, tough it out. You're doing the right thing!

Having a Romantic Relationship with Someone from Work

Romances happen in the workplace on a regular basis. Statistics show that almost half of all marriages are between people who met at work. Usually, everything works out: The lovebirds work comfortably with each other, and they live happily ever after. Occasionally, however, things don't work out: The dating couple is embarrassingly gushy at work; they sneak off for long lunches; they bring their personal troubles to work; or one of them promotes the other unfairly.

Flirting

Flirting is harmless unless the person you're flirting with doesn't want to be the recipient. But as you know by the time you're old enough to work, you don't begin a work relationship by flirting. You begin a relationship at work professionally, getting to know the person on a professional basis first. If he's single and you're single, and you think that your interest in him won't be rebuffed immediately, it's perfectly all right to ask him out for a drink after work.

If he says no and is not obviously disappointed that he can't make it, let the matter go. If, on the other hand, he seems disappointed that he can't accept, suggest that you reschedule for some other time. If he jumps at the opportunity, you'll know that your attraction to him is reciprocated.

If you're not interested in someone else's flirtations, you can inform the flirter of that fact by ignoring the suggestive remarks or by telling the truth: that you're not interested in having any relationship other than a professional one. Both strategies have risks, however. If you try ignoring flirtation, the other person may think only that you're obtuse and may increase the voltage; if you tell the truth, feelings may get hurt. Such is the stuff of adult life.

The best advice I have is simple: Try always to take the other person's feelings into account when you deliberate about what to do with an unwanted flirtation. If you end up hurting someone's feelings despite your best efforts otherwise, accept the situation and move on.

Dating

When you're dating someone in the office, remember two things: Check the company's dating policy, and keep your public displays of affection out of the office.

Also keep this advice in mind:

- ✔ If your company permits dating among coworkers and doesn't require disclosure, you're under no obligation to disclose an office romance. Some people prefer to keep their private lives completely separate from their professional lives. If the relationship looks as though it's going to last, however, you'd be polite to inform your supervisor.

- ✔ If your company doesn't permit dating, you keep either your job or the romance — or try to keep both by keeping the romance a secret. Know ahead of time, however, that the latter strategy probably will fail.

- ✔ If your company permits dating, but only on the condition that you disclose it to the appropriate person (a supervisor or someone in human resources), comply with the policy as soon as you can.

Having an office romance is thrilling. Anticipating the evening during the day can lead some people to distraction, however, and if distraction isn't curbed, it can result in embarrassment and even the loss of your job. Beware! Your excitement may be contagious to your loved one, but it's best ignored during the workday. Otherwise, you may find yourself out on the street after sending your lover a saucy memo. Remember these points:

✔ Closet and office trysts are mighty risky and will get you fired if they're discovered.

✔ Racy e-mails, like all other e-mails, are the property of the company.

Problematic romances

Many companies discourage romances between people of unequal rank. The reasons are obvious. People will suspect (and may be correct to suspect) that any promotion or special treatment of the person of lower rank is a result of the romantic relationship with the person of higher rank. And if the romance goes sour, there's simply too much risk that the person of higher rank will make life miserable for the person of lower rank. No company wants to put itself at risk of a sexual-harassment suit resulting from a failed romance.

Therefore, most companies require that relationships between superiors and subordinates be disclosed immediately, usually by the person in the position of power. (See the preceding section for more about disclosure.) In most cases, that disclosure immediately results in the superior's being taken out of the subordinate's evaluation loop. Another common consequence is that one of the two parties — usually, the subordinate one — is transferred to a different job.

One other problematic romance is that between a company representative and a client or customer. Take care that your romantic involvement with a client or customer doesn't entangle you in a conflict of interest in which you give the client preferential treatment because of the personal relationship between the two of you. In cases like this, you should ask to be reassigned rather than risk embarrassment and possible legal action.

Part V
Doing Business on a Global Scale

"The interpreter we had at that meeting made everything I said sound good. I wonder if he interprets expense accounts?"

In this part . . .

1 give you some universally helpful pointers on all facets of business travel, from knowing what to pack to handling the new challenges of airline travel.

This part explores the basic guidelines of adapting to another culture and gives you a better understanding of today's complex rules of business protocol around the world, from knowing how to present your business card properly to understanding the intricacies of dining etiquette in a variety of cultures. I cover social taboos in other countries and give you practical advice on ways to avoid committing the dreaded faux pas in a culture unlike your own. You learn how to navigate unfamiliar waters and come out an outstanding representative of your company.

Chapter 20

Pack Your Manners! Traveling for Business

*B*usiness travel doesn't have to be drudgery, and although some stress is inevitable, it doesn't have to make you miserable. The key is knowing that in all probability, something will go wrong: Your hotel will be next to a construction site, your luggage will be lost, your flight will be canceled, or you'll forget your favorite shoes.

Good travelers are ready for the unexpected. They take the inconveniences in stride, cope with the disasters, and are amused when something goes wrong in a way that they might really be able to laugh about later. In this chapter, you find out what it takes to be a good traveler.

Planning Your Trip

Your job may take you all over the city, country, or world. If you travel on a regular basis, you eventually learn what all good travelers learn: On the road, being self-reliant and having a routine are essential. Planning your itinerary, packing the essentials, and having a familiar routine help you cope better with the inevitable onslaught of new and unfamiliar people, places, and information.

Preparing your itinerary

When you travel, you may be making your own plans, relying on the in-house travel department, or using an agency.

You can begin to guarantee a good business trip by planning it as soon as you know the dates of the trip. Car rentals, airline tickets, train reservations, and hotel rooms don't get any cheaper the longer you wait, and they don't become more available. So get on the ball. Don't rely completely on your company's overwhelmed travel agent, either; some Internet research on your part may help.

When you're planning the dates of a business trip, either nationally or internationally, consider religious and local holidays, as businesses and restaurants could be closed. And don't forget about midsummer European vacations and spring break!

After you've made your travel and accommodation arrangements, put together an itinerary. In this itinerary, list the following:

- ✔ Flight information (flight numbers, departure and arrival times, departure and arrival cities, airline name, and airline telephone number)
- ✔ Ground-transportation information (such as car-rental agency name, telephone number, and reservation number; or limousine confirmation)
- ✔ Hotel name, address, telephone number, and reservation number
- ✔ Meeting times and places, with telephone numbers if possible
- ✔ Host names, telephone and fax numbers, and e-mail addresses
- ✔ Meal arrangements (research a few key cuisines and restaurants ahead of time)
- ✔ Scheduled entertainment

Give a copy of your itinerary to your supervisor or assistant, and give another copy to a friend or relative. If something goes wrong, and you don't arrive back when you say you will, someone will be able to initiate a search with accurate information about you.

Packing what you need

The rules are simple: Pack what you'll need, and leave everything else at home. You have to take your laptop, cell phone, PDA, reports, contracts, brochures, clothes, shaving kit or cosmetic bag, and vintage cowboy boots. Oops — leave that last item at home (unless they fit into your carry-on bag and you really like them). Don't forget your medication and your lens prescriptions if you wear glasses or contact lenses.

The key to packing travel clothing is keeping it simple, lightweight, and wrinkle free. You can achieve the first goal by taking no more than two changes of clothes per day; try to recycle clothes, if you can. To achieve the second goal easily, leave your heavyweights — the overcoat and ballroom gown — at home. And to achieve the third goal, take as many no-wrinkle items as possible.

Don't forget to take clothes for evenings and outings. If you're in doubt about what to bring, ask your host. Don't assume that because your company has casual Friday, the company you're visiting next Friday has one too. Ask your host whether his office has casual dress on Fridays.

Take a credit card with an open balance and cash if you'll be in a rural area. You may also want to bring traveler's checks. If you're on a business expense account, it's essential to keep precise records. If you have a laptop, consider using an accounting program showing all expenses, or keep an expense book with handwritten records and use it assiduously. Keep all receipts in a safe place. (See Chapter 18 for more about expense reports.)

If you're going overseas, be sure to have enough currency from your destination country to pay for small expenses before you get a chance to go to a hotel's or bank's exchange window. Also, ask your bank or host whether your ATM card is going to work for getting your destination currency at the hotel where you'll be staying or at a nearby bank.

Avoid exchanging money at airports. Airport exchange windows are more expensive than money exchanges at hotels or banks. You also can seek out independent money exchangers for a better rate.

No matter where you go, take identification that allows you to drive. You need your driver's license to board a flight, and you also may need it for additional ID when you're traveling. If you are a frequent overseas traveler, consider getting an international driver's license; it's quick and easy to obtain. For information on how to obtain an international driver's license or permit, visit the U.S. Department of Transportation at `ntl.bts.gov/faq/intdl.html` or the U.S. Department of State at `travel.state.gov/travel/abroad_roadsafety.html#permits`.

If you're traveling out of the country, double-check the expiration date on your passport. Renewing an expired passport can take weeks, and although you can rush the process, the fees are much higher. Also, some countries require that your passport be valid at least six months beyond the dates of your trip. Check with the nearest embassy or consulate of each country you plan to visit to find out that country's entry and visa requirements. For complete details, ask for information at any U.S. Postal Service office that issues passports, or visit `www.usps.com/passport`.

Traveling with your electronic tools

If you're like many professionals today, you own several beeping, blinking, ringing, buzzing, and/or musical plastic-encased gadgets that keep you connected to work, home, and all the information you need while you're on the road. These days, many busy people carry a phone, laptop, and PDA at the same time. Although these devices are useful, they can contribute to a cluttered, disorganized — and, therefore, unprofessional — look.

How can you survive on the road without these tools? One option is to consolidate gadgetry. Many phone/PDA combinations are available now, and more are sure to come. Also, most cell phones have numerous features that store phone numbers; allow text-messaging; and provide calendars, navigational tools, Internet and e-mail access, and digital cameras so that you can leave other gadgets behind.

When traveling with electronic devices, keep these tips in mind:

- ✔ Carry more than one electrical adaptor and converter to accommodate charging more than one device at a time.

- ✔ If you're carrying a laptop computer, try placing your bag on a wheeled carrier to get it through the airport instead of carrying it in your hand or over your shoulder. Specially designed laptop bags also work well, and some of them can be converted to regular briefcases for meetings.

- ✔ Airport security officials will ask you to turn off your laptop and other electronic gadgets. Comply pleasantly with their requests. After all, they're just doing their job, which is to keep you safe.

- ✔ Never talk on a cell phone while the flight attendant reviews safety information. In fact, you shouldn't talk at all during this presentation. Although you may be a seasoned traveler, other passengers may need to hear this potentially lifesaving information.

- ✔ If you're using your laptop on the plane, watch your elbows, especially if you're in the dreaded middle seat. If your typing causes you to intrude on other passengers' precious personal space, don't type. You won't be able to get much done while they're glaring at you anyway.

- ✔ If you have long fingernails, they may click on the keyboard while you're typing — a noise that can be extremely annoying to the passengers around you. If the clicking is unavoidable, you may want to check with those sitting near you to see whether they object.

Practicing Good Manners When You Travel By Air

Airline travel has never been more convenient (in theory) or more harried (in practice) than in the past few years. Pilots, staff, and ground crew are all stressed, which sometimes translates into rudeness and anxiety.

Most airport employees are trying hard to do their jobs, often under far-from-ideal circumstances. Weather, late connecting flights, problems at other airports, increased security, layoffs, consolidations, and labor disputes conspire to make flights late and people exasperated. In the following sections, I give you some guidance on how to keep your cool while you fly.

Following new security policies

In the constantly changing world of air travel, knowing just what to expect is impossible. If you haven't been to an airport recently, you need to update yourself on the latest airport security rules from the Transportation Security Administration (TSA). Travelers face tighter security and longer lines because of strict TSA regulations on carry-on items and required forms of ID. A little preparation, patience, and manners are required (along with a good deal of humor). No one is immune from scrutiny, so do your part to keep the skies safe.

Here are some guidelines:

- ✔ Be sure that your electronic devices are charged before you get to the airport. As you go through airport security, you could be asked to power up the devices to prove that they are what they seem to be.

- ✔ Empty your pockets of keys, loose change, pens, and other metal objects. Be prepared to remove your jewelry and your belt. If you're asked to remove items such as your shoes, do so graciously. Above all, keep your cool. Remember, this screening is for your safety and that of others.

- ✔ If possible, pay for your tickets with a credit card. Passengers who pay with cash are more likely to be pulled aside by security.

- ✔ Before you leave, know what is permitted and not permitted in your carry-on and checked luggage. To learn the latest rules and requirements, visit www.tsa.gov or www.dhs.gov/xtrvlsec.

- ✔ Never offer to watch someone else's luggage, and don't ask anyone else to watch yours. Doing so not only puts you in an awkward situation, but also involves a big security risk. Always keep your bags with you, and never carry anything onto the plane for someone else.

Planning well

As a traveler, you expect the airport to be efficient and the flight to go smoothly. Do yourself a favor: Modify your thinking. Be prepared for a flight that's delayed or an airline that loses your baggage. Being prepared means avoiding scheduling meetings within two or three hours of your arrival, and having enough money and food on your person that you can survive if the plane gets in after all the local banks, restaurants, and stores have closed. It means carrying all your luggage with you onto the plane, or at least carrying a bag with a change of clothes and your essential toiletries.

Have a reasonable checklist of information you want to bring on board, such as a backup airline schedule, a calendar for rescheduling flights or meetings, your itinerary, and your hotel and client phone numbers.

Double-check the number of pieces, size, and weight allowed for your carry-on and checked luggage. Be sure that the luggage will fit smaller carry-on limits, even when the suitcase is completely stuffed.

Staying calm and respectful

Air travel is stressful, no doubt about it. Unfortunately, some people seem not to be able to handle stress without lashing out. Everyone who has been in an airport or on an airplane probably has seen someone lose it at the check-in desk or on the plane. If you can't control your temper when you're stressed out, do what you can to prevent the conditions in which you get stressed. Confirm your reservation and seat number ahead of time. Get to the airport early. Most airlines require up to three hours of preboarding time for people traveling out of the country and two hours for people traveling nationally. To save time, take advantage of preprinting your own boarding pass from home within 24 hours of your flight time. Avoid the luggage check-in line by carrying your luggage. Avoid sugar; eat something with protein in it. Drink enough water. Take your medication. Breathe.

After the plane is in the air, you probably will be served drinks and may even be served food. Here, as much as anywhere, good table manners are in order (see Chapter 12 for details). Try to adhere to standard table manners as much as your tiny space allows. If you're lucky enough to be on a flight with food service, and you have dietary restrictions or preferences, you may want to request a special meal (such as vegetarian or kosher) when you book your ticket.

Keep these tips in mind when dealing with fellow passengers:

✔ At least nod and say "Hello" to your rowmates. You don't have to carry on a conversation if you don't want to, but it is polite to acknowledge others, especially in such tight quarters.

✔ Ask your neighbor whether working on your laptop computer will bother her.

✔ Keep your work off your neighbor's lap and tray.

✔ Occupy one armrest at a time. Spreading your arms and elbows across both armrests is rude.

✔ Be considerate to airline attendants, and thank them — and the pilots — when you deplane.

Avoid making these mistakes:

✔ Wearing heavy cologne or fragrance (but please shower before you leave!).

✔ Cutting in any line.

✔ Crushing or relocating other people's belongings in an overhead bin to accommodate your own baggage.

✔ Talking or laughing too loudly.

✔ Talking on and on to the person next to you while he's trying to work, read, or sleep.

✔ Grabbing the seat back in front of you when you're getting up from your seat. If doing so is unavoidable, let the person in front of you know ahead of time (and make sure that you don't pull his hair).

For the consideration of those around you, if you're on a long flight and you must remove your jacket and shoes, be sure that you have clean clothes and deodorant on and have clean socks with you. Sitting next to a passenger with body odor or stinky feet isn't too pleasant.

On the Road Again: Using Public and Private Transportation When You Arrive

When you arrive at your destination, you need to get from the airport to the hotel and check in at the hotel. If you've budgeted for them, hired cars or taxis are a convenient way to go. But be aware that taxi lines at busy airports are often very long. If you're in a hurry and are sufficiently familiar with the public transportation system, you may be able to shave time off your trip from the airport to the hotel by taking the subway or an express bus.

Keep these tips about taxis and public transportation in mind:

- If a dispatcher is available, let her get the cab. If your host has met you at the airport, and lots of cabs are around, the host hails; if cabs are scarce, both host and guest hail.

- The host or driver typically invites the guest to get in first curbside. If there are three or more people, the tallest or the heaviest sits in front. The host either gets into the back seat of the car from the street side or sits in the front passenger seat.

- Chief executive officers and other bigwigs rarely carry cash. If you're traveling with your superiors, be prepared to pay the bills.

- Be courteous to the driver, even if he snarls back at you. If so, continue to be polite but give a smaller tip.

  Most taxi drivers are perfectly nice people. Some aren't. Always have your wits about you when taking a taxi, and don't let anyone take advantage of you. For details on traveling by taxi abroad, see Chapter 21.

- On public transportation, you may ask people to move items on an otherwise-available seat so that you can sit.

- On public transportation, it is polite for both men and women to give up their seats to older people or people with disabilities if they aren't disabled themselves. Men should give up seats to women.

Whatever your destination and means of travel, if you know that taxis are hard to come by, prearrange a dependable car service. It's worth spending the few extra dollars to avoid the aggravation of waiting in the queue or hailing a cab. When you or your host hires a car, you can count on the driver to meet you at the arranged location, usually holding a little sign with your name or your company's name.

If you hire a limousine or sedan, remember that, as with taxis, the best seat is the rear seat closer to the curb, so that's where a Very Important Person goes. If you're a personal assistant or an associate sales representative for the company, you go in the jump seat or up front with the driver.

Here are a couple of additional tips for riding in a private car:

- Refer to a limousine as a sedan or a car, not a limo.

- If the car has been hired for you, you don't tip the driver unless she does something special for you, such as lugging your sample cases up four flights of stairs.

Knowing the Ins and Outs of Hotels

Most business people stay in commercial hotels, which are designed specifically for business travelers. They are less expensive than luxury hotels, because commercial hotels have fewer services.

This isn't to say that commercial hotels have no services. You can rely on commercial hotels to have meeting and conference rooms, computers, fax machines, copiers, and other business amenities. These hotels also have concierge desks, where you can get advice on things to do in town, look at menus from selected restaurants, purchase tickets for local entertainment, and make car-rental or child-care arrangements.

When you know what kind of hotel you're staying in, you'll know how many dollar bills you're likely to dispose of before you get a chance to lie down on your bed. Commercial hotels rarely have the staff of a luxury hotel. You're likely to find a maid and a concierge at a commercial hotel. But at a luxury hotel, you'll also find valets, door attendants, porters, bellhops, sometimes elevator and bathroom attendants, dry cleaners, tailors, and shoe-shiners. Here are my tips on tipping:

- Door attendant hails a cab: $1
- Door attendant carries your bag: $1 per bag
- Bellhop arrives at your room with your luggage: $1 or $2 per bag
- Parking valet retrieves your car: $1 or $2
- Maid cleans the room: $2 per night
- Concierge shows you a map of the downtown area: no tip
- Concierge gets you into the wildly popular restaurant you've heard so much about: $10 to $20
- Concierge gets you and your colleague tickets for opening night of an eagerly awaited opera production: $20 per ticket

When you're at the hotel, check in, find your room, and take a breather. If your host has done his job correctly and your flight was on time, you won't have to be anywhere for at least a few hours. Take the time to have something to eat, exercise, snooze, or prepare for your meetings.

Traveling with Colleagues

Traveling with colleagues, especially those you like, can add immeasurably to your trip. Conversely, traveling with those you merely tolerate or those you dislike can turn a pleasant trip into something trying.

You and your colleagues don't become friends just because you sit next to each other on a plane or share a hotel room. Sharing close spaces creates an opportunity to share other things as well, but you don't really want your colleague to know that you sleep with a stuffed monkey, do you? Probably not. Leave it at home. And you would be better off back at the office if you remain the model of discretion even as your colleague blathers on and on about her childhood pets after one too many in the hotel bar.

You may be tempted to go everywhere with your colleague when you're in a strange town, but your insecurity isn't an excuse to do something you probably wouldn't do at home. That means if your colleague wants to visit friends, you don't have to tag along just because you're lonely. And it means that if your colleague wants to go to a bar or find entertainment for the evening, you don't have to tag along just because you have nothing else to do.

If you're thinking about sharing a hotel room, find out ahead of time whether your colleague snores or walks in his sleep. Both situations can be unnerving and can lead to the loss of a good night's sleep. Make other arrangements if necessary — but be polite. If your colleague doesn't volunteer that he snores, you can ask, "Are there any reasons why we should get separate rooms?"

Staying Safe: A Special Word for Women Travelers

Differences still exist in appropriate behavior and dress for businessmen and businesswomen around the world. Sadly, women are also advised to be on guard for their own safety while traveling, either in the United States or internationally.

In the past and depending on the country, you may have had no reason to be afraid when traveling in a foreign country. Unfortunately, times have changed. Being open to new experiences and meeting new people are part of making yourself a successful international businessperson. On the other hand, although travelers of both genders should always be aware of their surroundings, women do need to be slightly more cautious.

This section isn't intended to scare you but to remind you of ways to keep yourself safe at all times while still having an enjoyable and productive trip. Even if you're a guy, reading this section can't hurt.

If you ever feel unsafe, there's probably a good reason. Follow your intuition, and do something to address your fear: Change your route, get into a taxi, go into a shop where lots of people are, or get off the elevator at the next floor if someone is making you uncomfortable. Don't let anyone tell you that you're being silly or overreacting.

Being safe at hotels

Safe travel begins during the planning process back home. If you're at all concerned about taking a taxi in your destination country, you or your travel agent should arrange for a car service to pick you up at the airport and take you to your hotel. Your peace of mind is worth the extra expense. (I discuss transportation from the airport earlier in this chapter.)

Your choice of hotel is also important, because your hotel is your home away from home, and you should feel comfortable there. A larger hotel that caters to business travelers probably will be safer than a smaller hotel. At least on your first trip to a place, until you become more comfortable there, you should err on the side of safety. Here are a few tips to keep in mind:

- The hotel should have a bellhop on duty at all hours to assist you with hailing a taxi or finding your way. Tip generously to ensure attentive service throughout your stay.

- When you're checking into the hotel, other guests shouldn't be standing close enough to hear your conversation. Many hotels will write your room number on the key envelope instead of saying it out loud. If someone at the front desk ever says your room number loudly enough that others can hear it, explain that you would like that information to be kept private and ask for another room assignment.

- Especially in a large hotel, ask for a room near the elevator so that you won't have to walk down a long hallway by yourself. Also avoid rooms on the first floor.

- Find your key while you're in the lobby, and keep it in your hand while you walk to your room. Having it in your hand prevents you from having to fumble for it in your purse while standing in front of your door.

- If you're nervous for any reason about walking to your room, ask for an escort. Again, generous tipping will ensure service with a smile.

- When you get to your room, lock the door immediately, and don't open it without looking through the peephole first. If someone claims to be from room service, but you haven't ordered anything, don't open the door.

- If you'll be using gym facilities or a parking garage, make sure that an attendant will be there at night. Be sure to park in a well-lit area, and look around you before you get out of the car. Before you get in the car, check the back seat to make sure that no one is in it. And always lock your vehicle, even if you're leaving it for only a moment.

Many hotels catering to business travelers are especially attuned to the needs of women. Some offer concierge floors, which not only provide extra services such as breakfast and evening cocktails, but also require a room key to exit the elevator on that floor. This amenity is well worth the extra money if it puts your mind at ease.

You shouldn't travel with jewelry that could be stolen; if you won't be wearing it every day, don't bring it. If you do have other valuables, however — including your passport and other important papers — lock them up in the hotel safe. That solution probably isn't workable for protecting your laptop computer, but you should lock the computer in your suitcase when you're out of your room. At minimum, don't leave it sitting out on the desk, where it presents an obvious temptation.

Moving around the city

If you were a mugger or a professional con artist, who would you look for: a confident, professional woman with spring in her step, or someone who looked as though she just fell off the turnip truck? Even if you feel uncertain, you can't let your uncertainty show. Take the time to learn what you need to know so that you'll look, if not like a native, at least like someone who can take care of herself. If you'll be walking somewhere, check the map before you leave, and confirm your route with the concierge. That way, you'll be able to walk confidently and look as though you know where you're going.

A cell phone has become a real traveler's friend over the past few years. If you get lost, help from someone you trust is just a phone call away. Keep important numbers — your hotel, the colleagues you're visiting, your credit card company — close at hand. If you need to make a call, step into an unobtrusive (but not deserted) place to do so.

Be wary of strangers who approach you on the street. Although you don't want to rebuff someone who's honestly looking for directions, you also don't want to seem overly friendly. If you feel uncomfortable for any reason, don't stop to speak with that stranger who's trying to get your attention.

Chapter 21

Now You've Arrived: Adapting to a New World

In This Chapter

▶ Behaving with tact and respect abroad

▶ Hitting the road in a foreign land

The ugly American is not just a creation of fiction. Perhaps no culture on Earth sends more rude or inconsiderate visitors overseas than the United States. The reasons aren't difficult to uncover: America is the most powerful nation on Earth, and Americans all too often assume that because ours is a powerful nation, our customs and codes of behavior are the best. Then we take those customs and codes overseas and are shocked when not everyone acts as we do and when some people have the effrontery to dislike us for acting as we do — which oftentimes can be loud and demanding. Americans also have been described as being too informal with their business dealings in other countries.

In this chapter, I show you how to develop enough awareness to avoid exposing yourself as someone with a lack of understanding of cultural differences. I also give tips for using transportation in a foreign destination.

Minding Your Multicultural Manners

Volumes have been written about how to behave in other countries, from attire to hand gestures to eating habits. In Chapter 22, I closely examine customs and etiquette by country and region. A few simple etiquette guidelines, however, can carry you through a variety of cultural situations without offending your hosts or damaging a business relationship:

✔ First off, erase from your mind any sense of xenophobia or cultural supe-
riority. If you were born in the United States, you may — as many
Americans do — believe that American culture is the best in the world.
Drop that attitude! To do business in other countries or with representatives from other countries, you must realize that their cultures are different, not inferior. In fact, words like *good* and *bad* really have no place at
all in describing cultural differences. Although your reaction to someone
else's culture may be positive or negative, the culture itself simply is
what it is.

✔ Along the same lines, never assume that you're doing someone a favor
by accepting his culture. Accepting and attempting to appreciate another
country's way of life and business are necessary for you to succeed —
just like learning to deal with other people in your office. The attitude
that people are lucky to have you around so that they can learn how to
act like Americans won't make you many friends around the world.

✔ You should avoid having heated discussions about politics anywhere —
in the United States, in the country you're visiting, or pretty much anywhere in the world. You never know when you may say something that
will offend, even a remark that seems harmless to you. If your associates
begin criticizing other countries or governments, you may find yourself
in a no-win situation. If you defend the country, you may end up offending someone. If you join in the criticism, your colleagues may lose
respect for you and wonder why you would ever say something so negative about your own country. Either way, this sort of conversation is
best avoided. If someone tries to engage you in a political debate,
politely deflect her. Saying something like this may work: "I've learned
never to discuss religion or politics. Now, what can you tell me about the
history of your city? It's so lovely."

In the following sections, I offer additional guidelines for minding your multicultural manners.

Keeping an open mind

In many cases, visitors to a foreign destination are eager to follow their hosts'
customs, and their hosts are eager to make the visitors comfortable by following the visitors' customs. American businesspeople may be practicing
their bows in anticipation of Japanese hosts, for example, while those hosts
are practicing shaking hands and making eye contact like their American
guests. Absolutely nothing is wrong with meeting your foreign counterparts
and finding out that everyone is trying to adopt other customs. In fact, knowing that each participant is interested in making the other comfortable is a
great way to start a business relationship. In general, however, businesspeople follow the customs of the country they are in.

Find out as much as you can about the cultures of people you work with. If you're traveling to another country for business, do some research. The U.S. State Department Web site (www.state.gov) is an excellent place to start, and plenty of other resources about customs and business around the world are available online and in bookstores. Many companies offer online courses for their employees traveling internationally. If someone at your company has visited the country you're traveling to, or if your company happens to have employees there, tap those resources for information.

If possible, begin reading online newspapers from your target country before you leave for your trip, and read daily newspapers after you arrive. Many major newspaper sites and news portals offer search services that allow you to specify search terms and get daily feeds of news about other countries.

Occasionally, a stranger or other visitor may ask you for directions when you're a visitor somewhere yourself. Congratulations! You must look like you know what you're doing. If you don't know the directions, simply say that you don't know — without explaining that you're a visitor too. You never definitely know the other person's intentions, and you don't know who might overhear you.

Even on your own turf, you have many opportunities to learn from foreign employees and visitors. Keep an open mind, and when you notice behavior that seems unusual to you, ask about it (respectfully and with humility). For example, say, "I noticed that women are reluctant to shake a man's hand; is this something that's customary and not done in Vietnam? I certainly don't want to cause offense by offering my hand to a woman." The more comfortable you make people feel, the more willing they are to explain. You may end up expanding your knowledge and becoming a better employee to boot.

Bridging the language gap

Even if the people you're visiting speak perfect English, it never hurts to learn at least a few words and phrases of their native language as a show of respect. Though they may snicker at your pronunciation behind your back (or even to your face), they will appreciate the effort.

You also should realize that English speakers around the world use very different words and expressions, not to mention different accents. With a little research, you won't be alarmed when someone offers you a rubber for your pencil or spotted dick for dessert, and you won't make your English hosts blush by describing your shag haircut.

Make yourself familiar with the various types of personal address used in a country. Many languages use forms of *you* that are singular or plural, masculine or feminine, and formal or informal. Even when you're speaking English, however, forms of address are often much more formal in other countries. Your pal Sol, the guy who writes the software in your office, may be Engineer Solomon in some other countries.

Never begin using first names until you're invited by the specific person to do so. Although telemarketers in the United States feel free to call and ask for Al, and physicians invite the elderly to "take off all your clothes, Peg, and put on this paper gown," most other countries are much more formal. Don't even ask someone's first name. *Mr.* and *Ms* are the norm until someone tells you otherwise.

Respecting religion

Religion is perhaps the most delicate of all subjects. Before you visit a country, find out what its major religions are, and learn at least something about those religions. When people around you begin pulling out their prayer mats, you shouldn't look stunned. It goes without saying that you should never, ever say anything disparaging about another religion, even if you consider something to be weird, and even if your religion advocates converting others. Remember, you're there as a businessperson, not as a missionary. Don't make jokes about religion, either. Just as many Catholics don't want to hear jokes about what happens when the president, the prime minister, and the pope are stranded on a desert island, your colleagues may not be amused by a joke that begins, "So Buddha walks into a bar. . . ."

You probably shouldn't ask any questions about religion, either, unless you know someone very well and are certain that she won't be offended. Though your curiosity may be genuine, questions such as "I don't understand why you pray so many times each day. Can you explain it?" may be interpreted as rudeness or criticism. If you're really interested, pick up a book on the subject.

Avoiding a dining faux pas

Dining is something to be careful about. You should brush up on the cuisine and dining etiquette of the country you're visiting so that you'll be ready, if necessary, to sit on the floor, eat with your hands, not eat with your hands, or swallow some new foods.

With all these opportunities for confusion, you're bound to make a mistake at least once in a while. That's where your humble and respectful attitude comes into play. Let the people you're around know that you don't know everything and that you would appreciate being corrected when you do something wrong. When you can tell from someone's expression or body language that you've made a mistake, address it immediately. Say, "I'm afraid I may have done something to offend you, and I'm so sorry. Please let me know if I've made a mistake so I can avoid it next time." If someone said this to you, wouldn't you forgive an offensive remark or two?

If you happen to be visiting with other Americans, agree to help one another out. Or ask your host to share a few tips ahead of time. When you make a blunder at the big dinner meeting, let your colleagues know so that they can avoid doing the same thing the next day. Although sharing your blunder may be embarrassing, you'll help raise the cultural literacy of the entire group, and your group (including you) will earn more respect from your hosts.

Dressing appropriately

In addition to helping you be an effective businessperson, dressing with respect for the local culture can help you stay safe, avoid embarrassing your-self or your company, and avoid offending others. In all cases, you should dress on the conservative side until you're very sure that you can branch out without embarrassing yourself. When in doubt, women are always correct with skirts that fall at or just below the knee and shirts with long sleeves. In some cases, you should wear a skirt or dress rather than pants. Depending on the occasion and the weather, men should wear a light, comfortable jacket or sweater, a shirt, and long slacks. And even if you're sightseeing on the weekends as part of your trip, leave your shorts and sandals at home. Women will be far better off with a roomy skirt in a breathable fabric, and men with lightweight khaki pants and a cotton shirt.

In Muslim countries, the rules regarding clothing for women are more spe-cific. Blouses with high necks and long sleeves are musts, and hemlines should be midcalf or lower. The rules are less strict in Israel, but if you ever visit a synagogue or a mosque, your knees and your elbows must be covered. Women also may consider bringing along a shawl-size scarf. It can keep you warm when used as a wrap and also cover your head if you're visiting a cathedral or doing business in Muslim countries.

For both professional reasons and comfort, women's shoes should have low heels and closed toes; men can wear a slip-on loafer or another comfortable leather shoe. Remember not to wear a brand-new pair of shoes for travel, and never wear tennis shoes unless you're on your way to the gym.

Both men and women should keep jewelry to an absolute minimum. Wearing your wedding ring is fine, but if your engagement ring is big and sparkly, you might think about leaving it in the safe-deposit box at home. The same goes for men and women's watches; wearing a flashy or expensive designer watch might attract criminals. Small gold, silver, or pearl earrings are good choices for women, and the same goes for necklaces; you can easily accessorize with a scarf, which is much less of a temptation for thieves. Whatever jewelry you bring, plan to wear all of it every day, or lock up valuables in the hotel safe. Don't leave anything in your hotel room.

In short, do your best to blend in so that you don't make a bad impression. This trip isn't the time to wear your flashy baseball tie or to paint your nails a garish color. The dress of other business professionals in the country you're visiting should be your guide. Check with other colleagues or the destination tourism bureau to find out what's considered the business norm.

Taking to the Foreign Road

Traveling around a new place by train, bus, or taxi isn't always easy, especially in an unfamiliar country. It's important to have a good understanding of the transportation system before venturing out.

The various modes of travel and the appropriate etiquette rules for each are fairly universal. A few exceptions to the rules occur, but most of the guidelines you should follow at home apply abroad as well.

Trains and buses

Regardless of the declining number of train and bus travelers in the United States in the past few years, in other parts of the world, trains and buses are still among the most efficient and comfortable means of transportation. Service between and around major cities is dependable and inexpensive, with most trains and buses arriving on schedule. The process of purchasing tickets and checking in usually is convenient and simple.

You still have the potential to offend your fellow passengers or create cultural clashes. The following guidelines will guarantee you a smooth ride no matter where in the world you travel:

- ✔ Bring aboard only what you absolutely need.

- ✔ Arrive early. You don't want to be running to board the train or bus as it's leaving the station.

- ✔ For long-distance travel, consider going in the middle of the week, when transportation normally is less crowded. Daily commuter trains are less crowded on weekends.

- ✔ If you're the chatty type, take notice of the body language of the person you want to engage. If it says, "I don't care to converse," pull out a good book or your music player (and listen to music with headphones).

✔ Be pleasant and considerate when you're speaking to a passenger seated near you. If no language barrier exists, many times these conversations can provide you interesting details of the city you're visiting or your destination location.

✔ If you use your laptop, check with your neighbors to make sure that the noise you make typing will not be an annoyance, especially if you're a woman with long fingernails.

✔ Keep the volume down. If you're speaking on your cell phone or talking to another passenger, avoid loud conversations or loud laughing. Though you may be enjoying yourself, the noise can be extremely irritating to those who may prefer to nap.

✔ If you plan to have a meal from the dining car on a train, wait until your seating time is called.

✔ When moving through the aisle, make sure to give way to passengers who are carrying luggage, passengers who have children, and elderly people.

✔ If you notice someone struggling with her baggage, offer assistance.

✔ Don't keep your carry-on baggage, work items, purse, briefcase, laptop, or other items on the empty seat next to you. If the train or bus is full, you'll just have to remove it for another passenger.

✔ If you're a woman traveling alone, if possible, sit next to another woman or a family rather than sitting next to an empty seat.

✔ Follow the smoking policy of the train or bus.

✔ Be aware of pickpockets. Keep important items such as your passport in a zippered compartment or purse that's held close to your body. You also can keep items in the inside upper pockets of your jacket.

✔ Always keep a close watch on your belongings, and don't ask anyone to look after your things.

Do your homework, and grab the city train and bus maps from the hotel before venturing out. Ask a hotel staff member to write down the location of where you're going and the return address in the appropriate language. Not only can train and bus schedules be confusing, but also, you may not find anyone who speaks English.

Taxis

If you're comfortable taking cabs in a foreign city, go for it! Often, a taxi is the most reliable and effective method of getting around in an unfamiliar city. In Europe in particular, taxis are among the most convenient means of transportation. Usually, it's more convenient to take the taxi from the taxi station than from the main streets. Almost all taxi drivers in France, Italy, and England are very familiar with the streets and can find your destination as long as you can communicate clearly or write down the address correctly. (Using a taxi in other parts of the world can be more of a challenge because of the population and traffic.)

Ask the hotel concierge how you can identify a legitimate taxi from the so-called "gypsy" cabs. In many countries, you could end up getting in the car with a perfect stranger who isn't licensed with any authority. The taxi may end up being perfectly safe, but you shouldn't take the risk. You might also check with the hotel about the approximate travel time to your destination and write down your hotel name and address if you plan to return.

Make an effort to familiarize yourself with where you are going and how long it should take to arrive. Don't rely on the taxi driver for this information. It also can't hurt to let a front desk staff member at your hotel know where you're going.

Normally, the front seat isn't for passengers, and one taxi is allowed to take three passengers. Act knowledgeable and relaxed after you enter the taxi. If the driver asks what route you prefer, never say, "You pick; I don't know where I'm going." Instead, say something like this: "Because you're the expert on driving in this area, please take whichever route you think is best." If a language barrier exists, avoid giving the driver too many specifics until you're closer to your destination, so as not to cause confusion.

When you're on your way, jot down the cab driver's name and medallion or badge number in the unfortunate event that you leave an item in the taxi or have a dispute.

As far as being a polite passenger goes, the rules are the same as they are for any other public transportation. Be respectful of the driver, keep your voice low, and don't eat or drink in the cab unless you ask permission first. You may alter your tip depending on the circumstances and the expected amount for the particular city. If the driver helps you with your luggage or goes out of the way to assist you in any other way, increase the amount.

If the driver seems to be going around in circles, ask him what he's doing, and ask him to stop and let you out if you think he's truly taking you for a ride! (You want to get out only in a busy area, of course, so you can easily find another taxi.) Stay in the cab while paying your driver; you don't want to be half in and half out while you have money in your hand. Finally, be sure to grab all your belongings before you step out of the cab; otherwise, your driver may drive off with your purse or briefcase.

For obvious reasons, it's best not to share a cab with strangers, either at home or abroad.

Chapter 22

Crossing Cultural Lines: Your Passport for Success

*E*ven if you're well on your way to bona fide expertise in American business etiquette, practices that pass as polite in San Francisco may be deemed downright rude in Seoul or Seville. Just knowing about your area of business expertise isn't enough any longer. Whether you travel internationally or do business with foreign clients at home, making a positive first impression is more important than ever.

Keep in mind that you are not only a company representative when you travel abroad, but a representative of your home country as well. It's critical that you always be respectful of other customs, cultures, and religions. To achieve a global perspective, try to put yourself in other people's shoes. Blending in and conforming to social norms is often a form of flattery.

In this chapter, I introduce you to some of the most common etiquette issues you're likely to face when you travel internationally. I cover general customs by region and discuss a few countries in detail.

The information in this chapter is a summary of tips on doing business in a variety of countries. An excellent resource for more information is www.executiveplanet.com.

Exploring Business Etiquette in Europe

Europe ranges from the cold northern countries of Norway and Sweden to the warm Mediterranean countries of Italy and Greece. Some customs and mores vary as much as the topography; others are shared across Europe.

Language

The European Union has 15 official languages, and though Europeans aren't going to give up their native languages anytime soon, English is fast becoming the business "communication" language. The recent move to English is coming from globalization and American cultural influence, and younger Europeans who have studied abroad and traveled are more comfortable using it. Even though most business professionals throughout Europe speak some English, it's always recommended to learn important key words of your destination's language.

Appropriate dress

For most businesses throughout Europe, business attire is formal, which means dark suits, subdued ties, and lace-up shoes. In some countries — Germany, Great Britain, and Denmark, for example — dress is ultraconservative and polished. In other countries — France and Italy, for example — greater personal style within the uniform is tolerated and appreciated. Women's clothing follows suit.

The Netherlands is an exception. The Netherlands is a famously egalitarian society, and this egalitarianism extends to business attire. Although you'll find plenty of conservative suits in some circles, you'll also find business casual up and down the hierarchy.

Greeting rituals

Handshakes are standard business-greeting gestures throughout Europe and usually are exchanged both before and after every meeting, no matter how many meetings you've already had. An exception is Great Britain, where (as in the United States) an initial handshake may be the only one you receive.

European handshakes are more formal and less buddy-buddy than those in the United States, with a quick grasp and release being the norm. In most European countries, handshakes are firm; an exception is France, where people prefer a lighter grasp. It's customary to let women and those of higher rank extend their hands first in Europe.

Europeans rarely use other people's first names immediately. Never assume that you'll immediately be on a familiar basis or that because the person you've just met is named Johann, you may call him that. Wait until he asks you to call him by his first name or uses a familiar form of address with you.

Titles, especially academic titles, are always used in Europe. In the United States, professors are rarely called "Doctor" or "Professor" outside the classroom, but in European countries, professors — along with lawyers, medical doctors, and other professionals — are introduced with their titles.

In Europe, the business card has a historical connection to the social card. As a result, the proper exchange of business cards at a meeting is significant. Most European businesspeople speak English, so your English business card probably will suffice for most places you'll go. You'll do yourself a real favor, however, by printing your business card in English on the front and in your host's native language on the back. Present the side printed in her language to your host. In countries such as France and Germany, any advanced academic titles you hold that are printed on your business card carry a certain cachet.

In some European countries, such as England, France, and Romania, business card etiquette is a bit more relaxed and involves little ceremony; however, business cards are exchanged frequently, so take a large supply.

The giving of business cards is typically done at the onset of a meeting, so the recipient will have something to refer to throughout the meeting. When you meet with several people, be sure to give your card to each person. Slighting any one person would be considered a faux pas.

Handling meetings

In general, meetings in the northern countries of Europe begin promptly, and the tone is businesslike, whereas meetings in the Mediterranean countries begin late and are prefaced by seemingly irrelevant banter. This banter is considered to be part of business, because it's the best opportunity for your host to get to know you — a prerequisite for business dealings in Mediterranean countries (and many other places, for that matter).

The fact that meetings in the Mediterranean countries typically begin late doesn't mean that you can arrive late; it means that your host typically will arrive late. Also, although your presentations should be precise, detailed, and logical everywhere, their reception will vary. In northern countries, you're unlikely to be interrupted. Don't expect the same elsewhere. Your beautiful presentations are likely to be interrupted regularly in Italy, Greece, Spain, Portugal, the Czech Republic, and the countries of the former Yugoslavia.

Dining and entertaining

Expect enormous variation when it comes to dining and entertaining in Europe. But one virtually universal practice exists: Europeans don't do business breakfasts.

Dining is taken seriously in most of Europe as an expression of generosity. In some countries, such as Italy and Greece, this generosity can reach stupefying levels; it can be virtually impossible to pick up a check in Italy and virtually impossible not to overeat or overdrink in Greece. Practically throughout all Europe, it's rude to refuse dinner invitations or any of the sumptuous items offered to you at a dinner. The Continental style of dining is used throughout most of Europe (see Chapter 12 for details).

In most of Europe, talking business over a meal isn't a violation of etiquette. In the Czech Republic, Italy, and Greece, however, you don't talk business over a meal unless your host initiates that discussion.

Giving and receiving gifts

Business and social gift-giving vary from country to country. In most countries, a small host gift is appropriate if you're invited to someone's home for dinner, but not in Great Britain, where no host gift is expected.

Across most of Europe, business gifts should not be too personal and should always be wrapped meticulously. Giving a gift unique to where you're from is appreciated; such gifts include a coffee table book about your state or city and local delicacies from home.

In some European countries, such as Belgium, France, Italy, Spain, Greece, and Portugal, you don't want to give a gift with your company logo, and it's best not to give a gift until after an agreement has been signed.

Social taboos

In many European countries, asking people what they do for a living or asking them a personal question as an opening conversational gambit is a serious mistake. Europeans are, for the most part, more formal and reserved about such matters than Americans are.

Watch out for these gesture-related mistakes:

- Showing your palm to someone is offensive in Greece.

- In Belgium, keeping your hands in your pockets when speaking to someone is considered rude.

- In England, never stare at anyone in public; privacy is highly regarded. Also, displaying a "V for victory" sign with your palm facing in is extremely offensive.

- ✔ Back-slapping is out of place in northern Europe.
- ✔ Having your hands below the table while dining is considered rude in most countries, especially France, Germany, and Austria.

Acting Appropriately in Africa

Parts of Africa have seen tremendous progress in recent years, especially in business growth. But as you find out in the following sections, Africa is immensely diverse, which can make business etiquette a little tricky.

General customs

Africa is so huge, so diverse, so complicated, and so rich that almost nothing can be said about shared etiquette across the continent. I can point out a few general customs, however:

- ✔ The northern countries bordering the Mediterranean are Islamic. The lavish generosity, indirect business discussions, expansive sense of time, and second-class-citizen status for women common to Arabic countries are common in these countries, too.

- ✔ In the countries with colonial pasts, inroads of European etiquette have occurred. Not surprisingly, these inroads follow the particular country's colonial affiliation. You'll see some English manners in Kenya and Nigeria, Dutch manners in various parts of South Africa, and Portuguese manners in Cape Verde.

- ✔ Soft handshakes are common across Africa. In countries with large post-colonial populations, such as Kenya and South Africa, expect European-style handshakes. In the Muslim countries of northern Africa, such as Morocco, you may find men holding handshakes so long that they become handholds. Don't be offended; this practice is common.

- ✔ *Conservative* is the keyword for business attire. In particularly hot countries, some easing up on the dark business suit is permitted. Your host won't be bound to Western dress, of course; he may show up in dressy traditional attire.

- ✔ Africans are justly famous for the pleasure they take in eating and entertaining and for their generosity. If you're invited to someone's home almost anywhere in Africa, be prepared: Your host will go all out to impress and please you.

In Muslim countries, don't eat with your left hand, which is symbolically tainted. Watch your hosts in other countries for similar taboos. When in doubt, do as your host does.

A multicultural mix: South Africa

South Africa is one of the most multicultural countries in the world. In addition to the indigenous black peoples of South Africa, colonialism and immigration have brought in white Europeans, Indians, Indo-Malays, Chinese, and many more. South Africa has been a political and economic success story since becoming a democracy. With a stable political system, South Africa is the financial, technological, and economic hub in Africa. In addition, South Africa's infrastructure, communications, and industries make it the leader in international trade in southern Africa.

Language

An estimated 2,000 languages are spoken in Africa. The languages of Africa are diverse and bear little relation to one another. South Africa alone has 11 official languages. The first is Afrikaans, which has its roots in 17th-century Dutch and has been influenced by languages such as English, German, Portuguese, Malay, French, and some African languages. However, even with 11 official languages, most businesspeople opt for English. English is the language of administration and is spoken throughout the country. South Africans often use metaphors and sports analogies to demonstrate a point.

Appropriate dress

In many companies in major South African cities, business attire has become more informal. For first meetings, however, dress conservatively. Women should wear business suits, dresses, or skirts with blouses and jackets; men should wear dark-colored, conservative suits.

Greeting rituals

You may encounter many greeting styles in South Africa, depending on the ethnic heritage of the people you meet. You can never go wrong by using last names and titles when you first meet someone; academic titles often add a great deal of luster. After you get to know someone well, switching to first names is appropriate.

When doing business with foreigners, most South Africans shake hands while maintaining eye contact and smiling. In South Africa, you can expect European-style handshakes from most businesspeople you meet. In general, handshakes between whites and whites, on the one hand, and whites and blacks, on the other, may differ. Although white people shake hands with another white person in much the same way as in northern Europe, whites and blacks shake hands with an additional flourish. After shaking the full hand, they grasp thumbs and then return to a full handshake.

Normally, women don't shake hands; they merely nod. Wait for a woman to extend her hand first, even in business settings.

Business cards are exchanged, but little or no ceremony is attached to the exchange. Reading the card slowly is considerate; don't rush to put it away.

Handling meetings

Major differences exist in communication styles, depending on each individual's cultural heritage. For the most part, it's important to maintain a harmonious working relationship and avoid confrontations. Most South Africans, regardless of ethnicity, prefer face-to-face meetings to more impersonal media such as e-mail messages, letters, and telephone calls.

Appointments are necessary and should be made as far in advance as possible. Scheduling meetings with senior-level managers on short notice is difficult, although you may be able to do so with lower-level managers. A more formal introduction will help you gain access to decision-makers.

Networking and building a relationship are crucial for long-term business success. Developing mutual trust before negotiating is imperative. The initial meeting often is used to establish personal rapport and to determine whether you're trustworthy. Deadlines often are viewed as fluid suggestions rather than firm commitments. Always follow up with a letter summarizing the meeting and the next steps.

Interrupting a South African while she's speaking is considered rude.

Dining and entertaining

A majority of business in South Africa is done while dining out, either at a restaurant or in someone's home. Expect to discuss business before the meal starts or at the conclusion of a meeting. Always arrive on time if you're invited out to eat, especially in someone's home.

You can eat many meals with your hands; it's important to use only the right hand. If you're dining from a communal dish, eat only from the side immediately in front of you.

Giving and receiving gifts

Business gift-giving isn't as common in South Africa as in Asian countries. If you're invited to a colleague's home, however, bring flowers, good-quality chocolates, or a bottle of good South African wine. Personalized office accessories with the recipient's company name and logo are appreciated. Gifts normally are opened when they are received.

Social taboos

Africans, as a rule, are religious, reserved people. Women should always dress conservatively, even if they're attending an evening event. Wearing revealing clothing is disrespectful.

Showing Respect in the Middle East

The Middle East is a region in which religion plays a significant cultural and social role. The dominant religions are Judaism in Israel and Islam in countries such as Egypt, Syria, Lebanon, Afghanistan, Kuwait, Syria, Saudi Arabia, United Arab Emirates, Oman, Yemen, and Jordan. Some Christians live in Turkey and Israel.

Because religion is so much a part of daily life in most Muslim countries, you can expect certain differences — some mundane, some extraordinary. Among them: Neither alcohol nor pork is consumed; the workweek in most Muslim countries runs from Sunday to Wednesday or Thursday morning; and prayers are said five times a day, during which time business stops. But the most extraordinary difference is the rigid separation of men and women in the vast majority of Muslim countries (Bahrain, Kuwait, and Oman being exceptions). In Arabic countries in particular, women rarely go out in public, and when they do, they're heavily veiled.

The countries of the Middle East have experienced a couple of decades with relatively little economic progress, and wealth is distributed unevenly among the countries, with United Arab Emirates and Israel offering the highest living standards for their entire populations, and Sudan and Yemen offering the greatest economic problems for their entire populations.

Language

Several languages are spoken in the Middle East. Two hundred million people speak Arabic in more than 22 countries, though the language varies from country to country. English is widely used in business throughout the Middle East and as the second language in most schools. Other languages include Turkish, Farsi, Urdu, and Hebrew.

Appropriate dress

In Israel, business casual is acceptable in a wide range of businesses. In Turkey and Arabic countries, go conservative, with dark suits and subdued ties. Businesswomen still have a hard time in the Middle East, in Saudi Arabia in particular, although less so now than ten years ago. Women must keep their knees and elbows covered at all times; a high neckline is required. Men shouldn't wear any visible jewelry, especially around the neck.

Greeting rituals

Business and personal greetings are given enthusiastically, with a smile and direct eye contact. Men shake hands and kiss each other on the cheek.

Among Jews, handshakes are standard greetings. Among Arabs, hugs and kisses are standard. If you're not Arab, you may get a handshake, but it's less like a handshake than it is a handhold, usually with both hands. Don't get nervous, and don't move away; Arab men often hold hands as a gesture of friendship. In business, men do shake hands with women; however, it's recommended to wait for a man to offer his hand. Muslims greet each other with *"Assalaam Alaikum,"* meaning "May peace be upon you and may God's blessings be with you." Learning and using a few Arabic greetings is polite.

Titles in the Middle East are important. Always use full names and all appropriate titles upon your first meeting; however, Arab people are fairly informal with names and normally address people by their first names, even in business. Use the honorific "Mister" and any academic or political title and the first name. Arab titles are *"Sheikh"* (an elderly man, leader, or scholar), *"Sayyid"* (a descendant of the Prophet Muhammad), and *"Hajji"* (one who has performed the pilgrimage).

Expect to exchange business cards with everyone. In Arab countries, it's polite and expected that your business card will be English on one side and Arabic on the other. Present your card Arabic side up. In Israel, real engraved business cards are preferred to printed ones. Raised-letter cards are less impressive. Always present and receive business cards with two hands, facing the person to whom you're giving a card, and make a point of studying the card before putting it into a business card holder.

Handling meetings

Morning meetings generally are preferred in the Middle East, and appointments are necessary; normally, business meetings aren't scheduled until you have arrived in the country. Be aware of religious holidays before scheduling meetings, and in Muslim countries, don't request meetings on Friday, which is a day of rest.

Meetings can be long, chaotic, and even pointless to an American sensibility. Interruptions (such as phone calls and people entering the room) are commonplace, and you'll have to refocus people back to the topic repeatedly. In Turkey and Israel, punctuality is prized, and meetings typically start on time. But "meeting time" is a rather loose term in Saudi Arabia, where you may wait an hour or more before your host appears.

When he (or, in Israel, perhaps she) arrives, you will begin with banter and conversation centered not on business but on many other topics. When you get down to business, you may be overwhelmed by the amount of argument and haggling. In Arab countries, you not only hear lots of discussion, but also many conversations occurring at the same time. Be patient. People in the Middle East love to talk, discuss, wrangle, and argue. If no decision is made on the spot, don't be disturbed. The decision will come later — sometimes weeks or months later.

The decision-maker in a meeting is most likely the person who's speaking the least (or who, at times, is only an observer).

Following are some general rules for meetings:

- ✔ Never say "no" directly; doing so causes shame. Find other ways to express disagreement.
- ✔ Age is important in Turkey. Defer to the oldest person.
- ✔ Decisions are reached slowly, so don't rush things; if you do, you'll give offense and risk your business relationship.

Dining and entertaining

Across the Middle East, hospitality is a means of demonstrating generosity, power, and wealth. As a result, Jewish and Arab hospitality sometimes appears extravagant to Americans. Accept the inevitable, and enjoy the prodigious feast to which you'll be invited.

Here are some tips for dining in Muslim countries:

- ✔ Meals are often served family-style. If a meal is served on the floor, you should sit cross-legged or kneel on one knee.
- ✔ It's polite to try a bit of everything that's served.
- ✔ Eat only with your right hand. Eating with your left hand is symbolically dirty.
- ✔ When you're finished drinking a cup of coffee or tea, turn the cup handle away from you to show that you don't want another serving.
- ✔ It's common for the person extending the invitation to pay. The invitee may decline the offer at first to be polite.

Giving and receiving gifts

Gift-giving is common in Middle Eastern culture, though gift-giving isn't the norm in Saudi Arabia unless you're invited to someone's home; then it's appropriate to take something small. Always reciprocate a gift with equal quality and value. Acceptable gifts are high-quality office accessories or gifts of silver, porcelain, and crystal.

In Jewish homes, a gift of flowers to the host is preferred, but gifts to the host are frowned on in Muslim homes.

Under no circumstances should you give a Muslim a gift of alcohol, a picture of anyone or any animal, or anything made from pigs. Never give a gift to the wife of an Arab colleague.

Social taboos

Here are some major social taboos in the Middle East:

- In most of the Middle East, it's bad manners for an outsider to discuss politics or religion. Don't ask personal questions about spouses and family, and never ask an Arab colleague about his wife or daughter.
- Crossing your legs and showing the soles of your shoes or feet are considered rude, as is openly disagreeing with someone, in Arab countries.
- Publicly holding hands with or kissing any member of the opposite sex is offensive.
- Under no circumstances should you slap anyone on the back or point at him with your finger.
- Refrain from looking at your watch when you're speaking with business-people; doing so is a sign of disrespect.
- The thumbs-up sign is rude in Muslim countries.

Behaving Gracefully in India

India is officially called the Republic of India, Hindi, or Bharat. It is the seventh-largest country geographically and the second-most populous country in the world.

India is composed of a multitude of religious cultures. The dominant religion is Hinduism, but significant numbers of Muslims, Buddhists, Sikhs, Jains,

Jews, and Christians also live in India. Onto this religious diversity is grafted a layer of British formality and good manners, resulting in a population that is as polite as it is distinctive.

In such a complex, diverse country as India, you must consider certain important factors when you're doing business — among them regionalism, religion, language, and caste. You may need to modify your behavior and approach depending on the person you are doing business with. You absolutely must research the cultures you expect to encounter so as to avoid making a major gaffe. You can't rely on logic or wing it.

Hierarchy plays a key role in the Indian business culture. Indians are sustained by extended family connections, which are maintained by socializing and mutual help. People in the United States aren't used to being so mindful of family hierarchy and ties, so they may underestimate the function and importance of those ties to people in India. Family matters may limit or expand an Indian person's field of action at any time. A family issue, for example, may take precedence over work.

For details and guidelines on doing business in India, I highly recommend *Doing Business in India For Dummies,* by Ranjini Manian (Wiley).

Language

Hindi is an official language of India. Many states have their own official languages, so Hindi might be less prevalent, especially in Southern India. English is the language of international commerce, but be aware of the differences. Indian English is more akin to European than to American English, which can create confusion.

In some parts of India, language can be a sensitive issue, so sticking to English is the safest bet, although learning some words in the language of your hosts and contacts is always appreciated and admired.

The Indian cultural values of harmony and of being agreeable at all costs translate into the inability to say "no" directly. For people who are direct and like to know where they stand, this linguistic pattern is most frustrating. Westerners' bluntness, impatience, and meaning of "no" can be harsh and blankly negative. On the other hand, the Indian "no" really means "maybe."

When you're conversing with someone from India, be aware of body language, especially nodding, which can be very confusing if you don't understand the meaning. People in the West nod to mean "yes." The same movement for Indians can mean "maybe" or "no." The shaking of the head from side to side, as in a figure eight, more often signifies a "yes."

Appropriate dress

Men should wear dark-colored, conservative, lightweight business suits for formal events and first meetings. Women should dress conservatively and modestly, wearing lightweight suits, skirts and jackets, or dresses; hems should be below the knee, and necklines should be conservative.

If the weather is very hot and humid, attire can be more casual. This means a long-sleeved shirt and a tie for a man, with long pants but no jacket. For women, a blouse with a light cotton skirt or slacks or a dress is acceptable.

In certain contexts, such as the high-tech and movie industries, dress is more informal, with people wearing tidy pressed jeans, T-shirts, and sports shoes. Casual dress is worn at informal social gatherings.

Because the cow is considered a sacred animal in India, leather belts or hand-bags shouldn't be used in general, though this prohibition isn't as strict in the business sector.

Greeting rituals

In general, Indians are formal on first meeting. Elders are respected and deferred to in many situations, business ones included. Caste rankings still play a role in a wide variety of social and business interactions, although they're not as pervasive as they previously were.

Handshakes between Indians and Westerners, women included, are the norm for most cosmopolitan areas. In areas of the country where religious traditions are still strong, however, Indian men may only put their hands together and make a slight bow to a woman. You may see one Indian bow slightly to another; that bow is a show of respect for age or for higher rank.

You can use the Hindi greeting throughout India. To do this, simply hold your palms together in front of your chest and say, *"Namaste"* (nah-mas-tay) or *"Namaskar"* (nah-mas-kar), with a slight bow. All Indian communities also have their own non-Hindi greetings of blessings and goodwill. Muslims say *"Assalaam Alaikum,"* to which you reply by saying, *"Wa alekum-Salaam,"* and Sikhs traditionally greet one another by saying *"Sat-Sri-Akal."*

The native language in southern India (such as Chennai and Bangalore) is Tamal. Learning a few words in this language will go a long way in winning new friends fast.

Use last names upon meeting people for the first time, and mention any higher academic or other titles. In the south, both Hindu and Muslim names identify a person first by given name, then "son of" or "daughter of," followed by the father's name. Northern Indian names (usually Hindu) have a surname and a given name. A married Hindu woman may drop her father's name behind hers and add her husband's first name instead. Sikhs collectively use the name Singh, used as a surname or between the first name and the surname.

India is so linguistically diverse, and English is so widespread, that you don't need to translate your business card into Hindi. If you're dealing with a focused group that doesn't speak English well, however, by all means translate your card into the language that the group uses. Indians publicly acknowledge academic degrees as well as any honors, so do add to your business card any degrees you have.

Business cards should be exchanged at first meeting and are presented without great ceremony. Be sure to present your card with your right hand. It's considered rude to put away a card you receive without exhibiting the courtesy of reading it (and thus acknowledging the giver). Take time to read any card given to you, and acknowledge the person's name and position by repeating it. Because Indian names can be difficult to pronounce, it's fine to ask whether you're saying the name correctly.

Handling meetings

Meetings should be scheduled at least two to three weeks in advance. Punctuality normally is expected, though being 10 to 15 minutes late won't have negative consequences; people in India have a tendency to be a little late. Family responsibilities take precedence over business, so last-minute cancellations are possible in business. Keep an open mind, and be flexible.

Indians of all religious backgrounds are wonderful speakers and take great pleasure in discussing their beliefs eloquently. Business is no different; you can expect a great deal of discussion of the details of a business deal. Negotiations can be slow until a business relationship has been built. Indians don't base their business decisions solely on data and statistics; they also use faith and intuition as guides.

Dining and entertaining

Business lunches are common, and it's perfectly appropriate to discuss business during lunch. Dinners at Indian homes are bounteous and delicious, and contrary to people in most other cultures, Indians consider it rude to show up on time! But you should be no more than 30 minutes late, either.

Most food is vegetarian. Hindus don't eat beef, and Muslims don't eat pork, so these aren't Indian specialty dishes. Don't ask for them if they're not on the menu. Even if beef and pork are on the menu, it's best not to request them if your business colleagues are vegetarians.

Meals throughout India are eaten with the right hand. When you eat, do so without using your left hand; as in Muslim countries, the left hand is symbolically unclean. If serving utensils are provided, you may use them with your left hand to serve yourself, but still avoid eating with the left hand. Eating correctly with your fingers involves a very specific etiquette, so I highly recommend that you do a little research on the Internet or purchase a book on etiquette in India and read up on the proper techniques; in a pinch, ask an Indian colleague for a few pointers. Then practice.

Many restaurants add a service fee to the bill, so you don't need to tip. Be sure to score through the gratuity line on your credit card so that you don't end up doubling on a tip.

Giving and receiving gifts

People in Western cultures try to counter materialism by saying, "It's not the value of the gift, but the thought that counts." Indians feel the same way. Many Indians believe that giving gifts helps one's path into the next life. For this reason, gifts don't have to be costly or large. Here are a few tips:

- Red, green, and yellow are lucky colors and good for wrappings. Black or white wrappings are for funerals.
- Don't give plumeria or white flowers, as they are used at funerals.
- Alcohol isn't an appropriate gift unless you know the person or business colleague well.
- Present your gift with both hands.
- Normally, you don't open gifts in front of the giver. The recipient of your gift will give you the same respect and not open your gift until later.

Social taboos

Here are some of the most general social taboos in India:

- The head is considered the seat of the soul. Never touch someone else's head, not even to pat a child's hair.
- Never point your feet at a person. Feet are considered unclean. If your shoes or feet touch another person, apologize.

✔ The right hand usually is used for cash transactions because it's considered auspicious; you also use it for giving business cards. Don't use both hands, as you would in China and Japan (which I cover later in this chapter).

✔ Indians don't show physical affection in public. Actor Richard Gere behaved inappropriately in 2007 when he spontaneously kissed an Indian actress during a public event; all India was in an uproar.

Adhering to Traditions in Asia

Asian countries often have radically distinct cultures with radically different etiquette. For Asia, more than any other region, it's best to consult country-specific books. Some similarities do exist, however.

The Pacific Rim countries — China, the Koreas, Japan, and Vietnam — have ancient cultures that are heavily influenced by the social and political views of the Chinese sage Confucius. Even where Confucianism isn't official state philosophy, many of its tenets are so deeply ingrained in the character and comportment of people that it serves as the basis of behavior.

Confucianism is an entire worldview — part philosophy, part religion, part etiquette manual, part political template, part economic treatise. It emphasizes respect for superiors, piety toward elders, love of family, duty to one's immediate society (village, town, and region), loyalty to friends and family, hard work, wisdom, courage, humility, and unfailing courtesy to all. The person who can embody these characteristics is a person of *jen* — the Confucian superior man.

You're less likely to be viewed as a jingoistic American if you recognize that some cultural traditions of the Pacific Rim countries are more than 2,000 years old and are sedimented so deeply into an Asian person's behavior as to be almost involuntary, like eye color.

In the following sections, I discuss the business etiquette rules in two Asian countries that are major business partners with the United States: China and Japan. Here are a few tips, though, that apply to countries throughout Asia:

✔ Additional deference to elders is expected. Never interrupt the senior member of the delegation.

✔ Always wait for a woman to initiate a handshake.

✔ Don't try to hurry any meeting. A meeting takes as long as it takes, and you can't do anything to change that.

✔ Business gifts are considered symbols of appreciation, and generosity is viewed as a valued personal trait.

An important destination: Mainland China

China is the world's second fastest-growing economy and one of the United States' largest trading partners. Economists predict this growth to continue — making the trade relationship increasingly central for both the United States and China. However, language, cultural, and political differences present significant challenges when doing business in China. For successful business transactions, it's imperative to make an effort to understand and respect the culture while building a relationship of trust.

For more on how to navigate China's business culture, see *Doing Business in China For Dummies* by Robert Collins and Carson Block (Wiley).

Language

The varieties of the Chinese language belong to the Sino-Tibetan family of languages. Each language has its own subdialects and dialects. More people (more than one billion) speak Mandarin than any other language. It's the main language of China's media, government, and educational institutions. In Hong Kong and Macau, however, very few people speak Mandarin; instead, they use English and other varieties of Chinese. More than 70 million people speak Wú in Zhejiang and Jiangsu provinces, in Shanghai, and in Hong Kong. More than 60 million people speak Cantonese, mostly in Guangdong and Guangxi provinces, on Hainan Island, and in Hong Kong and Macau.

Appropriate dress

Your default business wardrobe in China is conservative business dress, with suits, ties, and tie-up shoes for men, and conservative suits and dresses for women. Avoid flashiness of any kind.

Greeting rituals

Business greetings in China are easy; they're the same as those in the United States. You stand up, make a formal introduction, and remain standing during the process of introductions. It may be difficult to tell who the senior person is, so be very polite and forthcoming to everyone you meet.

Greet your Chinese contacts with a short nod or small bow. Many of them will offer to shake hands, but they won't give the robust handshake that Americans associate with confidence and integrity. This fact has nothing to do with being a wimp; it has to do with being respectful. Strong rules of respect forbid much physical contact between strangers.

A Chinese surname comes first, followed by a given name. The two names may be the same, however, as in Wei Wei; they may be hyphenated or joined, such as Yi-Yen or Yiyen. Some people use an English first name that's easier for foreigners to understand.

Traditionally, a married woman keeps the use of her maiden name. You know she's married through the use of the word "Madame" in front of her full name. However, on formal occasions, women have been known to use their husbands' names and then their maiden names, with or without their given names (for example, Mrs. Wang Hu). A woman also may just use her husband's name without her maiden name following, as influenced by the British in Hong Kong.

People get offended if someone consistently mispronounces their name. Even worse, you may innocently be calling a person a rude word and making him lose face in front of his own people.

It's prudent to politely ask a person which name is his family name. It's also good to confirm how people would like to be addressed, as many people like to be addressed with their business title. Government titles (such as chairman, general manager, or committee member) are important; use them when you address officials.

I cannot emphasize Chinese business-card etiquette enough. Make it a ritual: You're *presenting* your business card, not *handing it out.* Tossing your card, dealing cards like a bank teller, or displaying a casual attitude (such as placing a pile of your cards on a table and inviting people to take one) is disrespectful and will be noted.

You must give and receive a business card with both hands, with the writing up and facing the recipient. This is a formal ritual in China and most of Asia, so approach it with decorum.

Find out how your name would be pronounced phonetically in Chinese, and have it printed on your card or on a name tag for your lapel, if appropriate. Your card should have the information printed in Chinese on one side, even in gold ink. You should have this side facing up when you present the card.

Never write on a business card, which is considered an insult because it defaces the card. Also, under no circumstances should you put your counterpart's business card in your wallet and then put your wallet in your back pocket.

Handling meetings

In China, the beginning of the meeting follows a definite pattern. The top person from your host's country comes in at an appointed position in the flow of people. Normally, meetings have a brief prelude during which people get to know one another.

Some of your junior Chinese business associates will arrive early. You don't have to start the meeting ahead of time; they are there in case you need them for anything.

In virtually all Asian countries (China included), the conduct of the meeting is fairly structured. Enthusiastic sales jobs are out of place. Speak slowly and precisely, and give your host every opportunity to participate. Avoid saying "no" directly. Plenty of qualifiers are available for you to use; emulate the way your hosts disagree without disagreeing.

A written agreement isn't as important to a Chinese businessperson as the solidarity of his relationship with you. Chinese interpret rules in the context of your *quan xi* — that is, the quality and integrity of your relationship.

Dining and entertaining

Though business lunches are quite common, the events that occur after work are famous. You'll find that Asians in general love to entertain in restaurants and bars, and that the food is exquisitely flavored, prepared, and presented.

In China, expect a banquet — a long meal with innumerable courses served one after the other. Arrive on time, and get ready to eat. Try something from every serving dish, even if it's only a little amount, but never clean your plate. Symbolically, the meal's munificence means that you can't finish it.

Always offer food and drink to others before serving yourself, and don't take the last piece of food from the serving plate.

It's best to keep an open mind about food. If you're sensitive about what foods you eat, stick to dishes you know. Chinese don't always like Western food, so you may find yourself dining at many Chinese restaurants.

In the past, tipping was frowned on in communist China, and to some degree, it's still not accepted as part of Chinese culture. It's becoming more common, though, especially in large cities like Hong Kong and Shanghai, and in many Westernized hotels.

Giving and receiving gifts

Sometimes, you go to great efforts to prepare for your trip and forget to apply some thought to the gifts you'll give. You could arrive with a suitcase full of the wrong types of gifts, such as nice travel clocks with your company logo. Everyone can use a nice clock, right? Wrong!

Gift-giving in China and many Asian countries extends far beyond a gift to your host. In most Asian countries, gifts of some kind are appropriate even for a meeting. In Chinese culture, some people believe that certain numbers have significant meanings. For example, anything with the number 8 is a welcomed gift; the word for "eight" in Chinese is similar to the word for "prosper," "wealth," or "fortune." Other appropriate gifts are fine wine, liqueur (such as cognac), or whiskey; high-quality office accessories; lighters, if you know the recipients smoke; and technology gadgets.

Some gifts are considered offensive and should not be given in China, including the following:

- White flowers and chrysanthemums
- Straw sandals
- Depictions of storks or cranes
- Scissors, knives, or other sharp objects that imply the severing of a relationship
- Items that are white, blue, or black
- Clocks, which signify that one must prepare a funeral for an ancestor or dead person
- Cheese, which few Chinese eat

In addition, giving a gift with your company logo ensures that the gift won't be seen as a bribe but more as a form of advertising.

For gift wrapping, plain red is the best color to use, but pink, gold, and silver will do. Forgo yellow-and-black, plain black, or plain white paper. Have the gift wrapped locally, if you can; the shop will know the optimum colors, or do your research ahead of time and pack wrappings separately to use in your hotel room.

Present your gift with both hands and a low bow, murmuring, "This is a little something for you" or "A small token of appreciation."

Be ready to accept a gift from your host as well. In most cases, these gifts will be professional gifts. In China, politely refuse a gift at first and then accept it graciously.

Social taboos

Here are some of the most general taboos in China:

- Both men and women should keep their feet on the floor, not hooked under their chairs or crossed.
- Expansive hand movements are annoying and distracting to the Chinese sensibility.
- Being too talkative or too loud makes you seem undisciplined and undignified. To Chinese people, controlling one's emotion is polite, so as not to involve someone else in one's own turmoil.
- Don't be too "bubbly" and familiar, as in placing an arm around someone's shoulders or even patting her lightly on the shoulder, asking someone to call you by your first name, or calling someone "Comrade" (even if the Chinese do it among themselves).

- Don't put your hand in your mouth to dislodge food.
- Don't point when speaking.
- Stay calm if you're angry (with a waiter who spills food or drinks, for example, or an underling at work), in conflict, or experiencing a setback. Remember, only children cannot keep themselves in check; adults are supposed to be dignified.

The importance of dignity: Japan

In most countries, basic manners still apply, but in countries such as Japan, the customs are so strict that a simple mistake can cost you not only the deal, but also your dignity. The major religion is Shinto ("the way of the gods") and is woven into everything the Japanese do.

Language

The majority of the country speaks Japanese. You should use the language of your client in doing business. If you don't know Japanese, learn phrases like "Hello, my name is," "Nice to have met you," "Goodbye," "Thank you," "Please," "Excuse me," and "I'm sorry."

If you're fluent in Japanese and English, you should speak the language of the higher-ranked member. If you're using an interpreter or trying out Japanese, speak slowly and clearly, without using colloquialisms.

Saying "yes" is done with a nod. Saying "no" is done by placing a hand in front of the face and waving it back and forth. There is no word for "no" in Japanese.

Appropriate dress

Appropriate dress is a level above how Americans probably dress for work. Japanese business professionals are very careful in the way they dress, which is on the conservative side. Men should wear well-pressed dark blue or black suits and ties; businesswomen should also dress conservatively. Every item must be clean and in neat and good condition. No wrinkled clothing allowed!

You will encounter many opportunities to remove your shoes, so make sure that your socks or nylons are holeless, and have at least one pair of shoes that are tieless. Scruffy shoes aren't acceptable.

Greeting rituals

Most Japanese businesspeople shake hands and bow when greeting you. When you bow, the degree is as important as the action:

- ✔ The 45-degree bow, with palms in front of your knees, is offered to only the most senior members.

- ✔ The 30-degree bow, with legs straight and hands at your sides, is the most common.

- ✔ The informal bow, which is the quick bowing of only the head and shoulders, is used before you shake hands if your Japanese counterpart extends his hand.

Allow your Japanese colleagues to lead the way. If they shake hands first and then bow, you follow suit. Women normally don't shake hands, especially in social greetings, though today, this rule is changing among younger generations and in business.

Using titles and last names is important. In Japanese, the family name precedes the personal one. Yamaguchi Kazuo-san, for example, would be Mr. Kazuo Yamaguchi in English.

Dropping the *san* from a person's name is impolite. Simply refer to a person as Mr. Yamaguchi-san, and you'll be correct.

Business cards and their presentation are extremely important to the Japanese. Not only is there a ceremony around presenting them, but also, the Japanese view business cards as gifts.

Have your business cards translated into Japanese on one side, and change your title if what you do isn't clear. "Assistant manager" means very little compared with "assistant to the president."

Exchanging business cards involves a specific protocol:

- ✔ Take your card out of a nice holder. Men should carry a holder in the breast pocket of a jacket, not in a pants pocket. Women should carry a holder in a purse or a briefcase.

- ✔ Present the card Japanese side up, between the thumb and forefingers of both hands, while bowing slightly. Your fingers shouldn't cover your name, company name, or logo.

- ✔ When receiving a card, take it between the thumbs and forefingers of both hands at the top of the card.

- ✔ When you're given a card, immediately thank the person who gave it. View the card carefully. The longer you look at the card, the more respect you are giving the person. It's also acceptable to ask for the pronunciation of the person's name and to make a nice comment about the card.

- ✔ Never put the card away immediately. Putting it in a separate section of your card case is fine, but don't put away the case right away.

- If you are seated while a card is given to you, it's most polite to leave the card on the table until the meeting is over.

- It's impolite to write on a business card in the presence of the owner or to slip it into a pocket, especially a back pocket.

Handling meetings

Japanese interactions involve a heightened sense of formality. When you're doing business in Japan, your suitability with respect to conducting business will be assessed during a first meeting, so always maintain a sense of professionalism.

Business meetings usually take place for only one of three reasons: to build rapport, exchange information, or confirm previously made decisions. Decisions are rarely made in a meeting.

It's important to recognize that Japanese business society is group oriented. You'll always deal with a team as opposed to an individual. Each attendee will have a particular area of expertise, so either bring assistance or be sure that you're confident enough to handle all the questions you will receive.

The Japanese are very detail oriented. Expect lots of questions, repeated in different ways. Be sure to have the answers available, as failure to answer looks unprofessional. Bring as much written information on your company, service, product, or proposal as possible.

If you're meeting over a meal, wait until the meal is finished before initiating any serious talk of business. A few documents can go on top of the table, including a laptop computer, but only in a less formal restaurant. If it's necessary to have a number of documents and laptops, it's best to request a private dining area or private room.

Dining and entertaining

In Japan, business entertaining usually occurs after hours and rarely in the home. You'll be entertained often and many times with little notice. Be a gracious guest and enthusiastic while eating, and show great appreciation afterward.

Eating in Japan is simple and practical. Chopsticks are used as spoon, fork, and knife; toothpicks are supplied and used ceremoniously by men. As in most Asian cultures, chopsticks are used daily with each meal. Japanese food, such as sushi and sashimi, normally is cut into bite-size pieces so it can be eaten with chopsticks easily. There is a technique to using chopsticks, but you can master it easily with just a little practice (see Chapter 12 for tips).

Giving and receiving gifts

Gift-giving in Japan is deeply rooted in Japanese culture. It's important both socially and in business. Always bring gifts for new and old contacts. These gifts should be indicative of your rank with your company; the higher your rank, the higher quality of the gift. Don't give monetary gifts or gifts displaying company logos, though office accessories such as a good-quality pen are suitable. Wrappings should be natural paper with no paper ribbons. Use red and white for happy occasions, black and white for funerals, and gold and silver or gold and red for weddings. When you visit a home, bring candy, fruit, cake, cookies, or other specialty foods.

As with business cards and other rituals, presenting your gift properly is expected. Gifts are offered with both hands. Normally, the gift is set aside to be opened later. It isn't customary to urge the recipient to open it.

Social taboos

Be sure to avoid these taboos in Japan:

- ✔ Unless you know a person well, telling jokes and discussing private matters (such as spouse or children) is rude unless the other person offers first.

- ✔ Don't cross your arms when speaking or listening to someone.

- ✔ Avoid using American slang at all costs.

- ✔ When dining, never point, gesture, talk with your chopsticks waving in the air, or take food from another person's plate with your chopsticks.

Doing Business in Australia and New Zealand

Australia and New Zealand are separate countries, each with its own distinct national identity that includes particular customs and rules of etiquette:

- ✔ Australia is a casual country, and its people are friendly and open. You find overt formality in only the most rarified circles in Melbourne and a few other cities.

- ✔ New Zealand, on the other hand, is more like Great Britain, with greater formality and less instantaneous camaraderie.

Language

English is the official language of Australia; however, Australians' colorful vocabulary, accent, and slang can take a lot of getting used to. The two official languages of New Zealand are English and Maori. English is the language of day-to-day business within New Zealand — a remnant of ties to the British Commonwealth.

New Zealanders take great pride in their proficiency in the English language and hold anyone who also does so in high esteem. They are less forgiving of mistakes in spelling, grammar, and syntax made by Americans, Canadians, and Australians (other than those whose first language isn't English).

Appropriate dress

Men wear a conservative dark business suit, white or colored dress shirt, and tie. Always try to be tasteful and stylish, and lean toward the conservative. Women are advised to dress simply but elegantly, wearing a dress or a skirt and blouse for business.

Informal clothing is appropriate for working in the information-technology sector. Casual pants are fine for both men and women in this area.

Greeting rituals

Greetings are casual, often consisting simply of a handshake and a smile. Australian and New Zealander handshakes are firm and quick. Giving someone a limp handshake is referred to as giving someone a "dead fish," so keep it firm. Don't grasp the other person's hand with both of yours, and don't keep shaking. Women typically don't shake hands with one another in Australia but typically do in New Zealand. In both countries, women are expected to extend their hands to men first.

Australians and New Zealanders dislike pretense. Although you should call someone by his last name when you first meet him, this practice won't last long — especially in Australia, as you'll probably soon be invited to call your host by his first name. New Zealanders are more reserved when you first meet them, but they, too, will warm to you quickly. Announcing your title when you meet is offensive because it's perceived as showing off.

Business cards are exchanged, but little or no ceremony is attached to the exchange.

Handling meetings

Meetings start on time and get to the point at hand without many preliminaries in both countries. In fact, in New Zealand, arriving a few minutes early is polite. Business is conducted with respect, honesty, directness, and a trace of a sense of humor, but avoid showing strong emotions. Even though meetings generally are relaxed, they are considered serious matters. A brief amount of small talk is common.

If you make a presentation, keep it simple. Avoid making exaggerated claims and adding a bunch of bells and whistles.

Dining and entertaining

Lunch can be a business affair, but both the near-obligatory call at the pub and dinners are social events. Arrive on time in Australia and New Zealand.

Table manners are Continental style, with meals often served family style. Although both Australians and New Zealanders typically are casual in their manners, follow proper protocol on more formal occasions.

Meeting for tea is common. Afternoon tea is around 4 or between 6 and 8 p.m. and is an evening meal.

Giving and receiving gifts

Bringing a bottle of Australian wine, a box of chocolates, a book about one's home country, or some other small item to your host's dinner party is expected. Don't bring anything lavish, however. Recipients customarily open gifts when they're presented.

Social taboos

Being overly demonstrative with another man is a taboo for men in Australia and New Zealand. Also, trying your hand at saying "G'day, mate" is more likely to result in offense than anything else. The "V for victory" sign is given palm out; given palm in, it is offensive.

Certain national sensitivities are particular to New Zealanders. The term *mainland* isn't used for either the North or South islands of New Zealand; neither is it used to refer to Australia.

Building Business Relationships in Latin America

Latin America stretches from the Texas border to the tip of Tierra del Fuego in South America. Latin America's Spanish- and Portuguese-speaking populations are predominantly Catholic; its native inhabitants are primarily non-Catholic. The culture is patriarchal, with rigid divisions between work and home life: Men are in business, and women are at home with the family. As a businesswoman traveling to many locations in Latin America, you should be aware up front that this insistence on strict gender roles can be jarring and may be directed at you sometimes.

Anyone going to Nicaragua, Guatemala, El Salvador, Colombia, Chile, or Peru should know enough about the current political climate to avoid discussions that could skewer business dealings. These countries have faced serious political upheaval in the past quarter-century, and even where the wars are over, the scars are very deep.

In most Latin countries (particularly Mexico), people prefer doing business with those they know, like, and trust. Therefore, your success depends on your ability to establish rapport and maintain good relationships. Interpersonal skills are necessary to fit in; these skills can actually be more important than professional experience and know-how.

Brazilians, because of their Portuguese roots, have a relatively relaxed approach to life and business. They view business as being like any other sort of social interaction and place much more focus on relationships and business decisions than on profit margins.

Language

Spanish is the primary language spoken in Latin America, where people are proud of their language and aren't particularly eager to use English. You do yourself a favor by knowing Spanish; if you don't, at least learn a few key words and phrases.

Unlike most Latin American countries, Brazil uses Portuguese as its official language. Like other languages, of course, Portuguese has variations. Though nearly all the population in Brazil speaks Portuguese, English is now studied in schools and has replaced French as the principal second language.

Many Brazilians also understand Spanish, because Portuguese has many components that are similar. Also, the neighboring countries all consider Spanish to be their first language, so speaking some Spanish is practically a necessity, especially in border areas.

Both verbal and written correspondence is more formal in Latin America than in the United States. Latin Americans believe that the use of elegant language shows good manners and professionalism.

Appropriate dress

You won't go wrong by dressing conservatively: suits and ties for men, modest business suits and long dresses for women. Argentina probably is the most formal of the Latin American countries, and Brazil is the least formal. Venezuelans enjoy expensive accessories so long as they're in good taste.

Greeting rituals

Latin Americans generally are very friendly, very physical, and very good hosts. Normally, people get to know one another first and then do business. In fact, you probably won't get any business accomplished during your first meeting, and you may not get much done on your first trip, but you'll stay up late for dinners and parties.

Handshakes are firm and relatively brief. Constant eye contact during a hand-shake is crucial in Mexico and Argentina. In most countries, men shake hands with men, and women shake hands with women. In Brazil, Peru, and Mexico, men and women also shake hands, with the woman extending her hand first. After a relationship has been established, don't be surprised if you're met with a hug.

Male friends hug each other upon seeing each other. Female friends kiss each other on each cheek and touch each other's arms. Throughout Latin America, expect your conversational partner to stand close to you, and expect casual arm touching or shoulder patting. Don't move back, and don't waver in your eye contact.

When you meet someone for the first time, use your last name and whatever titles you have. If you don't know the other person's professional titles, use Mr., Mrs., or Ms *(Señor, Señora,* or *Señorita).* Common professional titles are doctor, teacher, engineer, and lawyer *(doctor, professor, ingeniero,* and *abogado).*

In business situations, you can generally plan on addressing others by last names only. First names are reserved for close acquaintances and family. It's best to avoid using a first name until you're invited to do so.

Latin American surnames are composed of both the paternal name, which comes first, and the maternal name. Only the father's surname is used when addressing someone. Be careful which name you choose to use, as the Spanish and Portuguese cultures are opposite.

Business cards are exchanged without much ceremony; presenting your card properly in American style will do (see Chapter 5). Your business card should be printed in both English and Spanish (or in Portuguese if you're in Brazil). Present your card with the Spanish or Portuguese side up.

Handling meetings

In some countries in Latin America, timekeeping can be a relaxed affair; meeting times are set but not respected. In Mexico, however, due to long-established business links with the United States, Mexicans are used to Western business-people being on time and try to do the same.

You're expected to arrive in a timely manner, but your host isn't, and the more important he is, the later he'll be. Meetings themselves follow the pattern of most Spanish-speaking countries, with lots of preliminary discussions designed to establish rapport. Business discussions occur only after rapport is established, and after they start, they're comparatively disorganized and subject to interruption. Decisions typically aren't made during first meetings.

Dining and entertaining

Business lunches are common throughout Latin America, and they're usually long, from 1 or 2 p.m. until 3 or 4 p.m. Dinner is a purely social event and can occur very late; it's not unusual to sit down to dinner at 10 or 11 p.m. throughout Latin America. Don't bring up business at dinner unless your Latin American host or guest does so first.

Because many different countries make up Latin America, dining styles and etiquette can differ by region. It's best to do a little research on your destination before you arrive. Generally, the Continental style of dining is used in business (see Chapter 12). It's not necessary to eat in the Continental style, though, if you're more comfortable using the American style. You should keep your hands above the table at all times while eating, and pass food and drink with your right hand.

Giving and receiving gifts

Gifts in most Latin American countries aren't expected on the first visit; however, gift-giving is more acceptable with subsequent visits and can help build stronger business relationships and friendships. Appropriate gifts include fine chocolates, a bottle of good wine or liquor (if you know the recipient drinks), business card holders, high-quality pens, or other office accessories. Flowers are a good choice when you visit someone's home; check with a local florist first for an appropriate bouquet to fit the occasion.

Venezuelans don't entertain at home very much. Being invited to someone's home is an unusual honor and shouldn't be taken lightly, so make sure that the host gift is something special.

Social taboos

Be aware that the following gestures can cause problems:

- ✔ The sign for "okay" formed by your forefinger and thumb is offensive in Brazil and Colombia.

- ✔ Don't cross your fingers (as a sign of good luck) in Paraguay; it denotes the act of sex.

- ✔ Putting your hands on your hips signals a challenge in Argentina.

- ✔ Putting your feet on a table is rude throughout Latin America.

- ✔ Raising your fist to head level is a gesture associated with communism in Chile. Also, slapping your right fist into your open left palm is viewed as an obscene gesture, and displaying your palm up with your fingers spread apart means "stupid."

- ✔ Putting your hands in your pockets is rude in Mexico.

Part VI
The Part of Tens

The 5th Wave   By Rich Tennant

"Very good answer! Now let me ask you another question..."

In this part . . .

If you're just looking for a few quick etiquette tips or a lesson or two, this part is for you! I first provide tried-and-true college-to-career tips to assist you in the transition from leaving school to beginning your job search. In this part, you also find ten interviewing-etiquette tips to help you feel relaxed and confident during the interview and make it easier for you to land that dream job.

Chapter 23

Nearly Ten College-to-Career Etiquette Tips

In This Chapter
▶ Transitioning from the dorm room to the boardroom
▶ Sharpening your newly acquired etiquette skills on the job

A re you about to graduate? How confident are you about your knowledge of Western business etiquette? Knowing the social graces in business can make or break your career, because no matter how brilliant a student or employee you may be, a lack of business protocol and social grace will hold you back in the corporate world. In a market that's growing more competitive every day, you certainly want to have every advantage. When you've followed the basic guidelines in this chapter, you can consider yourself to be a true professional.

A successful career doesn't come only to those who've worked longest or hardest or to those who have the most impressive résumés. These days, many corporations are unwilling to send people to the front lines unless they have a little polish, style, and finesse. A little finesse can give you a competitive edge over other applicants who may not be as polished as you are.

Start with Some Etiquette Research

For hands-on etiquette experience, graduating students need only to do a little research. You can find shelves of etiquette books, etiquette DVDs, and etiquette training companies across the United States. Check with your school to see what's available, and search the Internet for additional resources. For etiquette books and DVDs, go to www.amazon.com and search for the term *etiquette*. You also can check out www.etiquette survival.com for help.

Take an Etiquette Class

Consider attending an etiquette class before you graduate. In most large cities, you can find etiquette training and consulting businesses. Many college campus career centers also offer etiquette courses or workshops near graduation time.

Get Noticed with a Flawless Cover Letter and Résumé

Absolute accuracy in a cover letter and résumé is essential for making a positive impression on a potential employer. If your résumé contains glaring errors, potential employers will waste no time deleting it or throwing it out.

Writing a résumé and cover letter isn't an easy process. If necessary, hire a professional résumé service. Check your school's resources; most colleges have writing labs for additional assistance with cover letters and resumes. Also, try visiting a few job search Web sites such as www.monster.com and www.careerbuilder.com. Often these sites publish articles with practical advice that can help you with writing résumés and cover letters.

Present Yourself Professionally

Many people try to avoid passing judgment too quickly, but at first meetings, they inevitably assess other people by how they look. Ask yourself these questions:

- ✔ Does your work wardrobe help you present a confident, well-groomed image?
- ✔ Are the clothes suitable for the type of work you do (or want to do)?
- ✔ Do you have clothes that can take you from work to a social engagement?

Get a "college student to career professional" makeover. Try a new hairstylist, attend a wardrobe workshop, and have new makeup applied by a professional. Depending on the type of job you're interviewing for, you should conceal your tattoos and remove your body jewelry unless you know for certain that those adornments are acceptable to the employer. Build your business wardrobe as soon as possible, too. Fine apparel and accessories can be quite an investment, so shop wisely, and coordinate classic items for versatility.

See Chapter 4 for details on how to present yourself professionally.

Master the Art of Introductions

You may perform introductions all the time, but you may not realize that introductions create enduring impressions. Focus on these concepts:

- ✔ If a coworker or colleague isn't available to introduce you, it's proper to introduce yourself in business and social functions. Be sure to know the difference between a personal and business introduction.
- ✔ Find out the proper way to present and receive a business card.
- ✔ Don't forget to smile, and use good eye contact and a firm handshake.

Flip to Chapter 5 for full details on the art of meeting and greeting.

Communicate with Style and Confidence

Leave the slang phrases, jargon, and four-letter words in the dorm room. Trendy talk isn't appropriate in a professional setting or in the break room or cafeteria of your company. Master several ways to start conversations (Chapter 6 is a big help), and know how to end them gracefully. Always remember to listen more than you talk.

Experience the Magic of Networking

Attend career fairs while you're looking for a job, and network at special events even after you've scored a job. If you're interested in working overseas, you can make contacts and establish overseas networking by attending international exhibitions and conferences or by joining an international networking discussion group on the Internet. Networking events and groups can be fulfilling and produce results like these:

- ✔ Networking within your community increases your chances of finding publicized and unpublicized job openings. Mastering the art of networking can lead to solid employment referrals.

- Networking can provide ongoing support with business contacts.
- Networking can provide opportunities to develop your skills and knowledge in a specific industry as well as opportunities to share ideas.

Send a thank-you note to sources of new connections, and keep them informed of your progress. They may have a vested interest in your success and will probably want to support you as much as they can.

Chapter 13 has the scoop on networking at special events.

Make Yourself Clear on the Phone

Many times, the first contact you have with an individual is over the telephone, so the impression you make can be a lasting one. Therefore, you want to sound confident and professional — especially if the call is about a possible job. For complete details of how to make a positive impression on the phone, see Chapter 7.

Cultivate Contacts via E-Mail

Strive to communicate with colleagues from other countries who share your interests. If your company has offices internationally, check the employee directory and contact coworkers via e-mail. You also can search country-specific international job sites on the Internet (an excellent site is www. international-business-careers.com) or look for specific international companies that post job openings.

The rules that apply for e-mail communication at home are even more important when you're communicating with someone in another country. Here are some guidelines:

- Most cultures communicate in a more formal manner than people in the United States do, so use the proper title of individuals in your greetings.
- Avoid using slang terms or words that can take on double meanings.
- Consider the time difference and the day of the week before you send an e-mail. If you send an e-mail on Friday morning, it may be Saturday afternoon for the recipient. Or you may send an e-mail on a holiday that you weren't aware of and the recipient is off work.

Flip to Chapter 9 for more tips on e-mail etiquette.

Chapter 24

Ten Tips for Impressive Job Interviews

In This Chapter

▶ Preparing for an interview

▶ Sailing through an interview with flying colors

nterviews can be among the most challenging meetings you will ever have. Not only do you have to make certain that you're dressed appropriately, but you also must arrive on time, and you have to know what to say, when to say it, and what questions to ask. Being prepared will boost your confidence, and knowing how to behave should help calm your nerves and ease your anxiety. Heed the advice in this chapter, and you'll be on your way to the job you want! Flip to Chapter 2 for additional information on job interviews.

Do Your Homework on the Company

Get familiar with the overall company and the future it may hold for you. Test the products; research the company online by visiting its Web site, blogs, and press materials; and check out the company's ranking in the stock market, if applicable. Why is knowing all this stuff important? You'll be better prepared to answer questions and ask intelligent questions, which shows that you're well-informed and that you did your homework. It also shows that you have interest and enthusiasm in the company.

Practice Your Answers

It's a good idea to keep a log and draft your answers to the most commonly asked interview questions. These Web sites feature such questions:

- ✔ hotjobs.yahoo.com
- ✔ www.interviewup.com
- ✔ www.job-interview.net

Practice speaking the answers out loud into a tape recorder or to a friend or family member until your answers sound natural and not overly rehearsed.

Prepare questions of your own as well. Traditionally, at the conclusion of an interview, you have an opportunity to ask questions. Here are a few examples:

- ✔ "What are the opportunities your industry (or company) is facing?"
- ✔ "What are the challenges your industry is facing?"
- ✔ "Can you tell me the company's plans for future growth over the next few years?"
- ✔ "What have you found most rewarding about working at the company?"
- ✔ "How would you describe the corporate culture here?"

Dress the Part

Decide way in advance what you're going to wear. Conservative, tailored apparel usually is appropriate. Don't wear jewelry that makes noise (such as bangles or large earrings). In some cases, dress codes have relaxed, so check with others who know the company dress code to make sure that you aren't overdressed or underdressed (flip to Chapters 2 and 4 for ways to find out about company culture and appropriate dress). Your appearance makes or breaks what could be an enduring first impression.

Dress as though you already have the job. You may be interviewing for an entry-level job, but someday, you may want to run the place!

Arrive Early

Get accurate directions to the interview site. Make a dry-run trip to estimate the time you'll need to get to the interview on time. Plan where you park, what entrance to use, and where to go after you're in the building.

Being late is never acceptable! Arrive at least 10 to 15 minutes early.

Be polite to the people around you. A receptionist, security guard, or other employee can help you find the location quickly. Being overly friendly, however, can work against you if the other person is busy or not talkative.

Don't assume that the person who greets you is the receptionist. He may be a top executive or your interviewer.

Make a Lasting First Impression on the Interviewer

In first meetings, people may try to avoid passing judgment too quickly, but interviewers inevitably assess candidates on how they look and handle themselves. Here are a few tips to help you make that good first impression:

- ✔ Arrive with a smile. If you're seated, stand up to greet the interviewer by name, with a firm handshake and good eye contact.

- ✔ Confirm the pronunciation of the interviewer's name and her title in advance. Refer to the interviewer by her first name only if she gives you permission to do so.

- ✔ Do not chew gum, eat, or drink on the premises unless refreshments are provided, and sample them sparingly if they are available. Leave your own water bottle in your car.

- ✔ Tobacco use of any kind is not appropriate. If you do smoke, be sure to wash your hands and use a mouthwash or mints right before your interview so you're certain that there is no lingering cigarette odor.

Keep It Simple and Stay Focused

Here are some tips for keeping things simple and focused during an interview:

- ✔ Bring a nice notepad, crisp copies of your résumé, and a good pen.
- ✔ Don't fumble with a large briefcase or handbag.
- ✔ Turn off your cell phone (or leave it in the car) and alarm watch.
- ✔ Sit up straight, and never touch anything on the interviewer's desk.
- ✔ Try not to fidget with your clothes, play with your hair, pick your nails, tap your fingers on the table, or let your eyes wander around the room. Focus, focus!
- ✔ Did I mention turn off your cell phone?

Play It Cool

Be attentive, and give specific, concise answers to the questions. Allow yourself time to think about your answers. Don't rush to speak too quickly or interrupt the interviewer. And, of course, don't swear or use off-color language.

If you're asked a question that you did not anticipate, relax. Do your best not to say "uh," "like," or "you know what I'm sayin'." Being prepared with a clear understanding of why you're applying for the job will help you answer any unanticipated questions. And when you're asked a yes or no question, try to elaborate and provide additional information to support your response.

Use Your Best Table Manners

If you are interviewing in a restaurant, brush up on your table manners; this practice alone can give you additional confidence. How can you concentrate if you're worried about which fork to use? Two important guidelines:

- ✔ Don't order a meal that's difficult to eat, such as a big burger, spaghetti, or finger food.
- ✔ Don't drink an alcoholic beverage, even if it's offered.

See Chapter 12 for full details on dining etiquette.

End the Interview on a High Note

Always conclude the interview with another smile, a firm handshake, and eye contact, and thank the interviewer for her time. Walk out with confidence and a nice sense of relief. Whether you get the job or not, going through the process of an interview is a great learning experience.

Send a Thank-You Note

Immediately follow up with a handwritten note. Buy the paper and address the envelope in advance, if that helps. Express your thanks while the thoughts are fresh in your mind, and mail the note right away. You'll score points and make a good impression with your attention to follow-up.

Allow several days to pass before you call or contact the interviewer by phone or e-mail. Be patient. Follow up no more than once every week.

Index

• *U* •

BUSINESS, CAREERS & PERSONAL FINANCE

0-7645-9847-3

0-7645-2431-3

Also available:
- Business Plans Kit For Dummies
  0-7645-9794-9
- Economics For Dummies
  0-7645-5726-2
- Grant Writing For Dummies
  0-7645-8416-2
- Home Buying For Dummies
  0-7645-5331-3
- Managing For Dummies
  0-7645-1771-6
- Marketing For Dummies
  0-7645-5600-2

- Personal Finance For Dummies
  0-7645-2590-5*
- Resumes For Dummies
  0-7645-5471-9
- Selling For Dummies
  0-7645-5363-1
- Six Sigma For Dummies
  0-7645-6798-5
- Small Business Kit For Dummies
  0-7645-5984-2
- Starting an eBay Business For Dummies
  0-7645-6924-4
- Your Dream Career For Dummies
  0-7645-9795-7

HOME & BUSINESS COMPUTER BASICS

0-470-05432-8

0-471-75421-8

Also available:
- Cleaning Windows Vista For Dummies
  0-471-78293-9
- Excel 2007 For Dummies
  0-470-03737-7
- Mac OS X Tiger For Dummies
  0-7645-7675-5
- MacBook For Dummies
  0-470-04859-X
- Macs For Dummies
  0-470-04849-2
- Office 2007 For Dummies
  0-470-00923-3

- Outlook 2007 For Dummies
  0-470-03830-6
- PCs For Dummies
  0-7645-8958-X
- Salesforce.com For Dummies
  0-470-04893-X
- Upgrading & Fixing Laptops For Dummies
  0-7645-8959-8
- Word 2007 For Dummies
  0-470-03658-3
- Quicken 2007 For Dummies
  0-470-04600-7

FOOD, HOME, GARDEN, HOBBIES, MUSIC & PETS

0-7645-8404-9

0-7645-9904-6

Also available:
- Candy Making For Dummies
  0-7645-9734-5
- Card Games For Dummies
  0-7645-9910-0
- Crocheting For Dummies
  0-7645-4151-X
- Dog Training For Dummies
  0-7645-8418-9
- Healthy Carb Cookbook For Dummies
  0-7645-8476-6
- Home Maintenance For Dummies
  0-7645-5215-5

- Horses For Dummies
  0-7645-9797-3
- Jewelry Making & Beading For Dummies
  0-7645-2571-9
- Orchids For Dummies
  0-7645-6759-4
- Puppies For Dummies
  0-7645-5255-4
- Rock Guitar For Dummies
  0-7645-5356-9
- Sewing For Dummies
  0-7645-6847-7
- Singing For Dummies
  0-7645-2475-5

INTERNET & DIGITAL MEDIA

0-470-04529-9

0-470-04894-8

Also available:
- Blogging For Dummies
  0-471-77084-1
- Digital Photography For Dummies
  0-7645-9802-3
- Digital Photography All-in-One Desk Reference For Dummies
  0-470-03743-1
- Digital SLR Cameras and Photography For Dummies
  0-7645-9803-1
- eBay Business All-in-One Desk Reference For Dummies
  0-7645-8438-3
- HDTV For Dummies
  0-470-09673-X

- Home Entertainment PCs For Dummies
  0-470-05523-5
- MySpace For Dummies
  0-470-09529-6
- Search Engine Optimization For Dummies
  0-471-97998-8
- Skype For Dummies
  0-470-04891-3
- The Internet For Dummies
  0-7645-8996-2
- Wiring Your Digital Home For Dummies
  0-471-91830-X

* Separate Canadian edition also available
† Separate U.K. edition also available

Available wherever books are sold. For more information or to order direct: U.S. customers visit www.dummies.com or call 1-877-762-2974.
U.K. customers visit www.wileyeurope.com or call 0800 243407. Canadian customers visit www.wiley.ca or call 1-800-567-4797.

SPORTS, FITNESS, PARENTING, RELIGION & SPIRITUALITY

0-471-76871-5

0-7645-7841-3

Also available:
- Catholicism For Dummies
  0-7645-5391-7
- Exercise Balls For Dummies
  0-7645-5623-1
- Fitness For Dummies
  0-7645-7851-0
- Football For Dummies
  0-7645-3936-1
- Judaism For Dummies
  0-7645-5299-6
- Potty Training For Dummies
  0-7645-5417-4
- Buddhism For Dummies
  0-7645-5359-3

- Pregnancy For Dummies
  0-7645-4483-7 †
- Ten Minute Tone-Ups For Dummies
  0-7645-7207-5
- NASCAR For Dummies
  0-7645-7681-X
- Religion For Dummies
  0-7645-5264-3
- Soccer For Dummies
  0-7645-5229-5
- Women in the Bible For Dummies
  0-7645-8475-8

TRAVEL

0-7645-7749-2

0-7645-6945-7

Also available:
- Alaska For Dummies
  0-7645-7746-8
- Cruise Vacations For Dummies
  0-7645-6941-4
- England For Dummies
  0-7645-4276-1
- Europe For Dummies
  0-7645-7529-5
- Germany For Dummies
  0-7645-7823-5
- Hawaii For Dummies
  0-7645-7402-7

- Italy For Dummies
  0-7645-7386-1
- Las Vegas For Dummies
  0-7645-7382-9
- London For Dummies
  0-7645-4277-X
- Paris For Dummies
  0-7645-7630-5
- RV Vacations For Dummies
  0-7645-4442-X
- Walt Disney World & Orlando
  For Dummies
  0-7645-9660-8

GRAPHICS, DESIGN & WEB DEVELOPMENT

0-7645-8815-X

0-7645-9571-7

Also available:
- 3D Game Animation For Dummies
  0-7645-8789-7
- AutoCAD 2006 For Dummies
  0-7645-8925-3
- Building a Web Site For Dummies
  0-7645-7144-3
- Creating Web Pages For Dummies
  0-470-08030-2
- Creating Web Pages All-in-One Desk
  Reference For Dummies
  0-7645-4345-8
- Dreamweaver 8 For Dummies
  0-7645-9649-7

- InDesign CS2 For Dummies
  0-7645-9572-5
- Macromedia Flash 8 For Dummies
  0-7645-9691-8
- Photoshop CS2 and Digital
  Photography For Dummies
  0-7645-9580-6
- Photoshop Elements 4 For Dummies
  0-471-77483-9
- Syndicating Web Sites with RSS Feeds
  For Dummies
  0-7645-8848-6
- Yahoo! SiteBuilder For Dummies
  0-7645-9800-7

NETWORKING, SECURITY, PROGRAMMING & DATABASES

0-7645-7728-X

0-471-74940-0

Also available:
- Access 2007 For Dummies
  0-470-04612-0
- ASP.NET 2 For Dummies
  0-7645-7907-X
- C# 2005 For Dummies
  0-7645-9704-3
- Hacking For Dummies
  0-470-05235-X
- Hacking Wireless Networks
  For Dummies
  0-7645-9730-2
- Java For Dummies
  0-470-08716-1

- Microsoft SQL Server 2005 For Dummies
  0-7645-7755-7
- Networking All-in-One Desk Reference
  For Dummies
  0-7645-9939-9
- Preventing Identity Theft For Dummies
  0-7645-7336-5
- Telecom For Dummies
  0-471-77085-X
- Visual Studio 2005 All-in-One Desk
  Reference For Dummies
  0-7645-9775-2
- XML For Dummies
  0-7645-8845-1

HEALTH & SELF-HELP

0-7645-8450-2

0-7645-4149-8

Also available:
- Bipolar Disorder For Dummies
  0-7645-8451-0
- Chemotherapy and Radiation
  For Dummies
  0-7645-7832-4
- Controlling Cholesterol For Dummies
  0-7645-5440-9
- Diabetes For Dummies
  0-7645-6820-5* †
- Divorce For Dummies
  0-7645-8417-0 †

- Fibromyalgia For Dummies
  0-7645-5441-7
- Low-Calorie Dieting For Dummies
  0-7645-9905-4
- Meditation For Dummies
  0-471-77774-9
- Osteoporosis For Dummies
  0-7645-7621-6
- Overcoming Anxiety For Dummies
  0-7645-5447-6
- Reiki For Dummies
  0-7645-9907-0
- Stress Management For Dummies
  0-7645-5144-2

EDUCATION, HISTORY, REFERENCE & TEST PREPARATION

0-7645-8381-6

0-7645-9554-7

Also available:
- The ACT For Dummies
  0-7645-9652-7
- Algebra For Dummies
  0-7645-5325-9
- Algebra Workbook For Dummies
  0-7645-8467-7
- Astronomy For Dummies
  0-7645-8465-0
- Calculus For Dummies
  0-7645-2498-4
- Chemistry For Dummies
  0-7645-5430-1
- Forensics For Dummies
  0-7645-5580-4

- Freemasons For Dummies
  0-7645-9796-5
- French For Dummies
  0-7645-5193-0
- Geometry For Dummies
  0-7645-5324-0
- Organic Chemistry I For Dummies
  0-7645-6902-3
- The SAT I For Dummies
  0-7645-7193-1
- Spanish For Dummies
  0-7645-5194-9
- Statistics For Dummies
  0-7645-5423-9

Get smart @ dummies.com®

- **Find a full list of Dummies titles**
- **Look into loads of FREE on-site articles**
- **Sign up for FREE eTips e-mailed to you weekly**
- **See what other products carry the Dummies name**
- **Shop directly from the Dummies bookstore**
- **Enter to win new prizes every month!**